TOWTON
1461

The Towton Battlefield Cross marking the site where thousands perished in the snow on Palm Sunday 1461. (Author)

THE ANATOMY OF A BATTLE

TOWTON
1461

A.W. BOARDMAN
FOREWORD BY ROBERT HARDY

First published in 1994 by Sutton Publishing under the title *The Battle of Towton*
This fourth edition published 2022

The History Press
97 St George's Place, Cheltenham,
Gloucestershire, GL50 3QB
www.thehistorypress.co.uk

British Library Cataloguing in Publication Data.
A catalogue record for this book is available from the British Library.

ISBN 978 0 7509 9897 0

Typesetting and origination by The History Press
Printed and bound in Great Britain by TJ Books Limited, Padstow, Cornwall.

MIX
Paper | Supporting
responsible forestry
FSC® C013056

Trees for LYfe

For my family and those in it who
went to war before I was born

History is not the past. It is the present. We carry our history with us. We are our history. If we pretend otherwise, we are literally criminals.

James Baldwin
2017

Contents

Foreword

The late great Robert Hardy, actor and medievalist, kindly wrote these few words for me when this book, then called *The Battle of Towton*, was first published in 1994. His thoughts about battlefields are as true today as they were when we discussed Towton then. Therefore, I have left his foreword in this new edition as an introduction and a personal memorial to the man, and for anyone else who has ever questioned why we still pursue the abomination of war:

> Battlefields have a profound fascination for us. As a member of the Battlefields Panel set up by English Heritage to advise the government about the conservation of battlefields and battle sites, I have been trying to analyse the causes of that fascination. Mainly it is because, at a particular place and time, masses of men met together to settle their argument *à l'outrance*, to put it to the test of death. Battlefields are places where great skill, great loyalty, great courage, great perfidy, great coward-ice, great stupidity have been shown, where men have gone to their deaths because of passionate belief, uncontrollable rage, or in the control of a code and a discipline so powerful that it has seemed better to perish than to escape them. Whatever

frightfulness has happened, whatever idiocy perpetrated, whatever glory achieved, it has been done in the most absolute fashion, even when the action was not in the long run decisive.

A battlefield is also a tomb, holding the bodies of most of those who died there, in Towton's case a very great number; a perpetual shrine and memorial which should engage our thought and our reverence.

To know what really happened at Crécy, Agincourt, Poitiers, Patay, Castillon, Towton, that is the other fascination. It is impossible to reach the whole truth. Not even those who fought knew it all, but we can work towards the truth of the event. Known fact, reported fact, archaeological evidence, literary evidence and, under control, imagination are our guides. To that, add a passion and a dedication to the understanding of the event and the terrain and the personalities involved, and you may well glimpse truth.

It is a passion when another says or writes that one's own conclusions about the action of a battle are wrong, the response is fierce, and the re-examination intense. Andrew Boardman's account of Towton, one of the bloodiest and most raging battles of the medieval wars, is a marvel of evocation. He knows the history, which is extremely limited in particulars, and he has studied and discussed every possible clue. He knows the terrain both with exactitude and understanding, and he has a fine regard for what that great battlefield historian Colonel Alfred Burne called Inherent Military Probability. He is passionate in pursuit of the truth about this particular, this dreadful battle, and I believe that you will find in his vivid recounting of it more than fitful images of the grim truth about Towton Field, which lies today much unchanged since it lay in snow and blood on Palm Sunday 1461.

Robert Hardy, CBE, FSA.
Actor and medievalist
1994

Preface

Towton is Britain's bloodiest battle according to Google. It has also been called the longest and biggest battle fought on British soil. Like so many other close-quarter conflicts, there is no question about its place in history. But Towton was a particularly merciless event: a butcher's yard of revenge and violence that in a few hours (ten according to some chroniclers) developed into a no-quarter massacre that defies modern comprehension.

There is no doubt that Towton was pursued by Edward IV to 'cleanse' the monarchy of what he considered illegitimate rule. It was a battle of two kings and two dynasties fought in a driving northern snowstorm, bow against bow and hand-to-hand, by two overtly factional armies each seeking revenge on the other for crimes perpetrated earlier, in what we call today the Wars of the Roses. Above all, Towton changed Britain's history in a bitterly cruel way, prompting Shakespeare to liken it to the wind and tide of a mighty sea that set father against son and son against father.

They say every victory comes at a price, and Towton is comparable in effect (if not in actual casualties) to many other important battles in world history. Towton's death toll of 28,000 men, counted by the heralds, has been compared to British fatalities on the first day of the Somme in 1916. It has also been said that one per cent of the adult population of England fought at Towton and that a large proportion of its nobility was wiped out as a result. However, as with any battle in any era, there are alternative claims and more conservative estimates. Chronicles contain biased opinion about casualties, and even official court documents and contemporary letters of the period are liberally soaked in political propaganda. So, how do we uncover the truth about a battle like Towton?

There are many more bloodiest days to choose from if you are interested in figures and statistics, some of which cannot be verified due to similar problems of time and tide. But this book is not about calculating how many deaths were recorded on a bitterly cold Palm Sunday in North Yorkshire. Nor is it about comparing the size of medieval armies or the duration of the fighting at Towton (although these questions will be considered). Instead, this book is about a battlefield, how Towton continues to reach out to us across the centuries and how it raises profound questions about our acceptance of warfare as a continuation of politics. Above all, it explores the 'anatomy' and underlying significance of this largely forgotten battle from several different angles, and the results prove that Towton was, and is, significant militarily, socially and psychologically.

To search for the truth behind the myths and legends of Towton Field when all the rhetoric about numbers and time-scales are brushed aside is one way to approach the anatomy of a battle. But this is an impossibility and would, in my opinion, be the wrong approach. Given the historical significance of such a large death toll at Towton, we must take this into account. If we fail to do this, it would be like ignoring the impact of casualties on local populations after greater and more profound wars; and it is argued here that the effects of Towton on the north of England were considerable. In short, this was a great battle in an extraordinarily complicated and bloody civil war that pushed, commoners, nobles, and even kings, into a melting pot of internecine violence that has no modern comparison.

I have grown up with Towton since childhood. I have always lived within a few miles of the battlefield and have promoted it extensively whenever I can. To those who have read my various imprints of *The Battle of Towton* since 1994, I hope that another revised version of the book will add more flesh to the bone. I also wish to reach out to a new younger audience that may be unfamiliar with the subject while at the same time urging the converted to revisit the battlefield again and wonder at the kind of men who fought and died there more than half a millennium ago.

Why revise a book about Towton? For me, it is because, unlike any other historical site, a battlefield, in my opinion, is a living, breathing thing – a continually changing natural witness to the events that took place there – be it only briefly. In the case of Towton, this condition becomes more immediate if we consider that the battlefield has been relatively untouched since 1461. New evidence continues to emerge that challenges what we think occurred there. Medieval topographical features such as deserted villages, moated manor houses and period buildings, including chapels and churches, link past with present. Ridge and furrow field systems, the existence of ancient woodland and the discovery of medieval hedgerows remind us that the battlefield is a heritage site and must be preserved and protected at all costs. But above all this, there is one overriding survival of the battle that speaks volumes of the men who fought and died there in such a brutal way, and that is the fact that the whole site is an unmarked tomb. A stone wayside cross now marks the bloody meadows of Towton, but it is certain that once the fields 'betwixt Towton and Saxton' were littered with many mass graves, and despite the resistance of those who find the casualties at Towton over-egged, it is this link to remembrance that makes the site a place of 'sadness' and veneration for many.

Chroniclers' estimates of the Towton death toll vary wildly from the sensible to the ridiculous. However, since 1461, archaeologists have discovered numerous graves to highlight a much darker side of the Wars of the Roses than previously imagined. A terrible secret that Towton has cleverly concealed is gradually rising to the surface, and thankfully it is not the forgotten battle it once was. The mass killings and the slaughter perpetrated there is no myth or quaint legend anymore. Instead, the casualties remind us of our mortality and what we can do as a species when compelled to kill our fellow man.

Twenty-six years have passed since I first put pen to paper, and theories change with time. Since 1461 the fields between Saxton and Towton have attracted the interest of the royal, the pious, the academic and the romantic. In the Victorian era, the battlefield became the haunt of antiquarians. Towton inspired poets to write eulogies about the slaughter, and over the years, it has had its fair share of local historians who all perpetuated the legends told by farmers and villagers, stories that are still passed on today. Throughout the ages, mass graves were discovered in the now quiet fields of North Acres and bones were exhumed and re-buried in hallowed ground. The more famous areas associated with the battle became the subject of ballads and acquired bloody topographic names. More recently, walls of dead were found in cellars and even under the floorboards of local homes. Rivers became colourful receptacles of the great slaughter in certain histories and chronicles. And even a specific type of rose miraculously took root in a meadow to commemorate the 'white' and the 'red' of popular legend. These are some of the legends of Towton Moor – or are they merely persistent memories of even stranger tales lost in time?

Ever since the battle of Towton was fought, many myths have been perpetuated about what occurred there and where the actual fighting took place. A thin shroud of invention hid the truth of the battle for many centuries, and this is where my interest in a multi-disciplined approach began in earnest.

Following the work done by Brooke, Markham, Burne, to name but three battlefield detectives, I was lucky enough to write the first major work on the subject in 1994. But even I was not prepared for what was unearthed at Towton in July 1996 by the team of archaeologists from York and Bradford University.

War graves containing human bones became headline news, and like those discovered by the Tudors, Georgians and Victorians in their day, the human cost of warfare was expounded to the full by the media. The stark reality of dead soldiers who witnessed the battle of Towton still astonishes me. People interested in the dig demanded an interpretation, but even specialists in their field and modern research methods could not decode the whole truth about the graves and what they contained. A brutal death with an edged or blunt weapon leaves telltale marks on bone, and forensic tests can make a critical judgement as to how an individual died. With the help of anthropological science, approximate age at death can be revealed. A soldier's general state of health and proportions can be measured. But who are we to say under what circumstances a particular soldier died, and can we judge the tactical course of a battle from such a clinical post-mortem?

Other factors have caused me to revise my initial work concerning the strategic aspects of medieval warfare. The mechanics and devastating power of the warbow have been drastically modified and proven since 1994 to the extent that my theories about how the battle was fought have changed. In a test shot of a replica Mary Rose bow in 1996, the archer Simon Stanley shot a series of war arrows from beside the hawthorn tree above North Acres and achieved over 300yd. When retrieved, one replica arrow had split a block of magnesium limestone and penetrated the ground beneath, such was its power when it struck. In 2005 *The Great Warbow*, by Strickland and Hardy, exploded the extraordinary claims by some former experts that the bow of the late Middle Ages was largely ineffective and caused only disorder and confusion in the ranks at long range. However, conclusive ballistics tests since then have proved otherwise, and the implications of this research into the great warbow's killing power and consequently the duration of medieval battles, such as Towton, cannot be ignored.

Similarly, a reappraisal of the contemporary evidence reveals that the social impact of Towton was fresh in some people's minds long after the event. Whole shires refused to participate in further bloodshed or give support to the victors years later. There were even claims for compensation and evidence of economic collapse. Memorials, chapels, and official documents venerated the dead at Towton, much like in any age, and concerning the tactical, strategic, and political thinking of the time, the campaign was a model of propaganda. Chronicles and letters confirm my original claim that, in the second half of the fifteenth century, Englishmen waged a new type of warfare that was more advanced, purposeful, and devious than previously thought. More importantly, winning was not dependant on arbitrary tactics and (in the eyes of medieval man) God's judgement. Commanders sought a tactical edge over their opponents at the expense of the chivalric code. And at Towton it is apparent that the outcome of the battle was dictated by a sequence of events that caused already high casualty rates to increase out of all proportion far from the battlefield.

In pro-Yorkist letters and chronicles, one can detect the universal sigh of relief that Edward IV had triumphed. However, according to the evidence, Towton was a 'near-run thing' despite many contemporary writers inflating the death toll to suit their audience and political ambitions. Fear of foreign invasion, internal rebellion and quarrelsome nobles with private forces were dangers that could not be ignored, and the biblical casualties at Towton helped cement both crown and sceptre to Edward's warlike image when his newly acquired throne was far from secure.

As always, when dealing with historical events that have more than one scenario, this new reappraisal is highly controversial, and the image of the men who fought and died at Towton is far from romantic. The battle was regarded as a great tragedy at the time, and the death toll was mourned as a complete waste of life by contemporaries in England and Europe. But what is the significance of the battle of Towton today?

The visual evidence always produces a more direct response from anyone interested in the battle. But chronicled and written evidence such as wills, attainders and indentures are just as illuminating. As for battlefield treasure, some archaeological relics from Towton are predominantly difficult to authenticate, despite surfacing in great quantities to fascinate and spark heated debate among those who seek the truth. Some artefacts are things of incredible beauty and craftsmanship. They speak to us across time about the kind of soldiers that passed that way only once. Collections of arrowheads found on the battlefield summon up the ghosts of Yorkist and Lancastrian archers plying their deadly craft. Sword and dagger pommel heads re-animate weapons in our mind's eye that were originally designed to kill and maim. But are all these relics contemporary with 1461? We seek confirmation, and our elusive search for the truth uncovers more questions than answers with each new find. We may speculate what else could be discovered on the battlefield, what might have been dropped by soldiers or hacked from their bodies in the heat of combat, but this is not the end of the Towton story by any stretch of the imagination.

Admittedly many questions still arise about this unique battle. We can visit the 'living' battlefield of Towton and wonder at the unimaginable slaughter committed there. We can walk the site in all weathers – even snowstorms – to explore its topography. We can visit local churchyards and see memorials to the battle dating back centuries. We can read about the carnage in contemporary chronicles and letters. But have we got anything in common with the men who fought at Towton? Can we glean anything from their brutality and senseless slaughter? Indeed, is the battle of Towton at all significant in the twenty-first century?

In the foreword and preface to the 1994 edition of *The Battle of Towton,* the late Robert Hardy and I held the opinion that our indescribable fascination with the battle was a combination of several factors: a lifelong interest in the site, an affinity with the medieval period, a passion for military history and a personal search for the reasons why war is still pursued in an age of enlightenment. Battlefield conservation was also a significant issue at the time. But other than these passions, nothing tangible about the battle touched the present or changed our perception of the Towton story. The grave found in 1996 changed all that. It brought us face to face with the men who fought in 1461, and why and how they died raised questions about medieval man and his psychological attitude to violence.

It is perhaps worth reiterating my feelings in the first edition of this book that any place where great historical decisions are made must not be forgotten and that battlefields are among the most important of these. My personal search for the truth about Towton goes on, but as you read this account, it is perhaps worth remembering that civilisation has not moved on very far regarding warfare, apart from the technologies enabling armies to wage it more effectively. Perhaps education of past conflicts is the path away from violence? Maybe we are more civilised and law-abiding than the men who fought at Towton? But what would we have done if faced with a similar life or death situation?

I hope this new perspective revealing the 'anatomy' of the battle of Towton provides answers to some of these crucial questions and prompts further research into this unique conflict where contemporaries agree there was no quarter asked or given and no greater battle fought in a thousand years.

Andrew Boardman
2021

One

'O miserable and luckless race'

On 7 April 1461, George Neville, Bishop of Exeter and Chancellor of England, wrote to Francesco Coppini, the Papal Legate and Bishop of Terni in Flanders, that on Palm Sunday:

> there was a great conflict, which began with the rising of the sun, and lasted until the tenth hour of the night, so great was the pertinacity and boldness of the men, who never heeded the possibility of a miserable death. Of the enemy who fled, great numbers were drowned in the river near the town of Tadcaster, eight miles from York, because they themselves had broken the bridge to cut our passage that way, so that none could pass, and a great part of the rest who got away who gathered in the said town and city, were slain and so many dead bodies were seen as to cover an area six miles long by three broad and about four furlongs. In this battle eleven lords of the enemy fell, including the Earl of Devon, the Earl of Northumberland, Lord Clifford and Neville with other knights, and from what we hear from persons worthy of confidence, some 28,000 persons perished on one side and the other. O miserable and luckless race and powerful people, would you have no spark of pity for our own

blood, of which we have lost so much of fine quality by the civil war, even if you had no compassion for the French![1]

George Neville was writing of the battle of Towton, in which his brother Richard, the Earl of Warwick, had taken an active part. The document, preserved in the *Calendars of State Papers of Milan*, is evidence of what has become known as the longest, biggest and bloodiest battle on British soil. In the same letter, Neville gives his very opinionated view of the wars between the houses of York and Lancaster, known later as the Wars of the Roses, by lamenting the futility of civil strife in contrast with what he later points out might have been energies better directed 'against the enemies of the Christian name'.[2]

The bishop opened his letter by saying that he learned of these events from 'messengers and letters, as well as by popular report',[3] meaning, presumably, that his intelligence about the battle came directly from his brother Richard, Earl of Warwick, and King Edward IV, then in York, attempting to secure the area after their victory at Towton. Indeed, George Neville was commanded by Edward to join them in the north and help with this operation as soon as possible.

Other members of the clergy wrote about Towton that were equally dismayed about the death toll. On 7 April 1461, Richard Beauchamp, Bishop of Salisbury, wrote to Coppini that:

On Palm Sunday last King Edward began a very hard-fought battle near York, in which the result remained doubtful the whole day, until at length victory declared itself on his side, at a moment when those present declared that almost all of our side despaired of it, so great was the strength of our adversaries, had not the prince [Edward IV] single-handedly cast himself into the fray as he did so notably, with the greatest of human courage. The heralds counted 28,000 slain, a number unheard of in our realm for almost a thousand years, without counting those wounded and drowned.[4]

The Bishop of Elpin, Nicholas O'Flanagan, added to Coppini's reports by stating that 28,000 were killed in the battle, 800 being on King Edward's side.[5] Another letter from London to a Milanese merchant, Pigello Portinaro, on 14 April, claimed that 28,000 fell, 8,000 of them being Yorkists.[6] And yet another document from Prospero di Camulio, Milanese Ambassador to the Court of France, to Francesco Sforza, Duke of Milan claimed that:

> the combat was great and cruel, as happens when men fight for kingdom and life. At the beginning, fortune seemed to be on the side of King Henry and those banners of the queen, which are inscribed *Judica me Deus discerne causam meam de gente non sancta*, etc. They looked like conquering, and over 8,000 of the troops of King Edward and Warwick were slain, including Lord Scrope and Lord Fitzwalter among the nobles. However, subsequently the wind changed, and Edward and Warwick were victorious. On the side of Henry and the queen, over 20,000 men were slain along with the nobles mentioned below. In short, thirteen nobles perished and over 28,000 men, all counted by the heralds after the battle, including many other knights and gentlemen.[7]

Many such reports followed in the aftermath of Towton and, as newsletters, the above documents rate highly as containing unique facts about the battle from a mainly clerical viewpoint. However, we must remember that Francesco Coppini heard the news from two pro-Yorkists claiming that the Lancastrians were the aggressors, and that King Henry VI was a puppet in their hands. Indeed, Coppini was pro-Yorkist himself. The other letters seem diplomatically impartial, even though they may have received information about the battle from the same source. More important is that all the correspondence communicated the atmosphere and feelings in London in the first weeks after Towton and at a time when an anonymous author in the city claimed that 'I am unable to declare how well the commons love and adore him [Edward IV] as if he were their God' and that 'the entire kingdom keeps holiday for the event, which seems a boon from above'.[8]

Similarly, a private letter of the Paston family of Norfolk also communicated Edward's victory at Towton, confirming the casualty figures given above. In this case, William Paston reported to John:

> You will be pleased to know the news my lady of York [Edward IV's mother] had in a letter of credence signed by our sovereign lord King Edward, which reached her safely today, Easter eve, at eleven o'clock, and was seen and read by me William Paston. First, our sovereign lord has won the field, and on the Monday after Palm Sunday, he was received into York with great solemnity and processions. And the mayor and commons contrived to have his grace through Lord Montagu and Lord Berners, who, before the king came into the city, craved clemency for the citizens, which he granted them. On the king's side, Lord Fitzwalter was killed, and Lord Scrope badly hurt. John Stafford and Horne of Kent are dead, and Humphrey Stafford and William Hastings made knights, and among others, Blount is knighted. On the other side Lord Clifford, Lord Neville, Lord Welles, Lord Willoughby, Anthony Lord Scales, Lord Harry and apparently the Earl of Northumberland, Andrew Trollope and many other gentlemen and commoners, to the number of 20,000, are dead. [On a separate piece of paper attached to this letter, 28,000 dead were numbered by the heralds.][9]

So here was a great fellowship of death, even on the Yorkist side. Clearly, it shocked writers abroad and in England by its ferocity. But what of the Lancastrians, the main victims of the Towton carnage? What price their cause, and who reported for them, without bias, on the fateful day when the true anointed King Henry VI was ousted from his throne, and

William Paston's letter to his brother John, dated 4 April 1461, reporting the battle of Towton. (British Library)

20,000 of his adherents perished? What drove the contending houses of York and Lancaster to such a great and unseasonable conflict, in which the unusually high casualties presented unique accounting problems for the heralds? And why did the battle develop into a massacre resulting in rivers running red with blood and a rout that was mercilessly followed up to the gates of York?

The State Papers of Milan and the *Paston Letters* record only a small part of the Wars of the Roses story. The rest of its history is, of course, documented in the great, if sometimes inaccurate, chronicles of Britain, not forgetting writers in Burgundy and France, equal players in the drama. Edward Hall, John Whethamstede, Polydore Vergil, William Worcester, Philip de Commynes, Jean de Waurin and William Gregory – to name but a few writers – only light candles in history that illuminate the past. Eyewitness accounts of battles such as Towton sadly lack content and remain in the shadows due to their grim and provincial nature. Only a few sources speak the truth. Therefore, we must tread carefully and put other devices to work to illuminate the structure of historical events when source material contains biased opinion and falsehoods. Even where first-hand reports exist, one might argue, several accounts would have to be consulted to acquire an accurate perspective of a medieval battle, as each fighting man can only perceive his own immediate area of combat. Lacking an overall aerial view of the battlefield, the soldier's story would be limited to his own experience, which might prove tactically worthless when viewed with others.

Information on who was present at the battle of Towton and what motivated individuals to fight lies in attainder documents and the chronicles. The topography of the local area can be evaluated to answer such questions as to how terrain swayed the contending armies' movements on the day and to what extent the land precipitated victory or defeat. Archaeology can be helpful to locate graves and entrenchments, but, more importantly, relics may pinpoint personal regalia, which may confirm whose troops were present on the battlefield. Logistics can answer such questions as what influenced manoeuvres before and during the fighting, which troops were better equipped to survive combat, and, being thus armed, what disadvantages could overtake them when they ran. However, to conclude confidently why some men stood their ground and others fled during battles of any era, we must, in the end, evaluate the reasons for the armies being there, the effects of fatigue on morale and, of course, the human spirit. The late John Keegan, the author of *The Face of Battle*, one of the half-dozen best books on warfare to appear in the English language, suggests that:

The answer to some of these questions must be highly conjectural, interesting though that conjecture might be. But to others, we can certainly offer answers which fall within a narrow bracket of probability, because the parameters of the questions are technical. Where speed of movement, density of formations, effect of weapons, for example, are concerned, we can test our suppositions against the known defensive qualities of armour plate, penetrative power of arrows, dimensions and capacities of the human body, carrying power and speed of the horse. And from a reasonable assessment of probabilities about these military mechanics, we may be able to leap towards an understanding of the dynamics of the battle itself and the spirit of the armies which fought it.[10]

In my opinion, this methodology is valid when investigating any type of conflict. However, to investigate the battle of Towton, we must begin much earlier than 1461. In short, we must be aware of English history from at least 1399 when revolution stoked a dynastic 'fire pot' of uncertainty that was reignited time and time again until the last Plantagenets, and their pretenders, were killed off by the Tudors with numerous strokes of the pen and the headman's axe.

The history of the Wars of the Roses can be read in detail in many fine books on the subject. It is a veritable quagmire of noble titles, similar names and changing alliances. A real game of thrones and double-dealing. Therefore, my intention here is to give the reader some idea of the key events leading up to Towton and explain why through all the politics and cravings for power the wars became a dynastic conflict tainted with the blood of revenge in 1461. To quote Shakespeare, my aim is 'to turn the accomplishment of many years into an hourglass'.[11]

The Origins of the Wars of the Roses

Henry Bolingbroke, Duke of Lancaster, usurped the English throne from Richard II in 1399, and later, when Henry ruled and Richard was dead, a dangerous new precedent was set in motion to threaten English kingship from then on. This precedent, which had successfully unseated Edward II in 1327, meant that instead of a king ruling by lawful and legitimate right, he became more regarded as the first among equals by the princes of the blood. Henry Bolingbroke exploited this situation to the full when Richard II seized his lands after his father's death, and matters escalated first into regicide, then open rebellion, when he (then crowned Henry IV) inadvertently set noble against noble at the battle of Shrewsbury in 1403.

In becoming the first Lancastrian king, Henry IV also ignored another contender for the throne in Edmund Mortimer, whose father had been heir presumptive to Richard II during his reign. But Henry was a strong king, if somewhat fearful of his precarious position, and the Mortimer claims to the throne were never pressed until, in 1415, others tried unsuccessfully to usurp the crown. On the eve of Henry V's expedition to France, Richard, Earl of Cambridge, attempted to put his brother-in-law Mortimer on the throne and was executed for high treason. The plot was uncovered and revealed to the king by none other than Mortimer himself, in an act of betrayal, and when Henry V returned from France and victory at Agincourt, it was thought the winds of change had finally provided England with a model warrior king who could beat the French and win popular acclaim at home.

However, when Henry V died in 1422, he left his son a legacy of unfinished business in France. The trouble was that Henry VI of England and France was a nine-month-old child at the time, and others would attempt to rule England for him until he reached maturity. To quote a medieval political cliché, 'Woe to thee, O land, when thy king is a child'.[12] And when the Hundred Years War dragged on through lack of finance and mismanagement this forced Henry's council to reassess their position in France.

Henry V's French causes had been left in the hands of his brother John, Duke of Bedford, but when he died in 1435, two arguing factions emerged to contend if the war should be continued, or whether peace through a treaty was the answer to the drain on the English war chest. On the one hand, nobles such as King Henry's uncle, Humphrey, Duke of Gloucester, the Lancastrian heir apparent, violently opposed a truce, while on the other side, a party led by William de la Pole, later Duke of Suffolk, wished to negotiate with the French and silence Gloucester in the process. The Beaufort family, eventually acclaimed Dukes of Somerset, sided with William de la Pole to marry off Henry VI to a French princess, Margaret of Anjou. But what was the young king doing while others were manoeuvring for power?

There is little doubt that England hoped that Henry VI might someday emulate his warlike father. However, when Henry shook off his minority in 1437, this dream of strong kingship fell well short of the mark. Despite being tutored by the best civil and military minds in the land, Henry's political, marital and warlike shortcomings soon proved fatal for England. In adulthood, Henry of Windsor became a monkish king, an ineffectual monarch incapable of personal rule. And in an age of powerful men with dangerous ambitions, these failings inevitably and effectively helped undermine the English throne. Through gross negligence and the unchecked interference of devious ministers, Henry rapidly lost his father's military conquests in France, helped divide the nobility and, at least in part, caused the Wars of the Roses. In various parts of the country, people openly described Henry as a natural fool and no fit person to govern England. Yet this 'simple' king reigned for almost thirty-nine years, and soon after his death, thousands of pilgrims visited his shrine at Chertsey Abbey, attested to miracles there, and even revered him as a saint.

Unlike Edward II and Richard II, who were similarly manipulated by ambitious courtiers, Henry enjoyed

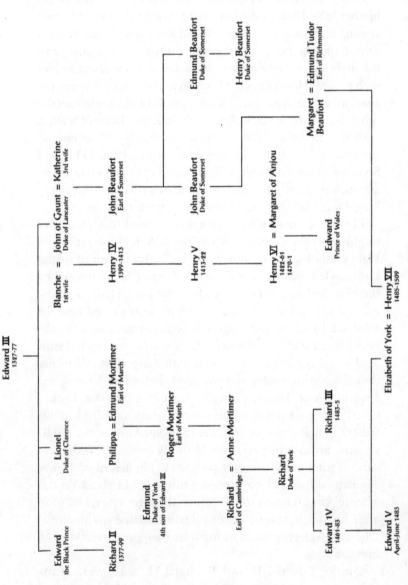

A simplified genealogical table of the contending houses of York and Lancaster. (Author)

martyrdom beyond the reign of his enemies. Even after the death of Richard III, who allegedly murdered him in the Tower of London, Henry's fame rivalled that of St Thomas Becket in popularity. However, Henry's apathetic character remained wholly evident to his contemporaries, despite subsequent efforts by the Tudor kings to sanctify his name for more selfish reasons. Historiography reveals that he was no more than a pawn in the hands of others. Indeed, the fact that Henry was tolerated for so long shows how docile he was as a ruler and how easily he could be controlled.

There is no doubt that Henry placed too much trust in his ministers, most of whom sought power for themselves out of political necessity, and aside from creating an unstable government, a firm wedge was driven between leading members of the nobility through favouritism. According to one contemporary, Henry was *simplex et probus* (honest and upright).[13] Still, this description must be weighed against a whole host of other kingly attributes that Henry did not possess. Apart from following a pious otherworldly existence that prevented him from dealing with affairs of state, the king could be highly vindictive, and after 1453 his reason became seriously impaired. Indeed, it is the measured opinion of most modern historians that Henry VI was a puppet in the hands of others and that Eton College and King's College, Cambridge, both products of his more pious interests, remain the only positive records of his reign.

When his minority ended, Henry was just sixteen years old. He had enjoyed a relatively trouble-free reign as King of England and France and was potentially on the verge of greater things. However, by 1447 military disaster abroad helped produce a power vacuum that caused various factions to emerge that the king was unable to control. Each aristocratic clique sought to influence Henry, and his lack of independent leadership aggravated the political situation so much that it worsened the family feuding that was already rife in England during the fifteenth century.

The most volatile and dangerous of these rivalries was that pursued by Richard, Duke of York and Edmund, Duke of Somerset. The Duke of York was Henry's Plantagenet heir presumptive while he remained childless, but as the king's main beneficiary York's greatest fear was that if his rival, the Duke of Somerset, could validate his own Beaufort claim to the throne, then he too could succeed Henry on his death. It was a tangle of families and shifting alliances that had its roots in the usurpation of 1399. Some individuals, like Henry VI, were born into a usurped throne and held the crown through right of conquest. Others, like Richard, Duke of York, could claim legitimate Plantagenet descent from Edward III's fourth son and through his father Richard, Earl of Cambridge, traitor to Henry V. Richard became Duke of York when his uncle died at Agincourt in 1415, but this was not his only claim. On his mother's side, through the dormant Mortimer line, Richard was also descended from Lionel, Duke of Clarence, Edward III's second son. The Beauforts, on the other hand, were equally placed to have a say in how England should be ruled, as they too had a claim to the throne, through John of Gaunt's third wife, Katherine Swynford. And when Edmund Beaufort became Earl of Somerset and received appointments and power from Henry VI, the Duke of York found only displeasure at court and bad debts through his own financing of the war in France.

What better recipe for disaster could fate have cooked up for England under a monkish king's weak and unstable rule? The answer can be found in what happened next. Along with Henry's queen, Margaret of Anjou, these three powerful men became a catalyst whereby only the strongest would survive.

To pinpoint exactly when the Duke of York became suspicious of the Beaufort family's manipulating hand behind the throne is difficult to judge. But in 1447, when York's lieutenancy of France was suddenly transferred to Edmund Beaufort,

The seal of Edmund Beaufort, Duke of Somerset, *c.* 1445. (Geoff Wheeler)

then only an earl, York must have had his suspicions. Worse still, the Duke of York was blamed for all the reversals in France and was appointed King Henry's lieutenant in Ireland, primarily to remove him from English affairs and help further Somerset's ambitions at court. In the same year, Humphrey, Duke of Gloucester, was accused of treason, imprisoned and probably poisoned to death by agents of the Duke of Suffolk, Somerset's ally. Soon afterwards, Suffolk himself was also murdered for similar crimes, and with Gloucester's death, the Duke of York suddenly found himself heir apparent. Suffolk, it seems, became the victim of his own high-handed intrigue. As for Somerset and his new-found appointment in France, when the English were defeated at Formigny in 1450, he dared not return to England and sought refuge in Calais until the storm clouds blew over.

A few weeks later, in the summer of that year, Jack Cade's popular rebellion highlighted the fact that reform was in the hearts and minds of many people in England, to the extent that London was for a time in anarchy. The rebels who entered the city were men of Kent and, as such, their grievances, although common feelings in the kingdom, were vented violently on some of the king's chief councillors, primarily those ministers who had offended their county. Hundreds of people were killed and murdered in the city, and the rebellion was only put down when Cade was caught and executed. However, the questions about the king and his 'advisers' would not go away.

With so much trouble at home, it is not surprising that Somerset, now furnished with a dukedom, chose to return to England from Calais to protect his own position. The Duke of York also stirred himself from Ireland, as insinuations were already being made that he had been responsible for Cade's rebellion. After all, York had been favoured in the commons manifesto, and Somerset branded as one of 'certain persons who daily and nightly are about the king's person and daily inform him that good is evil and evil is good'.[14]

The heated encounter between the two dukes in London was disastrous and occurred against a background of thousands of armed retainers bullying each other for position. It was clear to York that favour was still being bestowed by the king, and increasingly the queen, Margaret of Anjou, on his rival Somerset, despite his attempts to sway the king in the guise of being a true subject and champion of law and order. Disgruntled but firm in his resolve, York decided to canvass support from the Duke of Norfolk and the Earl of Devon, who were the only prominent nobles willing to go along with his open criticism of the court. Somerset by this time had been given the captaincy of the Calais garrison, the king's fickle but professional standing army abroad, and his military failure in France was soon forgotten. It seemed Somerset could do no wrong, and this situation, in the end, forced York over the precipice as, diplomatically, he had failed miserably.

Somerset and York's intentions were now clear, in so much as both were protecting their own political lives, there being no evidence that either of them was coveting the throne. Henry VI, removed from the feud in mind if not in body, watched the squabbling dukes with increasing tension, seemingly unable to comprehend either the gravity of the situation or the possible outcome of such a rift. Obviously, he did not think either noble was capable or wanted to dethrone him. If so, his ministers would have acted against such a threat immediately. Even considering his numbness to events, Queen Margaret, who became such a dominant influence behind the throne later in the wars, certainly favoured Somerset and did not suspect him of greater ambitions. However, from her point of view, the Duke of York was becoming her mortal enemy.

Richard, Duke of York, from a stained-glass window at Trinity College, Cambridge. (Geoff Wheeler)

The queen's gradual understanding of the king's short-comings, maritally as well as politically displeasing, made her suspect York, as heir to the throne, of being a typical over-mighty subject, bent on a course of ultimate power, and a threatening catalyst by which her own position and plans might be consumed. She misjudged the situation badly because England was not like France, fraught with generations of factional intrigue and war, although periodically it was to become so by her refuelling the situation through nobles who later became allied to her cause.

However, the Duke of York did not disappoint the queen's mistrust, and in 1452 he rose to the bait. In February, York marched on London from his castle at Ludlow to enforce Somerset's removal. He encountered the royal army at Dartford and quickly occupied a strong defensive position, which he fortified with guns. He made his position clear, declaring that he wished the king no harm but that 'he would have the Duke of Somerset, or else he would die therefore'.[15] However, as time passed, and under increasing pressure from the king's emissaries, a meeting was arranged to avoid the shedding of blood. The Duke of York was told he might present his grievances in person to the king. But, not for the last time in his career, York was tricked, and, after being escorted to London, he was forced into a humiliating upbraiding in front of his fellow peers. Somerset was vindicated of all charges raised against him, and at St Pauls in London, York was forced to swear a public oath never again to disturb the peace and he returned to his castle at Ludlow a bitter man.

It is interesting to note that in the king's army at Dartford, there were nobles, such as the Nevilles of Middleham, who were to become staunch Yorkists only a year later. This duality illustrates not only the effect of the king's mismanagement of the great magnates of the realm but also that the polarisation in England, caused by the quarrels between York and Somerset, was increasingly providing a convenient arena in which to settle local and ancient dynastic issues at the point of a sword. The Nevilles and the Percys offer classic examples of such behaviour, coming to blows across ever-shifting borders in northern England and occasionally mustering thousands of armed retainers to pursue their private feuds. Both sides saw distinct advantages in being on opposite sides in the Wars of the Roses, even if it meant their family suffered split loyalties.

By 1453 the Nevilles, specifically the two Richards, the Earl of Salisbury and his son the Earl of Warwick, were to be found siding with the Duke of York, as they too had come up against Somerset and the king in a dispute over land and titles. The king once again succeeded in putting leading nobles at each other's throats instead of defusing the situation as his predecessors might have done. However, the situation became worse for Henry when he received news of a catastrophe in France on his way to attempt to dislodge Warwick from Cardiff Castle. John Talbot, Earl of Shrewsbury, had been killed and his army routed at Castillon, and with this defeat, all lands won in the Hundred Years War were lost. Only Calais remained English. Even worse, on receipt of the news, Henry suffered a total mental breakdown, which rendered him incapable of personal rule. He was unable to speak, hear, or understand his actions or what was going on around him, and this, of course, left the kingdom effectively leaderless.

Henry VI probably suffered all his life from what might be called today catatonic schizophrenia, but this reversal in fortunes eventually caused an unexpected turnaround for the Duke of York. The Royal Council had to meet with him to discuss what should be done. York was in theory next in line to the throne, and it was a golden opportunity that York grasped with both hands. It was also the perfect moment when he might have staked his claim to the throne. However, York remained loyal to King Henry and was content to let the council imprison his enemy Somerset in the Tower of London until the king recovered his health.

England had narrowly averted a major crisis, but soon a more legitimate obstacle emerged to belittle York's ambitions when Queen Margaret gave birth to a son – an heir who would restore the status quo between York and Somerset and eventually give the Lancastrian dynasty added credibility. However, now the child's legitimacy became the focus of Yorkist attention, as in some circles the Duke of Somerset was named as the father, possibly giving rise to insinuations that this provoked the onset of the king's madness. The implications concerning Henry's pious and monk-like abhorrence of anything remotely sexual, and his depressive unwillingness to recognise the child when it was born, furthered these rumours considerably. But propaganda aside, it was thought imperative, as the king's illness became well known, that the Duke of York should be made Lord Protector, and this was confirmed by parliament when the north once again became a battleground of Neville and Percy feuding.

King Henry VI from an original dated *c.* 1450 in the Royal Collection at Windsor Castle.

The duke accepted the post grudgingly, we are told, but acted with venom, stripping Somerset of his captaincy of Calais, seating his friends in positions of power and quelling the northern dispute. However, the wheel of fortune was about to turn full circle once again, when at Christmas 1454, the king miraculously recovered his sanity, released Somerset from the

Tower and reversed all York's decisions. He also blessed his son, declaring that 'he never knew him until that time, nor what had been said to him, nor where he had been whilst he had been sick until now'.[16] An astounding accusation given the unique timing and circumstances of the child's birth.

With the Duke of Somerset free and the monarchy restored, the Duke of York's position became, not surprisingly, more dangerous and isolated. In short, York feared for his life, and after acquiring military support from the powerful Neville family, his next move was to remove his rival by force of arms. On 22 May 1455, negotiations broke down when Henry and his entourage were confronted by York and his Neville allies embattled outside St Albans in Hertfordshire. The Wars of the Roses were about to begin.

The Wars 1455–60

Some historians have regarded the battle of St Albans as a mere 'scuffle in the streets';[17] however, with approximately 5,000 men fighting in such a confined area, the battle can hardly have resembled a scuffle. Any armed incursion involving the king, and the leading nobles of the land with banners displayed in rebellion, must warrant the title of battle, despite how low the casualties might have been.

The Duke of York, with his Neville supporters, Salisbury and Warwick, embattled their retinues in an area known as Key Field to the east of St Albans, while the king's army, under the command of the Duke of Buckingham, occupied the town. Mediators were despatched to avoid battle several times and to accuse the Duke of York of high treason in answer to his scathing remarks about Somerset. However, this time, in difference to the Dartford affair, talks broke down, and the Yorkists launched an attack on the town's barriers, which Lord Clifford had hastily fortified.

The main assault failed, but 600 of the Earl of Warwick's troops under Sir Robert Ogle found a gap in the defences and they burst into the town 'through garden sides between the sign of the Key and the sign of the Chequer',[18] two of the town's ancient inns. The Yorkists proceeded to roll up the Lancastrian flank and then shot hundreds of arrows into the resulting confused mass. The king's standard wavered and was left abandoned in the main street, many in the royal army were routed, and the residue, finding themselves hemmed in, sought refuge and cover in the buildings that lined St Albans marketplace. Finally, finding the barricades weakened, more and more Yorkists pushed into St Peter's Street, and the end of the fighting was signalled when the Duke of Somerset, the Earl of Northumberland, Lord Clifford and others were butchered to death in the last throes of Lancastrian defiance. The king, wounded and shocked, his horror of bloodshed a well-known characteristic, was conveniently bundled into St Albans Abbey before the executions commenced. But it was no accident that the nobles marked for death were the Duke of York and the Nevilles' greatest enemies. It was a chance to change the face of government, and York made sure to renew his vows of allegiance as the king was treated for an arrow wound that had grazed his neck.

The battle of St Albans signalled not only the start of the Wars of the Roses but, more importantly, the unfurling of a bloody flag of revenge by the sons of the Lancastrian nobles killed there who vowed to kill the Yorkist lords thereafter. All three prominent nobles slain at St Albans had their name-sakes at Towton in 1461, of whom young Lord John Clifford, whose father had commanded the defences at St Albans, was to become probably the most vindictive one of them all.

After the fighting ended, York and his followers were absolved of all blame for the battle. Once again, the duke grovelled and renewed his oath of allegiance to King Henry, which, if nothing else, highlights his fear of the king's sanctity,

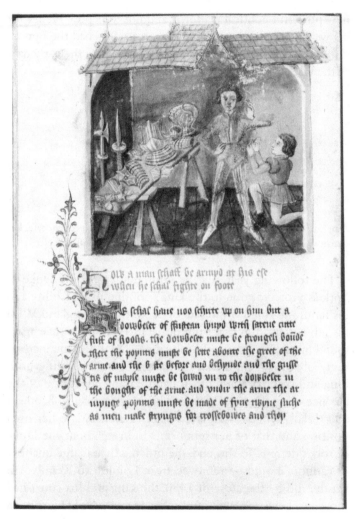

'How a man shall be armed at his ease when he shall fight on foot' *c.* 1480.

his sovereign's legitimate right to rule and his apparent acceptance of the Prince of Wales as heir to the throne. Also, now that Somerset was out of the way, York seemed content to right the wrongs of the land through his king, even from this new powerful political platform, and not to depose Henry for his weakness. As discussed earlier, he certainly had the opportunity to take the throne on several occasions in the early days of the Wars of the Roses.[19]

A petition presented to Richard of York during his first protectorate. His signature is prominent at the centre of the document. (Geoff Wheeler)

The following year saw the reinstatement of the Duke of York as Protector due to the king's continuing instability and his failure to quell disturbances in southwest England. With his subsequent dismissal from office in 1456, York once again found himself in a dangerous situation, and it became increasingly obvious to him that the queen was now ruling both king and country with a firm hand. Taking advantage of the absence of the Duke of York and his Neville allies in Scotland and Calais, Queen Margaret began to consolidate her own position and that of her supporters to bring about the Duke of York's demise. To this end, she ordered that a large quantity of cannon should be removed from London to Kenilworth Castle, and by the close of 1456, the king and his court had moved to Leicester, with most offices recently held by Yorkists filled with Lancastrians. However, the slide towards the next bout of the wars was gradual, almost as if no one except the queen and her allies really wanted to continue hostilities.

Conscious attempts to reconcile the two parties occurred in 1458 in the public charade known as Love Day, during which each faction walked arm in arm to St Pauls. This event was more than likely instigated by the king and had the effect of again bringing thousands of armed retainers to the city, almost igniting the political powder-keg and achieving nothing but further mistrust on both sides.

In May 1458, the Earl of Warwick was resorting to piracy. He had been appointed captain of the Calais garrison on Somerset's death and was predictably being squeezed by the Lancastrians, receiving less and less money from the Exchequer to pay the troops under his command. When he attacked the Hanseatic Bay fleet out of necessity, he was summoned to London to explain his actions before the queen, who demanded his arrest. But Warwick escaped back to Calais, claiming that there had been a plot to murder him. The Lancastrians, it seemed, were preparing for war. Therefore, it is not surprising that the Yorkists were conspicuous by their absence when, in June 1459, a Great Council met at Coventry where York and the Nevilles were indicted for their failure to attend the king.

Apart from the military and political defeats they had suffered since the battle of St Albans, the Lancastrians were now once again controlling events. And sensing this advantage, every attempt was made to mobilise their forces to act while the Yorkist lords were widely scattered. At the same time, the Duke of York made immediate plans to assemble his followers at Ludlow, sending messages to the Earl of Salisbury, in the north at Middleham Castle, and the Earl of Warwick, across the English Channel at Calais, to come to his aid. However, there is evidence that York was advised of Lancastrian preparations for war and the possibility of a trap in the Midlands much earlier. An Act of Attainder passed against the leading Yorkists later in the year claimed that York had planned another coup against the king; therefore, the duke may have changed his attitude to King Henry's right to rule at this time. He may also have been reviewing his own political position considering the queen's new pressures, causing him to pre-empt the possible Lancastrian move against him at Coventry.

However, on receiving word from the Duke of York, the two Neville earls prepared to march through gathering Lancastrian forces. Warwick, with men from the Calais garrison, narrowly missed Somerset's contingents and reached Ludlow unscathed. But Warwick's father, the Earl of Salisbury, was not so fortunate and was blocked by Lord Audley's army between Newcastle-under-Lyme and Market Drayton at Blore Heath. Here Salisbury ran into Lancastrian troops hoping to link up with the main armies of the king and queen nearby. Indeed, the Lancastrians had failed badly in concentrating their forces, considering that the king's army was within 10 miles of Blore Heath battlefield at the time of the action. Also, the situation was hindered by Lord Stanley, who, always the cautious player, sent only fair promises to join the royal army, echoes of a much later confrontation at Bosworth in 1485. At Blore Heath, Stanley failed to show, leaving Lord Audley to face the Yorkist forces alone.

The slope up which the Lancastrians charged the Yorkist battle line at Blore Heath. Lord Audley's Cross is situated part way up the ridge. (Author)

According to chronicles, when battle commenced, the Lancastrians had the edge in numbers. However, their resolve weakened when they failed to shake the Yorkists from their elevated position on the heath. Instead, they were soundly beaten after two cavalry charges and one infantry attack across a river and open terrain. Even though we have only meagre accounts of the battle from writers, it is said Salisbury secured one of his flanks with a wagon laager and succeeded in beating off the repeated Lancastrian assaults. However, when Audley was killed, unable to break the Yorkist line during yet another cavalry assault, one thing was certain – mounted knights were fast becoming redundant on the medieval battlefield.

As already stressed, the wars between York and Lancaster were not lucky in their chroniclers, so historiography is not as simple as we would like. The tactical aspects concerning the battle of Blore Heath typically illustrate the disparity of chronicled evidence, which is such a feature of the Wars of the Roses. The Towton storyline also shares this problem, as it too lacks concrete facts about the battle from the pens of early historians. William Gregory, writing some ten years after the battle of Blore Heath, and Jean de Waurin both had military experience; indeed, Gregory was a soldier in the wars, yet neither of their accounts of the battle can be trusted to the letter. The culmination of this frustrating lack of contemporary evidence is best summed up by the attitude of one author writing a history of England in that he would not include details of the battles of the period in his book because of the doubtfulness of available material.

Even though the Earl of Salisbury had driven Audley's force from the field, his own contingents were still in great danger because of the proximity of the main Lancastrian army. His retreat is reported to have been covered by a Friar Austin who 'shot guns all that night' to confuse the king's army.[20] Even though most of the Yorkists made good their escape, Salisbury's young sons were captured and imprisoned during the chase, highlighting the relentless pursuit of the unbloodied Lancastrian army and its firm resolve to rectify the embarrassing situation it had created. As for the Earl of Salisbury, he managed to cross the River Severn despite the king's forces and headed for Ludlow. Here, once united, the Yorkists despatched letters to the king explaining their actions, but by now, these petitions of innocence were becoming less believable and falling on hollow ground.

Among the professional soldiers that Warwick had brought to Ludlow from Calais, the Master Porter, Andrew Trollope of Durham, was, in my opinion, to become the most influential military brain in the Wars of the Roses up to the events at Towton. His later exploits and partnership with the new Duke of Somerset are somewhat of a legend in that eventually, as the duke's lieutenant, it is he who must be credited with changing the face of English warfare through tactical advantage and surprise during this period. His skill is something that his predecessors failed to grasp, being wholly preoccupied with the workings of chivalry, but chroniclers single out Trollope's cavalier exploits in the wars; therefore, they must have been highly unusual.

However, at Ludford Bridge, Trollope, then siding with the Yorkists, drew his troops up behind their defences of guns, carts and stakes in defiance of the king. And it was this act of defiance that forced Trollope into a difficult choice of loyalty, not to mention a dramatic decision that lost the Yorkists a crucial advantage in their struggle to keep their already fickle army in the field. In short, Trollope betrayed his Yorkist paymasters and joined the king.

A rumour spread in the Duke of York's camp that King Henry had issued pardons to all those who would not bear arms against him, and his forces arrayed for battle with banners displayed. Whether or not true, this hearsay certainly had the desired effect when Trollope, coming to England under the pretext that he would neither have to fight his sovereign nor commit treason, took his men and deserted to the Lancastrians during the night. What then became known as the rout of Ludford took place – an event that was to plague Trollope for the rest of his short life, branding him a traitor in Yorkist eyes and later placing a price on his head, dead or alive.

The result of his treachery weakened the Yorkist army considerably. The Duke of York was immediately forced to retreat. With his two sons, Edmund, Earl of Rutland, and Edward, Earl of March (later Edward IV), he fled the town via the quickest escape route into Wales. Warwick and Salisbury followed, breaking bridges down to slow the pursuing Lancastrians who were busy looting and pillaging Ludlow. The Duke of York took ship to Ireland, where he had served as a lieutenant in previous years, and he and his son Edmund resided here until September 1460 in enforced exile. Salisbury, Warwick and Edward fled to Calais, and subsequently all the Yorkists were attained by King Henry for their treasonable actions, their estates were confiscated, and their heirs disinherited.

The wheel of fortune had again turned against the Yorkists, it seemed. Their cause was in ruins. However, it was not the Duke of York but the three earls in Calais who now took centre stage in the unfolding drama. During the next few months, Warwick was to take the first steps on the road to what he considered his own political destiny and the grand title of 'Kingmaker', which history would later label him with.

Strategically, Calais, the Yorkist earls' refuge, was a crucial tactical position of strength in that the Lancastrians could not afford to ignore its commercial, political and military significance. The English had held the port and outlying districts for over a hundred years since Edward III's reign. Given its position at the crossroads of northern Europe for trade in wool, not to mention its proximity to France and Burgundy, the value of a permanently manned garrison of 2,000 men was an obvious boost to anyone who could pay and control them. The Yorkist occupation of Calais, therefore, threatened the Lancastrians not only commercially but also indirectly. An alliance with Burgundy, for

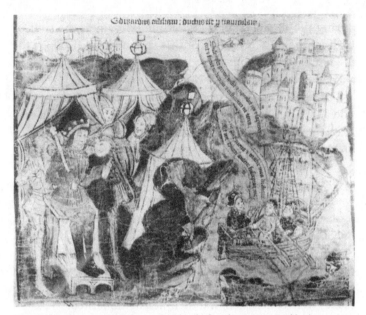

The Yorkists' escape to Calais and Ireland after the rout at Ludford.

instance, might prove disastrous for England. Thus, in response to this threat, the new Duke of Somerset, Henry Beaufort, was duly appointed Captain of Calais by King Henry and tasked with recapturing the port to remove the threat, which was growing stronger every day in favour of the Yorkist earls.

However, the Lancastrian preparations had not been good, and Somerset and his men were soon repulsed. They later resorted to a series of punitive actions against the Yorkists after securing the castle of Guines as a base for their operations. Meanwhile, the Earl of Warwick had also not been wholly on the defensive, and in January 1460, Sir John Dinham raided Sandwich, successfully attacking the town and thwarting another desperate attempt by the Lancastrians to recapture Calais. On the opposite side of the Channel, Somerset kept up his harassing tactics as best he could under the circumstances, but his hands were tied in so much as he could not afford to keep up the payments due to his men. Therefore, Warwick took full advantage of this lull in operations to sail for Ireland to confer with the Duke of York.

It is unknown what took place, or what was discussed, between duke and earl in the two months preceding Warwick's return to Calais. Of course, the obvious must have been stated, namely that an invasion of England must be attempted to reverse their attainders. But what was this to involve? We can only guess at what might have been contemplated to prevent such attainders from ever occurring again. Warwick may have even pushed for the Duke of York's eventual usurpation of the throne 'by his title of hereditary right',[21] purely out of his own lust for power at the expense of York's exposure to danger. However, by the end of their private conference, plans were laid for an invasion of England, and the Earl of Warwick set sail back to Calais to put this into practice.

In June 1460, the Yorkists embarked for England with a few thousand men, but not before their way had been paved by a well-executed propaganda campaign in Kent. A vital bridgehead had also been secured for them by the energetic Dinham, who this time captured Sandwich with the help of Sir John Wenlock and Warwick's uncle, Lord Fauconberg. Against all the odds and with the Papal Legate, Francesco Coppini, in their company to give weight to their enterprise, Canterbury was reached without opposition. Here Sir John Scott of Ashford and the notorious Kentish captain Robert Horne joined their ever-increasing numbers. Initially, the Lancastrians sent the two men to do precisely the opposite and prevent the Yorkists from reaching the town. Still, the recruiting drive towards London continued at pace, and Lord Cobham, the old ally of the Duke of York, was also welcomed into the fold as the main Yorkist objective came within striking distance.

King Henry, then at Coventry, received news of the Yorkist invasion, but not before the earls had entered London unopposed and bottled up the Tower garrison under Lords Scales and Hungerford. It seemed the Yorkists had gained the advantage for once. But it was apparent that the king, despite his lack of martial prowess, had wasted no time in marching south to counter the Yorkist threat; therefore, Warwick and Edward, Earl of March, moved against Henry before he could muster a widespread commission of array.

The success of the earls' invasion in 1460 gives more credence to planning and vigorous action rather than luck. Propaganda must be given credit for the means of invasion, and, as with some other more important strategic gains in the Wars of the Roses, disinformation alone gained the Yorkists footmen and support from the main counties of Kent, Surrey and Sussex, which allowed their invasion plans to succeed. However, a further element of cohesiveness must also be considered, in that a Yorkist *esprit de corps* had been created in Calais. With the help of the Earl of Warwick, the young Edward, Earl of March, had gained confidence in his own abilities free from the restrictions placed on him by his father. No doubt, Edward attracted great respect and also recognised the skill of his senior commanders who had led and carried out the successful invasion of England against the odds. Therefore, it is no accident that the same men would be chosen to lead some of Edward's contingents into battle at Towton the following year.

But not everything went well for the Yorkists. Before departing from London, the nobles had to reaffirm their earlier oaths to the clergy. They were forced to swear not to harm the king but instead free him from his enemies, and to this end, various bishops, including Coppini, who was turning more and more Yorkist every day, were sent with the army. All of this was brought about by the Yorkists' own earlier propaganda campaign to appeal to the people. The same people who were now accidentally being bombarded from the Tower by Lancastrian artillery firing on Yorkist positions left in command of the Earl of Salisbury. London too had become a battleground it seemed, and while this had a detrimental effect on the population, it turned the citizens against the king's men, while

Warwick, Edward and Lord Fauconberg marched out of the city in the guise of being its saviours.

After leaving his wife and son at Coventry, the king's army advanced to Northampton and fortified a camp just outside the town on the banks of the River Nene between it and Delapré Abbey. Here he endeavoured to muster more men to the royal banner, and, with the support of the Duke of Buckingham and Lords Grey, Beaumont and Egremont, he awaited the Yorkist challenge.

Edward IV in full armour, as depicted in the Rous Roll.

The battle of Northampton saw the last time in the Wars of the Roses when a major attempt to avert bloodshed was made through mediators and heralds. However, the failure of the lofty prelates of the realm, who tried to negotiate a settlement, including the Archbishop of Canterbury, not to mention the Pope's Legate, shows just how far the nobles were prepared to go in their quest for supremacy and control of the king. The battle of Northampton was also the first time that Warwick, March and Fauconberg, the battle commanders at Towton, saw joint action. However, it was not the abilities of the Yorkist leaders that were victorious this time, as again luck and, more crucially, treachery helped them win the field; and at the same time it brought to the Wars of the Roses commander a new fear to contain within his army.

Resolute and confident in their fortified position, the Lancastrians despatched a defiant message back to the Yorkists and took their positions behind a formidable array of guns. Lord Grey of Ruthin was given charge of the Lancastrian defences, and the Yorkists began their attack. However, the Lancastrian artillery, thought to have been operational, had succumbed to waterlogged conditions and would not fire. And this disaster allowed the Yorkist army time to scramble up the slippery embankments of the Lancastrian defensive earthwork and attempt to gain entry to the camp.

In what could have been a very bloody and costly assault by the Yorkists, the tide turned when Lord Grey and his men changed sides and, as one chronicler recorded, aided the struggling Yorkists over the redoubt. Once inside, with the help of Grey's treachery, the Lancastrian army crumbled. Buckingham, Beaumont and Egremont were killed defending the king near his tent, while the remaining Lancastrians were routed, many drowning as they tried to escape across the River Nene.[22]

It is highly likely a prearranged plan was executed at the battle of Northampton between Lord Grey and the Yorkists, possibly allied to feelings of genuine disloyalty. The evidence to support this is overwhelming, considering that a frontal assault on a strong position would have been, to say the least, foolhardy. At the ill-fated battle of Castillon in France, John Talbot was rendered almost unrecognisable by injuries when his English army attempted a similar assault against gun emplacements. In fact, his herald only identified him after the battle by the characteristic gap in his teeth.

With the battle now won, the king once more fell into Yorkist hands, and, on their triumphant return to London, Lord Scales and the defenders of the Tower surrendered. Some were executed on Warwick's orders, and consequently, when news of this reached Somerset and Trollope, still defiantly in possession of Guines near Calais, they also capitulated, handing the castle over to the Yorkists in return for their freedom.

All now awaited the return of the Duke of York from Ireland, but even the staunchest Yorkists were unprepared for the next act that Richard Plantagenet was about to spring on them so rashly. Certainly, Warwick was not pleased with the way York dived headlong into a very embarrassing scene in Westminster Palace on his return to London. John Whethamstede takes up the story:

And when he arrived there, he [York] advanced with determined step until he reached the royal throne, and there he laid his hand on the cushion or bolster, like a man about to take possession of his right, and he kept his hand there for a short time. At last, drawing it back, he turned his face towards the people, and standing still under the cloth of state, he looked attentively at the gazing assembly. And while he stood there, looking down at the people and awaiting their applause, Master Thomas Bouchier, the Archbishop of Canterbury, came up and, after a suitable greeting, asked him whether he wished to come and see the king. At this request, the duke seemed to be irritated and replied curtly in this way: 'I know of no person in this realm whom it does not behove to come to me and see my person, rather than that I should go and visit him.'[23]

In this vivid account, the Duke of York seems to have 'died' in the best traditions of the theatre. Nevertheless, there was no doubt that York was claiming the throne. He then put forward his title through his ancestor Lionel, Duke of Clarence, the second son of Edward III, as opposed to King Henry's right through Edward III's third son, John of Gaunt. But after being unable to get any response to this petition either, he stormed out of the assembly hall, burst the bolts of the king's private apartments in a fit of rage and resided there for some time, brooding over his dynastic failure.

A portrait of Anjou on a profile medallion by Pietro di Milano. (Geoff Wheeler)

Everyone was shocked, and the questions the Duke of York had raised were put before the Lords, who claimed that such a matter was beyond their learning. In turn, the problem was passed on to the judges, who were equally baffled, in that it was beyond the law to say who should, or should not, rule England. Eventually, however, a compromise was reached, and the so-called Act of Accord called for Henry's right to rule, as he was the anointed king, but after that, the Duke of York and his heirs were to succeed him. As one might expect, the Earl of

Warwick and his brother, the Bishop of Exeter, George Neville, were involved in the settlement. But it would not be surprising if there existed bad feelings between Warwick and York thereafter, possibly because the duke did not follow Warwick's plans as discussed during their meeting in Ireland. Certainly, there were angry words between them, which may have turned the Earl of Warwick to favour Edward, Earl of March, to fulfil his kingmaking ambitions, as Edward, being the Duke of York's eldest son, was now second in line to the throne.

The Lancastrians were equally vexed with York's dynastic advances, especially Queen Margaret. For example, where did the new arrangements leave her son, the Prince of Wales, now that the Yorkists were heirs to the throne? Unlike the king, who it seems agreed to the settlement, the queen was not prepared to let this indignity occur without a fight. And from her new base in Hull, she set about gathering a large army to crush the Duke of York once and for all, reinstate King Henry, and secure her son's inheritance.

The motivations of the two warring factions by the end of 1460 had reached fever pitch. None had gained the upper hand, but the king was even more under the thumb of those that controlled him. In assuming this authoritative role, the queen was, along with young Prince Edward, now more a focus of Lancastrian hopes and strength. The old Duke of Somerset's sword had been picked up at St Albans by his more militarily able son. And the Duke of York, probably lacking credibility and, now in his fifties, divested of some of his earlier gusto and sound judgement, had become a victim of his own impetuosity. York had done the unthinkable and imitated Henry Bolingbroke's usurpation of 1399, emerging from this theatrical blunder a bruised, unstable and bitter man. The war, because of these events, had also undergone a significant change. It had turned from a quarrel between two men who sought control of the king for financial and political reasons into a dynastic issue and a battle for the right to wear the crown itself. However, the very same war was now about to undergo a further metamorphosis and become, in some ways, a war between the north and south of England.

Queen Margaret's resolve to punish the Yorkists for their attacks on the crown and her son was unflinching. After conferring with her followers in Hull, she sailed to Scotland to consult Mary of Guelders and the young James III. The Scots promised Margaret arms and men on condition that Prince Edward would be married to one of James' sisters and that the important garrison town of Berwick-upon-Tweed would be handed over to them. However, despite Margaret's efforts to woo England's oldest enemy, harsh terms were suddenly replaced by unbelievably good news for the Lancastrians in the shape of a Yorkist disaster at Wakefield.

Two

'Yet it rotteth not, nor shall it perish'

In December 1460, Lancastrian movements in the north and Wales caused the Duke of York to assemble his forces to aid his Yorkshire tenants who were being harassed by the queen's troops. He despatched his eighteen-year-old son, Edward, Earl of March, to collect support from the western marches, and after gathering approximately 5,000 men and 'a great ordinance of guns and other stuffs of war'[1] from the Tower of London, York set off north with his younger son, Edmund, and the 'prudent' Earl of Salisbury.

York's first disaster was hitting bad weather, and because his artillery failed to cope with the rain and muddy roads, it had to be turned back. Then on reaching Worksop, the duke came upon the advance guard of his army cut to pieces by an unknown enemy, which prompted him to head for Sandal Castle near Wakefield, of which he was both lord and owner. It was here that he, and many of his followers, spent their last Christmas.

It is certain that this localised harassment was a ploy to lure York into mainly staunch Lancastrian territory. But the skirmish at Worksop may have been a pure chance encounter with forces commanded by the Duke of Somerset and the Earl of Devon, marching from the west to join the assembling army of the queen. Indeed, the array of Lancastrian peers gathered at Hull and later at Pontefract Castle in opposition to the Duke of York's meagre army was considerable, as it included the Dukes of Somerset and Exeter, the Earls of Devon and Northumberland, possibly the Earl of Wiltshire, and numerous other powerful northern lords such as Clifford, Roos, Neville, Dacre, and the instigator of the Ludford rout, Andrew Trollope. Their combined forces are said to have numbered 15,000 men, a vast army by the standards of the day.

It was now quite clear that the Duke of York was isolated and cut off from his allies. Without the help of Warwick, who was guarding London, and Edward, far away recruiting in Shrewsbury, the duke had all too easily walked into an untenable situation that, in the end, would force him to commit a series of military and logistical blunders in the face of the enemy.

The excavated remains of Sandal Castle, Wakefield, looking across the barbican towards the keep. (Author)

Trusting in the promise of a truce between the two armies that would last until after Epiphany, York received Lord Neville at Sandal Castle. *Davies' Chronicle* relates what could happen in the Wars of the Roses when commissions to recruit were granted to unscrupulous nobles:

> Then the Lord Neville, brother to the Earl of Westmorland [a Lancastrian branch of the family] under a false colour went to the said Duke of York, desiring a commission of him for to raise a people for to chastise the rebels of the country, and the duke it granted, deeming he had been true on his part. When he had his commission, [Neville] raised to the number of 8,000 men, and brought them to the lords of the country, that is to say, the Earl of Northumberland, Lord Clifford and the Duke of Somerset, that were adversaries and enemies to Duke Richard.[2]

Given the above evidence, it is reasonable to assume that, because Neville had double-crossed him, York was by this time an angry and desperate man. To make matters worse, the Christmas festivities had taken their toll on the food supplies available to his army at Sandal. To keep even a small force in the field during times of plenty was always a problem in the fifteenth century, and living off the land, especially in friendly territory, was not always considered the best policy as this was the only pool for levying recruits and support.

The Yorkists were certainly in a desperate position, and it was this lack of food supplies that forced them into a corner. They took advantage of the brief respite in military operations, in accordance with the truce, to try to rectify their situation. William Worcester gave the basic details, if not the correct date, when the Duke of York made the fatal decision that would eventually lead to the imminent disaster at Wakefield and his defeat in battle:

> On the 29th day of December at Wakefield, while the Duke of York's people were wandering about the district in search of victuals, a horrible battle was fought between the Duke of

Somerset, the Earl of Northumberland and Lord Neville with
a great army, and the other party, where there fell on the field
the Duke of York, Thomas Neville, son of the Earl of Salisbury,
Thomas Harrington and also many other knights and squires,
and 2,000 of the common people.[3]

The battle of Wakefield had been brought about by the Duke
of York failing to grasp the situation he and his followers were
in, that his enemies were no longer prepared to keep faith with
him, and that all through December 1460, he had continually
committed a cardinal military sin – the underestimation of the
enemy. Although the battle was over in a short time, due to
minute planning by the Lancastrians, its actual story can sadly
never be told because many chroniclers failed to understand
why the Duke of York left the protective walls of Sandal Castle to
encounter a vastly superior Lancastrian army in the fields below.
However, Andrew Trollope, now a staunch Lancastrian, seems
to have been the brains behind the lure and successful ambush
that followed. One reason suggested for the Duke of York's
rash action is that Trollope dressed 400 of his men in Warwick's
livery in the guise of reinforcements to lower the duke's guard.
This deception may be true, but would such a trick entice the
duke's whole force out of the castle to greet them? Therefore,
it is more probable that a Lancastrian army of equal strength
to the Yorkists presented itself before the castle the day after
the foraging party, mentioned by Worcester, had been attacked,
and blockaded York's supply line to Wakefield. No doubt this
would have forced the duke to act with as many men at his
disposal,[4] which is highlighted by Sir David Hall's cautionary
words before the engagement. The Tudor chronicler Edward
Hall, Sir David's grandson, gave his understanding of events:

The Duke of York with his people descended down the hill in
good order and array and was suffered to pass forward towards the
[Lancastrian] main battle, but when he was in the plain ground

between his castle and the town of Wakefield, he was environed on every side, like a fish in a net, or a deer in a buckstall, so that manfully fighting, he was within half an hour slain and dead.[5]

Here then is the cause for the Yorkist defeat: an ambush executed by two Lancastrian forces emerging suddenly from woods on either side of what was then Wakefield Green or 'Pugneys', while the main force was fully engaged and drawing the Yorkists away from the castle. A modern ploy, attributed to Andrew Trollope, carried off with precision by Lancastrians who were no longer prepared to keep faith with the Duke of York and the accepted codes of chivalry.

The site of the battle of Wakefield, taken from opposite the memorial commemorating where the Duke of York was slain. (Author)

If we are to believe what is said about where York fell during the battle (a small triangular piece of land marked by three ancient willow trees in hollow boggy ground, according to Daniel Defoe)[6] it seems probable that the duke was struck down almost immediately, as the main battlefield graves are to be found near Portobello House, close to the River Calder. Human remains, swords and bits of armour were unearthed here in 1825, placing the end of the battle and the rout some way from Sandal towards Wakefield.

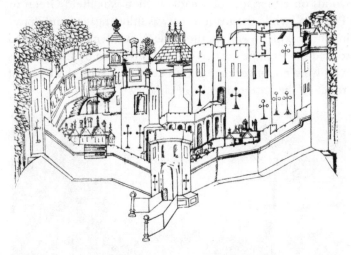

Sandal Castle from a drawing made *c.* 1562. (Geoff Wheeler)

Attempting to escape the massacre, many chose to flee to the town, including the Duke of York's seventeen-year-old son, Edmund, Earl of Rutland, who crossed Wakefield Bridge in panic, with Lord Clifford in hot pursuit. Clifford, whose father had been killed at St Albans in 1455, soon caught up with him, killing him in cold blood. Rutland was later pictured in some accounts as a small boy who was murdered as he tried to gain access to a house in the town 'a little above the barrs beyond the bridge'.[7] Clifford is also supposed to have stabbed Rutland in the presence of his tutor, which was probably Rutland's tutor in arms, shedding a different light on the whole episode. William Gregory described Rutland as 'one of the best-disposed lords in this land'[8] and consequently his judicial 'murder' by Clifford later stirred Yorkist avenging angels to perform similar acts of revenge in their turn.

However, even worse Lancastrian recriminations were to follow. And as the heralds and gravediggers got to work at Wakefield, the Yorkist prisoners taken after the battle brooded over their fate behind the infamous walls of Pontefract Castle. The Earl of Salisbury, who had been captured by a servant of Trollope, was to have been ransomed for his life, but it was said that the common people who bore him a grudge dragged him out of prison and cut off his head. His death was also said to have been the work of the Bastard of Exeter.[9]

A much romanticised version of the death of Edmund, Earl of Rutland, at the hands of Lord Clifford on Wakefield Bridge.

Other prisoners, including John Harrow, a Yorkist captain of foot, shared a similar fate at the block, and their bodies were all interred at the nearby priory. Salisbury, Rutland and the Duke of York's decapitated heads were removed to York where the Lancastrians spiked them on Micklegate Bar, York's head being adorned with a derisory paper crown mocking his regal aspirations.

The Duke of York's title and hereditary right, however, was not so easily severed, and, as he had once claimed when he returned from Ireland, his royal blood was perpetual and 'for though right for a time rest and be put to silence, yet it rotteth not, nor shall it perish'.[10] Edward, Earl of March, now Duke of York, was about to take his father's words and claim literally and exact a terrible revenge.

The Yorkist defeat at Wakefield left the Lancastrians drunk with success, even more so when Queen Margaret arrived with additional troops from the north, and now that the London road was open, final victory seemed to be only a matter of time and occasion. The superior tactical expertise shown at the battle of Wakefield and the resulting extermination of the Duke of York, members of his family, and some of the more valued Yorkist captains, gave the Lancastrians new hope amid almost continuous defeat in the field. Since 1455 the royal army had suffered no less than three major defeats, not to mention the battle for the control of Calais in 1460. Only the non-battle of Ludford can be credited to them. It, therefore, seems probable, because of this sudden turnaround at Wakefield, that the northern command now relied more on the professional talents of men like Andrew Trollope in military matters rather than divine intervention. Indeed Jean de Waurin, the Burgundian chronicler, rated Trollope's competence highly above other nobles. Therefore, it is equally likely that he masterminded the Lancastrian strike south in a midwinter campaign that would eventually sweep the Yorkists into panic, disarray and retreat.

With this intention in mind, a concerted plan of action was put into operation that involved the victorious northern army of the queen and another pro-Lancastrian force commanded by Jasper Tudor and the Earl of Wiltshire in the west. It is recorded that the Earl of Wiltshire landed in southern Wales with a force of Bretons, French and Irishmen, and united with Tudor in the hope of joining forces with the main Lancastrian army marching on London. The earl, however, is something of an elusive character, renowned especially for his feats of battlefield escapism and considering his disappearance from the battle of St Albans in a monk's habit, and other engagements, including Towton, it is certain Wiltshire was continually reviewing his own personal situation.

Meanwhile, at Shrewsbury, Edward, Earl of March, learned of the deaths of his father and brother at Wakefield. According to the Act of Accord, he was now the new Duke of York and heir to the throne. But this must have been secondary to Edward's feelings of revenge, and this is illustrated by his speedy advance north, towards the murderers of his family, and then west, to encounter the Welsh Lancastrians marching on Hereford. His castle at Wigmore was ideally placed to counter this threat as it protected one of the main routes into England and the marcher lands of his ancestors the Mortimers. Here he was able to gather contingents on his own ground, many of whom would fight for him later at Towton, and like his father before him, Edward was fully aware of his Plantagenet ancestors and how the crown had been stolen from them in 1399.

In retrospect, Edward, now Duke of York, was probably the ablest commander of his day. His later exploits show that his skill in timing, speed of recruiting and moving large armies great distances in adverse weather conditions were far in excess of his peers. He did not lack courage either, fighting all his battles on foot in the English manner and always at the head of his contingents urging his men on. However, like his counterparts, the Lancastrians, he recognised the abilities of

The Wars of the Roses, 1455–64. (Author)

the great captains in his army, using their knowledge to good effect, and rewarding them with annuities and titles when they pleased him. Many authors have belittled Edward's ability on the battlefield and, in contrast, highlighted the experience of such men as Warwick and the sixty-year-old campaigner Lord Fauconberg.[11] However, before and after the battle of Towton, Edward consistently demonstrated his prowess as a commander and copybook medieval warrior, unlike the Earl of Warwick, who was soon to fail miserably in a second battle at St Albans, and later at Barnet in 1471.

However, in 1461 Edward's army at Wigmore were nobles keen not to see their estates overrun by their enemies, and this must have been a daunting test of credibility for an eighteen-year-old to overcome. In the presence of doughty marcher lords like Sir William Herbert, Walter Devereux and Richard Croft, who were entrusting their lands and estates into Edward's care, the new Duke of York's limited military experience may have been questioned before the arrows started to fly near a little-known crossroads beside the River Lugg.

The Battle of Mortimers Cross

Various dates have been given for battles in the Wars of the Roses, and the 1st, 2nd and 3rd of February 1461 are all probable dates for the battle of Mortimers Cross. However, like so many other conflicts in the wars, the whole truth behind Edward's victory on the Welsh border is shrouded in legend due to conflicting and limited evidence. Indeed, Mortimers Cross is more famous for a natural weather phenomenon rather than the actual fighting. It is no wonder chroniclers were confused. William Worcester had this to say about the battle, although the strength of the Yorkist army is wildly exaggerated, and details of how Edward managed to gain victory are not given:

> On the vigil of the Purification of the Blessed Virgin [1 February 1461] a battle was fought near Wigmore at Mortimers Cross when the Earl of March advanced with 51,000 men against the Earl of Pembroke with 8,000, and from the field fled the Earl of Pembroke, the Earl of Wiltshire and many others.[12]

William Gregory recorded that 'Edward, Earl of March, the Duke of York's son and heir had a great victory at Mortimers Cross in Wales the 2nd day of February'[13] and Edward Hall, writing in the Tudor period, agreed with this date, the battle recorded as being fought on 'Candlemas Day in the morning'.[14] Other writers and chroniclers suggest 3 February, the feast day of St Blaise, although 2 February 1461 is more probable, not forgetting that the year was still 1460 as the new year in the fifteenth century began on 25 March.

King Edward IV from the Royal Windows in Canterbury Cathedral. (Geoff Wheeler)

Most historians say Edward's army met the Earl of Wiltshire and Pembroke's mixture of Welsh and Irish levies at the junction of four main routes on the banks of the River Lugg. Recent research by Glenn Foard and Tracey Partida places the battlefield further south of Mortimers Cross near an original intersection of roads that led through the marches. However, aside from the location, it must have been a cold, crisp morning with a weak wintry sun in the sky because as the two opposing forces approached each other a strange sight was witnessed in the east. William Gregory gave a brief description of this event in his chronicle, but Edward Hall expanded on the story he heard by saying that the Yorkists led by Edward:

> met with his enemies in a fair plain, near to Mortimers Cross, not far from Hereford East, on Candlemas Day in the morning, at which time the sun, as some write, appeared to the Earl of March like three suns which suddenly joined all together in one.[15]

Gregory recorded that 'over him [Edward] men saw three suns shining',[16] giving rise to a legend and heraldic symbolism. However, more important on the day was that the suns were allegedly changed by Edward's quick thinking from a portent of medieval doomsday into religious symbolism. In explaining the first recorded parhelion (ice crystals refracting in the atmosphere) as the Father, Son and Holy Ghost, who were conveniently on the Yorkist side, Edward raised the morale of his awestruck troops and attacked with a renewed sense of purpose.

Legend has it that, during the fighting, one Lancastrian 'battle' (division), thinking it had done enough, sat down while others engaged the enemy. However, the lie of the land may point to not so incredible an event if both armies could not deploy or bring all their forces to bear on such a narrow front. Indeed, the present battlefield monument, at Kingsland, some distance from the modern crossroads, marks the southern edge of a narrow strip of land, running between hills in the west and the River Lugg in the east. Therefore, it may be safe to assume that the fighting occurred somewhere in this restricted area, possibly with the river securing the flanks of both armies and the hills the other. Equally plausible is the assumption that, because the Yorkist army was more experienced, confident and larger than their opponents, the battle was over almost immediately and therefore deployments and manoeuvres may have been arbitrary.

Gregory graphically depicted what happened when the Lancastrians broke and were routed under increasing pressure from the Yorkists and what vengeance Edward dealt out to his enemies:

> And there he took and slew knights and squires and others to the number of 3,000. And in that conflict Owen Tudor was taken and brought to [Hereford] and he was beheaded at the marketplace, and his head was set on the highest pinnacle of the market cross, and a mad woman combed his hair, and washed away the blood off his face, and got candles, and set about him burning more than a hundred. This Owen Tudor was father to the Earl of Pembroke and had married Queen Katherine, mother to King Henry VI. He thought and trusted all along that he would not be beheaded until he saw the axe and block, and then he trusted on pardon and grace until the collar of his red velvet doublet was ripped off. Then he said 'That head shall lie on the stock that was want to lie on Queen Katherine's lap', and put his heart and mind wholly on God, and very meekly took his death.[17]

Other Lancastrian captains were also executed in the rout towards Hereford, and thus Edward decisively disposed of the first threat to his dynastic ambitions in ruthless fashion despite the escape of Pembroke and Wiltshire, undoubtedly his two main targets.

As for the parhelion (or sun dog), the aptly named 'Sun in Splendour' became central to Yorkist symbolism for years to come. Elements of this semi-religious event may have greatly encouraged Edward to become king, and his interpretation of the 'vision' later became central to Yorkist propaganda, not

The battle of Mortimers Cross and the vision of the three suns from the Genealogical Roll of the life of Edward IV.

to mention inspiring the suns and roses livery badges of his reign. God was on Edward's side, it seemed, and men like Sir Walter Devereux, Lord Fitzwalter and Sir William Hastings were later to become Edward's right-hand men because of their victory at Mortimers Cross. They had gone into battle with confidence, and this must have weighed heavily against the mixture of mercenaries and Welsh squires opposing them. However, the Yorkists had also won the battle due to the high calibre of their troops. Marcher lords were trained to defend the border, so were their men, and as for Edward, now Duke of York, the battle validated his bid to usurp the throne. It proved that the Lancastrians were the aggressors in the eyes of God. The west was secure, but Warwick in the east was yet to be tested.

Thirteen days after the battle of Wakefield, unruly contingents commanded by Lord Neville pillaged the Yorkshire town of Beverley, setting the tone for the Lancastrian advance south. The army's ferocious reputation ran before it, causing fear and panic up and down the country. Many of the northerners who plundered their way towards London were Scots, brought by Queen Margaret and allegedly promised that all lands south of the River Trent was fair game in lieu of wages. But by giving these soldiers a free hand, the queen had inadvertently set wheels in motion that she would later be unable to control, even though the plundering troops may have been in the minority. The Prior of Croyland Abbey was among the most fearful of the Lancastrian *chevauchée*[18] and wrote, almost reminiscent of Viking invasions, about defensive measures around his abbey:

The Northmen swept onwards like a whirlwind, and in their fury, attempted to over-run the whole of England. Also, at that time, paupers and beggars flocked forth in infinite numbers, just like so many mice rushing forth from their holes and abandoned themselves to plunder and rapine without regard to place or person. What do you suppose must have been our fears dwelling here in this island [Croyland Abbey] when everyday rumours of this sad nature were reaching our ears, and we were in the utmost dread that we should experience similar hardships to those which had been inflicted by them upon our neighbours? In the meantime, at each gate of the monastery, and in the village adjoining, both at the rivers as well as on dry land, watch was continually kept, and all the waters of the streams and weirs that surrounded the village, by means of which a passage might possibly be made, were rendered impassable by stakes and palisades of exceeding strength, so much so, that those within could on no account go forth without given leave first, nor yet could those without in any way effect an entrance. For really, we were in straits when word came to us that this army, so execrable and so abominable, had approached to within six miles of our boundaries. But blessed be God, who did not give us for a prey unto their teeth![19]

Croyland Abbey, along with many other religious houses, had much to protect in the way of wealth from the advancing Lancastrian 'whirlwind' from the north, so much so that some of the wealthier, well-connected prelates paid professional soldiers protection money. The Bishop of Ely, for instance, hired thirty-five Burgundian mercenaries to guard his cathedral when news reached him that the queen's army had already looted towns like Grantham, Stamford, Peterborough and Royston. Luton fell to the ravages next, and by 16 February, the defenders of Dunstable, captained by a local butcher, according to Gregory, were also beaten out of the town.

Taking all this unruly behaviour into account, we may safely assume that, by this time, the Lancastrian army was severely depleted. Most of the Scots may have deserted with their plunder, and the massive force that had driven south with such speed and confidence may by now have resembled the size of the army mustered before the battle of Wakefield.

The Second Battle of St Albans

The Earl of Warwick had by this time, at last, moved lethargically to the attack, but only after cautious defence measures had been put in place first. These measures were, in the end, to prove useless, chiefly because the Yorkist propaganda, which included scaremongering, backfired. In fact, fear of the northerners before they reached London made many wavering midland and southern lords join the Lancastrians instead of alienating them. In the face of a victorious, powerful and pillaging army, this was an easier option than defending land in the Wars of the Roses.

The Dunstable Swan. Part of the 'livery of swans' given by Edward, Prince of Wales, before the second battle of St Albans, and probably lost by one of the nobles on the Lancastrian side.

Eventually, however, the Duke of Norfolk, dragging King Henry with him, moved out of London on 12 February, linking up with Warwick on the outskirts of St Albans just before the Lancastrians attacked Dunstable. William Gregory, who was probably in the Yorkist army and therefore an eyewitness, recounted in his chronicle the confusion, not to mention indecisiveness, of Warwick's command when news was received of the Lancastrian approach to the town:

> The lords in King Henry's party [the Yorkists in this case] pitched a field and fortified it very strongly, and like unwise men broke their array and field and took another, and before they were prepared for battle the queen's party was at hand with them in the town of St Albans, and then everything was to seek and out of order, for the scouts came not back to

them to bring tidings how near the queen was, save one who came and said that she was nine miles away.[20]

It seems from the evidence above that Warwick, unsure of the Lancastrian line of march, had not received good intelligence from his scourers (scouts). Consequently, his battle array, most probably stretching like a dashed line from the Great Cross in the middle of St Albans over Barnet Heath and Nomansland Common, had to be hastily moved when news arrived of an attack up the Dunstable road. Equally annoying for Warwick's troops was that this necessary realignment involved moving the fortifications they had set up to redress the inequality between themselves and the Lancastrian force. It was a long-drawn-out manoeuvre, by all accounts. And Abbot Whethamstede, who probably watched the second battle of St Albans from his abbey tower, explains what happened when Lancastrian soldiers advanced up the hill towards the Great Eleanor Cross in the centre of the town under a hail of Yorkist arrows:

However, they [the Lancastrians] were compelled to turn back by a few archers who met them near the Great Cross, and to flee in disgrace to the west end of the town, where, entering by a lane which leads from that end northwards as far as St Peters Street, they had there a great fight with a certain small band of people of the king's army. Then, after not a few had been killed on both sides, going out onto the heath called Barnet Heath, lying near the north end of the town, they had a great battle with certain large forces, perhaps four or five thousand, of the vanguards of the king's army. The southern men, who were fiercer at the beginning, were broken quickly afterwards, and the more quickly because looking back, they saw no one coming up from the main body of the king's army or preparing to bring them help, whereupon they turned their backs on the northern men and fled. And the northern men seeing this pursued them very swiftly on horseback, and catching a good many of them, ran them through with their lances.[21]

Abbot John Whethamstede, who was probably an eyewitness to some of the action at the second battle of St Albans in 1461.

When the Lancastrians reached the Yorkist position on Barnet Heath, the 5,000-strong division, and especially their Burgundian gunners, were still in the process of turning to face their flank. Gregory, possibly involved in the main battle at Sandridge with Warwick, saw the defensive contraptions they had to move and realign into position and the confusion that resulted from the manoeuvre:

> And before the gunners and Burgundians could level their guns, they were busily fighting, and many a gun of war was provided that was of little avail or none at all, for the Burgundians had such instruments that would shoot both pellets of lead and arrows of an ell in length with six feathers, three in the

middle, and three at one end, with a very large head of iron at the other end, and wildfire, all together. In time of need, they could not shoot one of them, for the fire turned back on those who would shoot these three things. Also, they had nets made of great cords of four fathoms long and four feet wide, like a hedge, at every second knot there was a nail standing upright so that no man could pass over it without the likelihood of being hurt. Also, they had a pavise [a large wooden shield] borne as a door, made with a staff folding up and down to set the pavise where they liked, and loopholes with shooting windows to shoot out of. And when their shot was spent and finished, they cast the pavise before them, then no man might come over the pavise because of the nails that stood upright unless he wished to do himself a mischief. Also, they had a thing made like a lattice full of nails as the net was, but it could be moved as a man would, a man might squeeze it together so that the length would be more than two yards long, and if he wished, he might pull it wide, so that it would be four square. And that served to lie at gaps where horsemen could enter in, and many a caltrop. And as the real opinion of worthy men who will not dissemble or curry favour for any bias, they could not understand that all these devices did any good or harm, except on our side with King Henry. Therefore, they are much neglected, and men betook themselves to mallets of lead, bows, swords, glaives and axes.[22]

Gregory's graphic contempt for the innovative defences and temperamental handguns of Warwick's mercenaries is plain enough, yet if they had not been hastily realigned, the Lancastrians might have lost the battle, or alternatively found it very difficult to come to grips with their enemies. However, Gregory does not explain why the Yorkist mainward at Sandridge did not support their hard-pressed vaward at the crucial moment, which, according to Whethamstede, stood idle, watching the outcome of the battle. However, the

Yorkists were not the only ones with problems at St Albans, as Gregory's observations highlight that, on the Lancastrian side:

> The substance that got the field were household men and feed men. I ween there were not 5,000 men that fought in the queen's party, for the most part of the northern men fled away, and some were taken and spoiled out of their harness by the way as they fled. And some of them robbed ever as they went, a pitiful thing it is to hear it.[23]

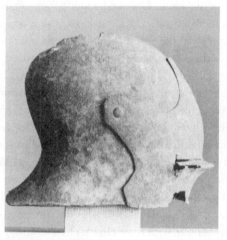

Sallet, *c.* 1460. (Royal Armouries)

So how did the Lancastrians, with such desertion problems of their own, break the Yorkist four-mile-long battle line at St Albans? From Gregory and Whethamstede's eyewitness accounts, and given the unique details of the battle, it is possible to explain why the Earl of Warwick failed if we consider three main factors. First, at least some of the queen's army was an already bloodied and confident force last engaged at Wakefield. Second, the Lancastrians were mainly northerners determined to rescue their king from captivity, and third, that speed of movement and lack of communication was chiefly responsible for turning Warwick's carefully prepared defensive position into a panic-stricken running mêlée.

Three separate attacks are mentioned, each Yorkist detachment receiving little or no information from scourers or messengers about where the enemy was at a given time. The first attack by the Lancastrians at the Great Cross probably caught the Yorkists by surprise. But then the indomitable Trollope sent a larger force to attempt to dislodge the Yorkist archers, thereby outflanking them farther up the street. Here the Lancastrians met with another Yorkist contingent, which was scattered after a 'great fight', which in turn made their archers' position at the Great Cross untenable.

After clearing the town, the Lancastrians approached the turning Yorkists on Barnet Heath, who initially offered stiff resistance. However, the battle-hardened veterans of the north broke them quickly due to the Yorkist mercenaries whose malfunctioning weapons and forced realignment caused Warwick to panic. One can only assume that 'the Kingmaker' commanding the mainward was some distance from the vaward when it was attacked, and that, by the time he reached Sandridge from his original position at Nomansland Common, the unfortunate Yorkists were already looking over their shoulders and on the verge of collapse.

Thinking it wise to save what troops he still had left, Warwick may have decided to quit the field facing overwhelming odds. With darkness falling, the chronicles recorded that he had little option. He abandoned his routed army to the mercy of Lancastrian cavalry, who quickly cut them up in a frenzied cull of revenge.

The queen's highly disciplined force of 'household men and feed men' containing the retainers of such well-known nobles as Somerset, Exeter, Northumberland, Devon and Shrewsbury, and many other fierce northern lords such as Clifford, Roos, Greystoke, Gascoigne and Welles, had proved their worth to the queen. They had defeated the less experienced Yorkists under Warwick who had suffered from bad intelligence in the face of an overwhelming enemy on too wide a front.

After the second battle of St Albans, Warwick attempted to blame his defeat on the treachery of a man called Lovelace, caught at Wakefield and given his life by the Lancastrians on the pretext of playing the traitor to the Yorkist cause. But the whole Lovelace story seems apocryphal, coming from the pen of Jean de Waurin, who, meeting with Warwick sometime after Towton, may have been fed lies by the Kingmaker to embellish his history. Also, if Warwick needed additional security for this kind of fabrication, most of the men who fought at St Albans, such as Norfolk and Fauconberg, were conveniently dead by this date, not to mention some of the lords instantly beheaded by the Lancastrians after the battle in the usual reprisals that now became commonplace in the Wars of the Roses.

When Warwick's forces capitulated, the queen saw to it that the young Prince of Wales judged and witnessed the executions of Lord Bonville, a mortal enemy of the Earl of Devon, and Sir Thomas Kyriell, a veteran of the French Wars. Lord Montague, Warwick's brother, was spared, but the queen was no doubt hoping to dissuade her son from assimilating the feeble nature of her husband despite him being just seven years old at the time.

When the king was eventually found, laughing and singing under a tree, Andrew Trollope, limping from a wound received from a Yorkist caltrop, was knighted for his services. Trollope is reputed to have nonchalantly exclaimed, 'my lord, I have not deserved it for I slew no more than fifteen men. I stood still in one place, and they came unto me, but they stayed with me.'[24] A fitting, if not cavalier-like, end to a battle that was won, in part, due to Trollope's tactical advice in combination with the Duke of Somerset's authority.

With the Earl of Warwick on the run and the road to London open at last, the sweet smell of success lifted Lancastrian spirits, even though reports were coming in daily that Edward, Duke

Richard, Earl of Warwick, from the Beauchamp Monument.

of York, was marching on the capital at the head of an army fresh from his victory in the west. Queen Margaret, noting this, wisely withdrew her main army to Dunstable, as by now the reputation of the 'northmen' was preceding all before it, and she sent a contingent of hand-picked knights to London's Aldgate, where they demanded admission in the king's name.

However, the mayor refused to open the gates, as the citizens 'living in mykel dread'[25] of the pillaging stories of Warwick's earlier propaganda campaign were in no mood to fall for such a trick, even though it was their king who craved admittance. Earlier, the commons had destroyed some carts carrying food and supplies to the Lancastrian army and had also risen against certain knights at Westminster on the queen's behalf. The fickle citizens reacted to the mayor's orders that everyone was to stay indoors under curfew. At length, the queen ordered the hard-pressed city to proclaim the Duke of York a traitor when news of his army and victory at Mortimers Cross became widespread.

With the queen's army on the verge of total desertion through lack of victuals and the mayor steadfast against the northern lords, the ambitions of the Lancastrian house sadly crumbled. If London had been taken by force of arms, the Wars of the Roses would have been a different story altogether. But the queen chose not to press the issue, possibly due to the dispersal of her Lancastrian contingents, and perhaps because to disband and reform her army afresh was a much better option than to conduct a battle and ultimately a siege with such an unruly and pillaging mob.

By the end of February 1461, the royal family and the remnants of their scattered forces were on their way back to Yorkshire. As they went homewards, they continued plundering the country – taking carts, horses and cattle so that, by all accounts, men of the shires had almost no beasts left to till their land. It is also reported that some towns ravaged by Queen Margaret's troops found it very difficult to recover from this midwinter foraging. However, it is difficult to assess whether the scale of the disaster was a product of Yorkist propaganda.

The war between north and south was to continue, but with a new slant in the form of a man who was prepared to usurp the English throne with the help of his followers. Unlike his late father, Richard, Duke of York, Edward was no longer prepared to keep faith with his enemies and the king. Now he saw the means, with Warwick's political prowess, if not his military ability, to assert his own formidable character on the

Londoners in the guise of a medieval saviour. The citizens were desperate for deliverance, and he would not disappoint them. He was not only about to bring his father's claims back to life using the precedent of 1327, but also to surpass them, fighting the fiercest and bloodiest battle in living memory.

Three

The Rose of Rouen

After the second battle of St Albans, the Earl of Warwick, and the remnants of his beaten army, immediately marched to link up with Edward, Duke of York, who had received news of the Lancastrian threat facing London because of the earl's defeat. William Worcester recorded where the two men met, who was present in the Yorkist army (the named lords all fighting at Towton) and how, with the political help of the Nevilles, Edward was acclaimed King of England and France:

When he heard this news, Edward, the new Duke of York, who was then near Gloucester, hastened towards London, and at Chipping Norton, in Oxfordshire, he met the Earl of Warwick. And then there were in the army of Duke Edward, Walter Devereux, William Herbert, John Wenlock, William Hastings and many others of the Welsh Marches, with 8,000 armed men. And they entered London with him, and Edward stayed at his home at Baynard's Castle. On the Sunday following [1 March], after midday, in the big field at Clerkenwell, the populace of the city congregated together with the army of the duke to the number of 3,000 or 4,000, whom the said reverend father George Neville, then Chancellor of England, ordered to stand in the field. And he caused to be proclaimed the title by which the said Edward could claim the crown of England and France, and at once all the people shouted that Edward was and should be king. I was there and heard this, and I went down with them at once into the city.[1]

It takes little imagination to visualise what happened in St John's Field when:

Unto the host was proclaimed certain articles and points that King Henry had offended in, whereupon it was demanded of the said people [in the presence of the army] whether the said Henry were worthy to reign as king any longer or no. Whereupon the people cried hugely and said 'Nay, Nay'. And after it was asked of them whether they would have the Earl of March for their king they cried with one voice 'Yea, Yea'.[2]

Stage managed by the chancellor and his brother Warwick this might have been, but in the eyes of the people of London, it was a blessing after everything they had endured over the past few weeks. However, Edward's position was still far from secure, chiefly because many English nobles were with the king and queen in the north. Also, even though London was prepared to acknowledge a new monarch, the threat of Lancastrian forces looming on the horizon could seriously undermine London's fears if Edward did not strike at once to eradicate it. To this end, Edward wasted no time in accepting the crown at Baynard's Castle. Worcester described the speed at which all this took place:

On 3 March, the Archbishop of Canterbury, the Bishops of Salisbury and Exeter, and John, Duke of Norfolk, Richard, Earl of Warwick, Lord Fitzwalter, William Herbert, Lord Ferrers of Chartley [then Sir Walter Devereux] and many others held a council at Baynard's Castle, where they agreed and decided that Edward, Duke of York should be King of England. And on 4 March, the Lord Edward, Duke of York, went publicly to Westminster with the lords and was received with a procession. After the declaration of his title, he took the crown and sceptre of St Edward and caused himself to be proclaimed Edward IV.[3]

Baynard's Castle in about 1649, where Edward, Duke of York, accepted the English throne. (Geoff Wheeler)

The new king began his reign on Wednesday, 4 March 1461. However, the enthronement ceremony was deferred until a later date, as, according to George Neville, more important things had to be put in order first. In fact, in true medieval fashion, some chronicles tell us that Edward wished to be judged worthy of the crown, by God himself, in battle. But it is more likely that, quite simply, the Yorkists did not want to waste any time, and instead decided to strike at the Lancastrians as soon as possible rather than keep nobles in London who might be better employed gathering recruits for the march north.

To this end, on the Saturday after the *Te Deum* was sung at Westminster Abbey, King Edward despatched Warwick northward 'with a great band of men', after already sending the Duke of Norfolk 'into his country [East Anglia] with all diligence to prepare for the war on the party of King Edward'.[4] Norfolk was sent to recruit troops on the first day after Edward was proclaimed king, a clear indication of the urgency placed on the forthcoming campaign, not to mention Edward's unabated thirst for revenge.

According to George Neville, Edward, Warwick, Norfolk, and Lord Fauconberg 'took different roads'[5] to their agreed meeting place in the north, suggesting that soon after Warwick and Norfolk left London on 11 March, Fauconberg, commanding the bulk of the Yorkist army, was next to leave the city. *Hearne's Fragment*, which describes some events in the Towton campaign, gives details of the Yorkist order of march:

> Whereas on the Wednesday next following the king's footmen assembled in a great number, of the which the most part were Welshmen and Kentish men. Then on the Friday ensuing, King Edward issued out of the city in goodly order at Bishopsgate, it then being the 12th day of March [13th according to George Neville] and held on his journey, following these others.[6]

The footmen assembled on Wednesday and captained by the veteran Lord Fauconberg were to become the vaward or front advance guard of the army. This division, usually containing the most men, was, in this case, a day's march ahead of the main body commanded by the king due to the long snaking supply columns that must have accompanied armies to war in the medieval period.

Estimates on the length of baggage trains and how vulnerable and unwieldy they were, is illustrated (in the extreme) by a Hungarian historian, G. Perjes. Using his calculations, based on large armies of the seventeenth century with provisions to last for a month, an army of 60,000 would require a wagon train of 11,000 carts, 22,000 drivers and helpers and 50,000 to

70,000 draught animals, all in a single file exodus calculated as stretching 198km, with the rear being behind the head of the column by eight days. Dividing this by six to approximate the 10,000[7] troops in Fauconberg's vaward (based on Worcester's calculations), we may surmise that the resulting 33km baggage train was a great burden on the march.[8]

A fifteenth-century army on the march. (From *Essenwein's Medieval Handbook*)

However, as John Gillingham points out in his military study of the Wars of the Roses, an army probably only had a few days' food supply to carry in far fewer wagons, with most being provided by paid victuallers travelling with the army. In some instances, men naturally resorted to pillaging, and it was inevitable that some soldiers committed war crimes when they scoured communities for food and supplies. By medieval standards, this was acceptable behaviour when on campaign in a foreign country. Still, this practice always proved a significant problem for army commanders at home as it could lead to the risky dispersal of foragers and troops scouring the countryside. As we have already seen, at the battle of Wakefield in 1460, foraging played a large part in the Duke of York's defeat. And in extreme cases, alienation and rejection, like that experienced by Queen Margaret's northerners in the winter of 1461, could spell utter disaster.

Therefore, it is apparent that towns and villages were essential staging posts to marching Wars of the Roses armies because they provided better billeting facilities for troops and supplied them with what they needed to continue their journey. This sudden appearance of an army, as one can imagine, was equally problematical for a town's citizens and officials when such a vast number of men and animals presented themselves at their gates. To ease this burden, it is recorded that King Edward secured immense loans to pay his men and buy food and supplies on the march north. Indeed, his troops were ordered to refrain from robbery, sacrilege and rape 'on pain of death', in great contrast, if not clever Yorkist propaganda, to counter the Lancastrian scorched earth policy a few weeks earlier.

Edward's own line of march took him through St Albans and Cambridge, with what appears to have been a north-westerly change of direction in response to the news, according to *Jean de Waurin's Chronicle*, that Henry VI was based at Nottingham. One would have thought that the direct road to the north through Newark would have been a more natural route for the Yorkists, but, according to the Burgundian chronicler, Edward's army reached Nottingham on 22 March and here received further reports that the Lancastrians had retreated into Yorkshire beyond the River Aire.[9] Judging by the earlier news that the enemy was near, it may be safe to assume that Edward IV linked up with the forces of the Earl of Warwick before he reached Yorkshire in anticipation of a Lancastrian army in the vicinity. However, the Duke of Norfolk's forces were still recruiting and were some distance behind them both at this time.

The Armies

The *Rose of Rouen*, a Yorkist political poem of the Wars of the Roses, alludes to which nobles, towns and shires fought for the Yorkists at the battle of Towton. Livery badges identify the nobles in the opening verses, but later in the rhyme, virtually every flourishing municipality that sent a contingent to Edward's aid is mentioned. 'The Rose' symbolism is used to describe Edward IV, who was born on 28 April 1442 at Rouen in France, and from the biased tone of the poem, we can be sure this personal analogy of a flower with thorns had a double meaning:

> For to save all England The Rose did his intent,
> With Calais and with London with Essex and with Kent,
> And all the south of England up to the water of Trent,
> And when he saw the time best The Rose from London went.
> Blessed be the time, that ever God spread that flower!
>
> The way into the north country The Rose full fast he sought,
> With him went The Ragged Staff [Earl of Warwick] that many men there brought,
> So did The White Lion [Duke of Norfolk] full worthily he wrought,

Almighty Jesus bless his soul, that their armies taught.
Blessed be the time, that ever God spread that flower!

The Fish Hook [Lord Fauconberg] came to the field in full
eager mood,
So did The Cornish Chough [Lord Scrope of Bolton] and
brought forth all her brood,
There was The Black Ragged Staff [Lord Grey of Ruthin] that
is both true and good,
The Bridled Horse [Sir William Herbert], The Water Bouget
[Viscount Bouchier] by The Horse [Earl of Arundel] stood.
Blessed be the time, that ever God spread that flower!

The Greyhound [Sir Walter Devereux], The Harts Head [Lord
Stanley] they quit them well that day,
So did The Harrow of Canterbury and Clinton [Lord Clinton]
with his Key,
The White Ship of Bristol he feared not the fray,
The Black Ram of Coventry he said not one nay,
Blessed be the time, that ever God spread that flower!

The Falcon and the Fetterlock [Edward IV as Duke of York]
was there that tide,
The Black Bull [Sir William Hastings] also himself would
not hide,
The Dolphin [Lord Audley] came from Wales, Three Corbies
[Sir Roger Corbie] by his side,
The proud Leopard of Salisbury gaped his eyes wide.
Blessed be the time, that ever God spread that flower!

The Wolf came from Worcester, full sore he thought to bite,
The Dragon came from Gloucester, he bent his tail to smite,
The Griffin came from Leicester, flying in as tight,
The George came from Nottingham, with spear for to fight,
Blessed be the time, that ever God spread that flower![10]

In addition to the nobles mentioned above, we must include such men as Sir John Wenlock, Sir John Dinham, Sir Walter Blount, John de la Pole, Sir Humphrey Stafford, Lord Grey of Wilton, Lord Saye and Sele, Lord Abergavenny, Lord Dudley, Lord Cobham, Sir Robert Ogle, Lord Fitzwalter, Lord Stourton, Sir Richard Croft, Sir Roger Tocotes, Sir Thomas Vaughan, Sir John Dunne, Sir John Say, Sir William Stanley, Sir James Strangeways, Sir John Scott, Robert Horne Esquire, John Stafford, Sir Thomas Montgomery, Sir John Howard, Sir Thomas Walgrave, Sir John Fogge, Sir Laurence Rainsford, Sir Robert Harcourt, Sir John Paston, and the rest of the Bouchier family, notably William and Humphrey.

Stained-glass window of Lord Wenlock at Luton. (Geoff Wheeler)

A significant proportion of these men received their advancements after Towton. However, before this, we may wonder what motivated such men to join one side or the other in Yorkist and Lancastrian armies. Political ties obviously played a large part in their choice of camps, but, because of this, their retainers and consequently the troops that their followers recruited rarely had this choice during the fifteenth century; in general terms, they were tightly bound by feudal ties some of which stretched back generations.

Along with their retinues, the nobles and knights formed the backbone of a typical Wars of the Roses army in an age when loyalty in the field was a matter of payment and allegiance. It was loyalty in this form that made or broke a battle line when, in some instances, as we have seen, treachery and double-dealing could be bought or sold without warning. But when battle was joined, commanders could do very little to alter the inevitable except lead their contingents by example and display personal feats of arms to encourage their troops. It was generally the calibre of their men that dictated whether they fought or ran, according to their status or their loyalty. However, this apparent loyalty did not deter some men from tempering this allegiance. In other words, working on both sides of the fence until a favourable turn of events presented itself, namely being on the winning side. The Stanley brothers were particularly adept in this area, as at the battle of Blore Heath and later at Bosworth Field, but it was a dangerous game which could be construed treasonous if luck was not with them.

Most knights, including the king, were trained in the use of arms from an early age by henchmen, and it was this training that, in the end, would be put to the test on the battlefield at the pinnacle of their careers. In fact, this act of violence in battle was longed for by the knight, it being the culmination of his life, through which he might be noted and receive rewards and advancement on the social and political scale.

Chivalry dictated that this was a noble's reason for being in a battle on the right side and, if he needed it, the justification for unlawfully killing his fellow Englishman when lawful killing was only condoned by the church against the king's enemies. However, to explain why the nobles took one side or the other in the wars, or neither in some cases, we must look at the methods of raising English armies in the fifteenth century, as part of the answer lies there.

To begin with, the strong king, in the eyes of his followers, was the epitome of the medieval knight of Arthurian legends and the great sagas, pious in his beliefs and strong in battle. He was also the rallying point for his subject's loyalty, greed and ambition. In 1341 Edward III reorganised the structure of medieval armies that left England to fight in France. He instituted a system of written indentured contracts between the crown and the prominent nobles of the land. These nobles would then subcontract with knights and men at arms who were their friends, tenants and neighbours and so on. Some of these captains were, even in 1461, 'of the war of France', meaning that they were experienced professional fighters who were valued leaders not only as veterans of other battles but also as military tacticians.

The above system of recruitment was called Livery and Maintenance, which also involved, by the time of the Wars of the Roses, a contract clause stating that, in return for a noble's protection, his retainer in gratitude had to take the field under his banner and wear his livery. Some of these adherents were paid, others served out of personal loyalty, but most soldiers were driven by greed. In short, there was no standing army to rely on in the Late Middle Ages. The Wars of the Roses were civil wars. Therefore, skill with weaponry was limited (apart from the warbow). In short, it was only the aristocrats whose lives were filled with professional violence, or the practice of it, while common soldiers were largely regarded as 'arrow fodder' and the scavengers of battlefields.

Men such as the veteran William Neville, Lord Fauconberg – aged sixty at the battle of Towton – were therefore regarded as indispensable assets to the army and, as such, Edward IV must have relied heavily on their knowledge. It also shows how important these men were when Englishman fought Englishman at home, in the fact that some veterans had already been systematically killed during the wars to deprive the other side of further help in military matters.

In the Hundred Years War, the system instigated by Edward III worked well under strong kingship, but when the English lands in France were overrun, and King Henry VI showed his inability to rule, disaster struck the system a heavy blow. England was at first infiltrated by disgruntled soldiers returning home from the war to find employment in the only trade they knew. They took the opportunities offered by Livery and Maintenance and sought employment, payment and protection with the great nobles, whose resulting private armies became powerful forces, extremely dangerous to the king and weakening his authority. The king's only defence in such a volatile situation was to gain as much military support from his nobles as possible through patronage and advancement, which sometimes bred discontent similar to the York and Somerset feud in the early days of the wars. As explained earlier, these divisions between the nobles counterbalanced the equilibrium of law and order in England and created the polarities that became a cause and such a feature of the wars when one noble received greater favouritism than the other.[11]

Thus, there was no clear-cut reason why each noble or knight chose York or Lancaster, as it was the more complicated question of retaining that caused one side to be favoured more than the other. In such a predicament, ancient land quarrels, such as those pursued by the Nevilles and the Percys, even turned local issues into miniature wars and forced both families onto opposing sides. Some nobles, however, chose not to obey the rules of Livery and Maintenance. The Paston Family, whose letters still survive, fought for the Duke of Norfolk as retainers, and in 1485 the duke summoned John Paston to do him service. As with every indenture, we can see his call to arms bears all the hallmarks of master and servant in an age when survival was a case of pressure or gangsterism:

> Wherefore I pray you that ye meet with me at Bury [St Edmunds], for, by the grace of God, I purpose to lie there upon Tuesday night, and that ye bring with you such a company of tall men as ye may goodly make at my cost and charge, besides that ye have promised the king; and I pray you ordain them jackets of my livery, and I shall content you at your meeting with me.[12]

However, in 1485, according to the evidence, it is unlikely that Paston complied with the order because, soon after Bosworth and the death of the Duke of Norfolk on the battlefield, Paston was appointed sheriff of the county. Here then, we have an instance of a knight not obeying his lord in a risk that might have turned out quite differently if Richard III had defeated Henry Tudor in battle and later sought Paston out to punish him.

Apart from these complicated and unsavoury methods of Livery and Maintenance that were used to recruit support, another 'official' way that a Wars of the Roses army raised men was to call out the militia and local shire levies under commissions of array. The *Rose of Rouen* gives details of which towns and counties sent contingents of troops to fight for Edward IV at the battle of Towton.

When the Earl of Warwick left London in early March for the north, he was given the authority by the king to raise levies from Northamptonshire, Warwickshire, Leicestershire, Staffordshire, Worcestershire, Gloucestershire, Shropshire, Nottinghamshire, Derbyshire and Yorkshire, thereby corroborating some of the details in the poem. These commissions gave Warwick, and other Yorkist captains, the power to recruit

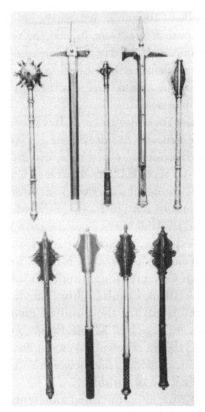

Contemporary weapons used by the nobles in hand-to-hand fighting. (Royal Armouries)

all men between the ages of sixteen and sixty years from the shires in defence of the realm. This raising of troops was Anglo-Saxon in origin and involved every man's promised allegiance to the king. Failure to respond in some instances and in times of great need meant forfeiture or death. In fact, such large armies were engaged at the battle of Towton because two kings (Henry VI and Edward IV) used their equal powers of array to supplement nobles' retinues. If we take a Lancastrian array, for instance, when the City of York sent a thousand men to 'the lamentable battle of Towton',[13] we may be able to understand just how large both armies were. Indeed, the Yorkist army was huge by the standards of the day, and it is recorded that Edward raised more men than any English king had ever put in the field before. The Lancastrian force was even greater aside from Yorkist tales of propaganda.

Men from the Yorkshire town of Beverley also fought at Towton on the Lancastrian side. Flagons of wine were given to the town's armed men as they rode towards the advancing Yorkists, state civic records.[14] The charters of Canterbury mention that their contingent under the banner of 'The Harrow' was also present. On 2 August 1461, Edward IV praises 'the faithfulness and laudable services of the citizens to the king, and the costs, expenses, labours, jeopardies, and hurts of our said mayor and citizens' given at the battle of Towton.[15]

Soldiers from Coventry fought on both sides under their standard of the 'Black Ram'. Eighty pounds was collected throughout the wards for the hundred men 'which went with our sovereign liege lord King Edward to the field in the north'.[16] And so the list of town and city militias goes on, with little or no political dividing line between York and Lancaster even in the same town or parish.

The City of York also contained adherents to both York and Lancaster. York is said to have been the centre of a strong party formed in the north under the Earl of Westmorland and Lords Dacre, Clifford, and Egremont. Here Henry VI and his queen, Margaret of Anjou, assembled their forces commanded by the Duke of Somerset, and the north and parts of Scotland responded dutifully to the royal call to arms. But the battle of Towton must have been an anxious time for many, especially the citizens of York, for no doubt many of their townsmen who fought on Palm Sunday must have wondered whose side they were on.

So, what did these ordinary Lancastrians feel when they lost a battle and were on the run? Collective fear obviously, exhaustion, shock, but also we can glimpse in certain documents the threat of social collapse. The Yorkists were hungry for revenge after the battle of Towton, there were orders of no quarter in the air, and this wider fear of local anarchy is chronicled in *York Civic Records*. Even several years after the battle, Towton was a memory the citizens remembered with sadness and fear:

> Many were slain and put in exile; the said King, Queen, and noble prince, their son, resident within the said city, where they to the utter jeopardy would have suffered them to have been during their pleasure; and then after the coming of King Edward into your said city, the inhabitants of the city for their truth unto their said sovereign lord, such as abode was robbed, spoiled, and ransomed, and the other so extremely impoverished that few of them was ever after of power to defend themself living in the said city, but utterly constrained to depart out of the same by reason whereof the two parties of the said city was within a few years after the said battle utterly prostrated, decayed and wasted.[17]

One thing is certain, during the Wars of the Roses, towns and cities did not remain immune to the dangers of national disorder or abject poverty. However, traditionally Wars of the Roses armies were much smaller than fought at Towton, at most about 5,000 to 10,000 men, sometimes a lot less, who resulted from a combination of the above recruitment methods.

Typical of shire and city levies of the era is the Bridport Muster Roll, which formed part of a commission of array in 1457, mustering in all over 12,000 men from southern England for Henry VI. The individuals listed for Bridport in Dorset provide a rare glimpse of our medieval ancestors' state of military readiness against the king's enemies – in this case, French raiding parties on the English coast.

Of armed men, by far the greatest proportion was equipped with the warbow, the most devastating weapon of the day.

Most of these men carried a sheaf (twenty-four) or part sheaf of cloth yard (30in) arrows and a buckler (a small round shield). Second only to the bow and arrow was a sword, buckler and dagger. Most men wore various styles of sallet and kettle helmets. Even an earlier type of helmet, a basinet, was owned by one man. Wealthier men were ordered to provide more weapons or armour to supplement the rest of the militia deficient in arms. Other kinds of weapons were also inspected at Bridport, such as various polearms, including glaives, spears, bills and the lethal two-handed knightly killing tool the poleaxe. Even a primitive handgun was noted. 'Harness', meaning the complement of a recruit's military equipment, also included full defensive plate armour. However, it is clear from the muster roll that bits and pieces of the full suit of armour, or *cap à pie*, had been acquired by the soldiers along the way, while on their travels, as family heirlooms or, more recently, on the battlefields of France. For example, in Bridport, leg harness, gauntlets, chain harness and the more popular padded 'jack' and brigandine of the period were all in use. A few pavises, similar to the ones used at the second battle of St Albans, were also recorded in the muster, and more were ordered to be made.

The traditional medieval shield was absent, in preference to the buckler, which is significant given that most soldiers would have required two hands to fight on the battlefield, such as draw a bow or wield a cut-and-thrust weapon. The knight or man at arms on foot, usually encased in armour plate, eventually rejected his trusty shield because of this, favouring the two-handed pole weapon and greater manoeuvrability in combat. The notion that a mid-fifteenth-century man in armour was an immobile automaton shuffling aimlessly around the battlefield is a well-worn untruth. A medieval manuscript of the period depicts a knight in full armour plate doing a cartwheel to illustrate the point.

The Bridport Muster of 1457 also questions how large Wars of the Roses armies were at the time. We can see that, on this occasion, the southern counties alone were able to raise 12,000 men between them in defence of the realm. What size of army was then available to the Yorkists and Lancastrians in 1461, when the whole of England, and parts of Wales, Scotland and the continent were involved?[18]

In summarising the different ways of raising troops in the fifteenth century, the hardest area to pinpoint, and thus wholly understand, is the role of mercenaries employed in both Yorkist and Lancastrian ranks during the wars. Whether Burgundian, French, Breton, Flemish or German, these soldiers of fortune were specialists with their chosen weapons, but they would only fight while the money lasted. As we have seen so far, ad hoc units of mercenaries had failed badly in some engagements. At Mortimers Cross, for example, various nationalities of men were present in the Lancastrian army, which in the end may have suffered defeat because of them. However, Warwick's gunners and Burgundians at the second battle of St Albans were unlucky, as flakes of snow may have caused their handguns to malfunction, some backfiring and killing their operators in the process. A contingent of Burgundians is also said to have been present at Towton, commanded by Seigneur de la Barde, who may have had the same problem due to adverse weather conditions rendering gunpowder weapons useless.

Later in the wars, Edward IV found his alliance with Burgundy highly advantageous at a crucial stage in his reign, in that the force with which he invaded England in 1471 contained as many as 300 Flemish hand gunners, almost a quarter of his entire force. Even later, French mercenaries were present in the army of Henry Tudor at the battle of Bosworth in 1485. But the most heroic last stand of mercenaries occurred in 1487 at the battle of Stoke, when German and Swiss contingents in the Earl of Lincoln's army, commanded by Martyn Schwartz, were destroyed to a man by Henry VII's forces in a vain attempt to put a Yorkist pretender on the throne.

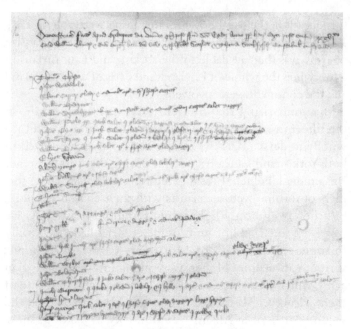

Part of the Bridport Muster Roll, 1457, recording the town militia and listing various weapons that were used in the Wars of the Roses.

Along with the addition of the standing Calais garrison and the other border strongholds, this gives the reader an idea of the kind of men who fought the Wars of the Roses. As discussed, the reasons behind why each man became part of one contingent or another varied according to their status, loyalties, the effect of medieval press-ganging or just downright greed or hatred for the opposition. However, the impact of certain recruitment methods on the common soldier is significant when assessing a medieval soldier's morale, and this was a contributing factor at the battle of Towton in 1461.

We know quite a lot about the aristocracy who fought in the Wars of the Roses, but who were the largely unknown soldiers caught up in the struggle between York and Lancaster?

Various contemporary sources provide glimpses of the kind of men that marched off to war during 1455–87, but it is evident most armies were far from united. Some contingents were contracted by feuding nobles and gentry; others fought as part of official commissions of array. Many tradespeople and artisans joined town or city militias, and a smaller proportion of soldiers were paid thugs, mercenaries or garrison troops, well versed in arms from other countries.

The depth of research into this subject is problematic, and the sources are minimal. However, the battle of Towton does provide the best glimpse of armies during this period when loyalty in the field was a matter of payment or allegiance. It was loyalty in this form that made or broke a battle line when, in some instances, treachery and double-dealing could be bought or sold without warning. Commanders could do very little to alter the inevitable once battle was joined except lead their contingents by example or personal prowess. Therefore, contrary to modern popular opinion, those men in the lower echelons of medieval feudal society dictated the outcome of battles, even if their captains were well-versed in warfare.

Much like other wars in other eras, including the present day, it is not just a commander who influences his soldiers' feelings and reactions at the maximum point of danger. A more direct effect on a soldier is his questioning why he is there in the first place, what peer pressure he is subjected to, and who fights beside him. It is these factors that encourage a man to fight or flee when the tide of battle turns. Local kinship was the heart and soul of Wars of the Roses armies. And if we must make a comparison about medieval battlefield cohesion, perhaps we need to look no further than the parochial recruitment practices and fighting abilities of the long-suffering 'Pals' regiments of the First World War.

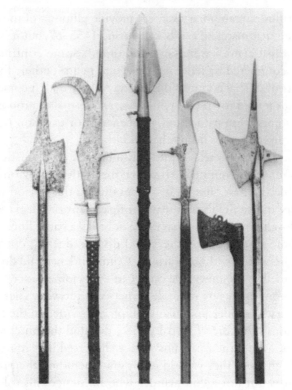

Contemporary weapons including bills and polearms used by the rank and file in the fifteenth century. (Royal Armouries)

The March North

When Edward united with the armies of Warwick and Fauconberg on the road to York, he learned that Warwick the Kingmaker had already disposed of his own father's killer while recruiting in Coventry. Warwick arrested the Bastard of Exeter there and promptly had him executed for the death of the Earl of Salisbury after the battle of Wakefield, which may have greatly encouraged the town's burgesses to supply him with eighty militiamen, promising that forty more would follow.

John Benet's Chronicle tells us that Warwick marched to Lichfield with his recruits and then Doncaster to link up with King Edward, who Benet says had advanced through Newark (which, as stated earlier, is a more reasonable assumption if we must make a judgement on Edward's route north).

At a Yorkist council of war, still deficient of one prominent captain, John Mowbray, Duke of Norfolk, it was decided to advance without further delay into 'enemy' territory, where Edward may, in theory at least, still have been able to recruit more support (although this is doubtful considering the massive Lancastrian presence in the area). However, Edward's scouts had been thorough in their intelligence. The north was massing another large force in the name of King Henry, and Edward marched on to Pontefract Castle, knowing the next formidable river behind which the Lancastrian strength might gather was the Aire. Using Pontefract's great fortification as a base, Edward may have chosen to wait for the Duke of Norfolk's contingents here because the greatest concern in Yorkist minds at this time must have been his lateness. Possibly even his loyalty was questioned too, not to mention that he was terminally ill. What price the Yorkist cause before a major encounter with the Lancastrians if Norfolk died on the march? And could the Yorkists compete with the royal army if he failed to show?

It was a dilemma that must have haunted Edward as his army marched deeper into Lancastrian held territory and winter closed in. However, according to tradition, the Yorkists reached Pontefract sometime on 27 March 1461 and made camp on a triangular piece of land below the castle on the Knottingley road known as Bubwith Heath. This tract of land is still visible and was situated behind what was Bubwith House. Relics of the period are said to have been found there during the last century, although what was unearthed is not documented. As for Edward, Warwick and Fauconberg, Pontefract's high keep was an ideal vantage point for viewing the surrounding countryside. The crossing over the Aire at Ferrybridge could be seen from its battlements, and Edward's first act must have been to view this, place a substantial guard there, then visit the priory below the castle walls where his father and brother's headless corpses had been buried after the battle of Wakefield.

Unfortunately, we have no contemporary accounts of Lancastrian movements at this time other than plans had been put in place to harass the Yorkist advance. No documents survive like the *Rose of Rouen*, other than those mentioned earlier, nor indeed do Henry VI's commissions of array, except for the City of York, Beverley and some isolated townships, which detail Lancastrian recruiting drives in 1461. However, we know that the Lancastrian headquarters was in York or its immediate area, as might have been expected, and that men must have been flocking to the king's standard since the second battle of St Albans on 17 February. The Lancastrians, however, would not have kept such a large army standing for all that time, and promised allegiance would have been the order of the day up to the time when news came in that the enemy was near.

Thankfully, as an alternative means of assessing King Henry's chief captains at Towton, we have Edward IV's Act of Attainder on the then defeated Lancastrian host, dated in the first year of the king's reign, 1461 (see Appendix 1). The attainder gives the names of those who lost their lives on Palm Sunday and includes the Duke of Somerset and others who were still on the run after the battle. The main protagonists for the king were the Dukes of Somerset and Exeter, the Earls of Devon and Northumberland, Viscount William Beaumont, Lord Roos, Lord Clifford, Lord Welles, Lord Neville, Lord Willoughby, Sir Thomas Grey, Lord Rugemond-Grey, Lord Dacre, Sir Humphrey Dacre, Sir Philip Wentworth, Sir John Fortescue, Sir William Tailboys, Sir Edmund Moundford, Sir Thomas Tresham, Sir William Vaux, Sir Edward Hampden, Sir Thomas Fyndern, Sir John Courtenay, Sir Henry Lewes,

Sir Nicholas Latimer, Sir John Heron, Sir Richard Tunstall, Sir Henry Bellingham, Sir Robert Whitingham, Sir John Butler, Sir William Mille, Sir Simon Hammes, Sir William Holland, Sir Thomas Butler and Sir Thomas Everingham. We may also assume from other evidence that the Earl of Wiltshire, Lord Scales (later made Earl Rivers by Edward IV), Lord Hungerford, Lord Mauley, Sir Ralph Grey, Sir Robert Hildyard, Sir William Plumpton, Sir Nicholas Harvey, Sir William Gascoigne, Sir Andrew Trollope and his brother David Trollope were also present on the field. In some cases, such as that of Sir William Gascoigne, there is no evidence of his fighting on the day. However, in Gascoigne's case, this point is debatable, given that most of the Lancastrian strength was gathered and that the Earl of Northumberland had only just knighted him after the battle of Wakefield. He was also present at the second battle of St Albans, and it is entirely likely that Gascoigne perished at Towton in the service of his master the earl (see Appendix 4).

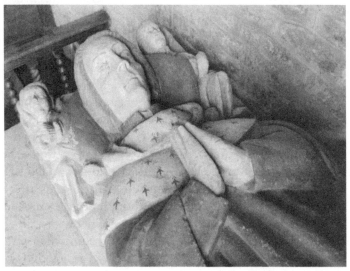

The tomb of Sir John Fortescue, who was attainted after Towton. (Geoff Wheeler)

A surviving letter from King Henry VI to Sir William Plumpton, dated 13 March 1461, attests to this Yorkshire knight's presence at Towton at the cost of the life of his eldest son (see Appendix 2). The presence of other nobles, like the Earl of Wiltshire, can be confirmed due to their later captures, executions and subsequent attainders. It is at least safe to assume that anyone who had Lancastrian sympathies and personal scores to settle with the Yorkists was at Towton on Palm Sunday 1461.

The Lancastrian force mainly comprised northerners, but, judging by the nobles and the lesser-known squires listed in the Yorkist bill of attainder, men from all over the country were present in King Henry's army, including soldiers brought by the Earl of Devon from his own county and Dorset, men from Nottingham, some from London, and others from Calais, France and Scotland. In fact, if Edward did arrive at Nottingham during his march north, it may have been apparent that Lancastrian commissioners had deprived the Yorkists of some, if not all, of the town's expected recruits. This makes the point that authority through commissions of array was by this time a lottery, and the Lancastrians were lucky insomuch as the north was fully united to King Henry's cause.

As stated earlier, the City of York was no doubt the Lancastrian main muster point in Yorkshire. However, soon the royal army, commanded by the Duke of Somerset, marched south-west, leaving the king – more at home with a bible than a poleaxe – the queen and the young Prince of Wales safe in the city. As might be appreciated, Henry VI had been wounded once and captured twice by the Yorkists in the wars and this may have prompted a decision not to jeopardise his safety again. Queen Margaret and the Lancastrian high command may have thought Edward would show no mercy this time? Either way, having the King of England leading men into battle was a great morale boost in the medieval period, and we may assume the same was expected in the Wars of the Roses.

The king's father, Henry V, had fought at Agincourt, therefore his son's absence at Towton may have affected the Lancastrians in more ways than one. It was certainly a concern, in that each soldier must have looked to their immediate superior for orders, example and support in the forthcoming battle rather than the absent king, who was becoming more of a figurehead by this time.

Micklegate Bar, York, where both Yorkist and Lancastrian heads lined the battlements before and after the battle of Towton. (Author)

However, we can visualise that, as the Lancastrian dukes and lords strutted out of York beneath Micklegate Bar to fight for their king, their morale must have been high if not over-confident, both in their numbers and their purpose. The late Duke of York's decomposing head still spiked above them after the battle of Wakefield likely added to their confidence in that it was they, the nobles, and not the king, who had placed it there so decisively in December 1460. To support this, Lancastrian accounts suggest that the queen had ordered that room be left in this grisly company of trophies rotting on Micklegate so that Edward and Warwick's heads might join them in time to come. Stories such as these were intended to promote morale in the army, making it apparent that the Lancastrians were fighting on the right side, that Henry VI was the anointed king, and that the Yorkist usurper was not fit to wear his crown.

As the two armies marched towards each other, it must have been apparent that each side was fighting for a cause. But of greater concern to the soldiers must have been more basic feelings of survival. William Gregory, the soldier who had witnessed medieval army life, gave an account of his open contempt for the horsemen in the army and the race for supplies of food before the second battle of St Albans:

> As for spearmen, they are only good to ride before the footmen and eat and drink up their victuals, and many more such pretty things they do. You must hold me excused for these expressions, but I say the best, for in the footmen is all the trust.[19]

Some of these footmen may have been worried about payment for their services when much depended on money owed at the end of their contract. Issues such as how long they were to serve, how far they were to march, what would happen to their dependents while they were away and, ultimately, whether they would live or die, must have been fears visualised by veterans and raw recruits alike. Therefore, because of these fears, their commanders' thoughts were firmly fixed on seeking a battle before these men, with their fickle ways, deserted when their forty days service, or thereabouts, expired.

With this point in mind, the Lancastrians advanced to Tadcaster from York sometime prior to the 27 March. Certainly, by this date, they had crossed the bridge over the River Wharfe, which, according to George Neville, was broken down in the process.[20] Then, the army took the London road over the River Cock to Towton, where they camped for the night. Wading over this natural obstacle, which some authorities say was in full flood, the Lancastrians gained the high ground immediately above and around the village of Towton. Most likely, a watch was placed on the edge of the high plateau overlooking Saxton village and the road from Ferrybridge, and at some point, Lord Clifford was sent out with his retainers (The Flower of Craven) to report on Yorkist movements further afield.

It is certain that the ridge between Towton and Saxton was the Lancastrians chosen place to fight. It is difficult to argue otherwise, as the tract of land that became the battlefield on Palm Sunday offered distinct advantages, as it was, and is today, the highest point between Pontefract and York.

Four

'Let him fly that will, I will tarry with him that will tarry with me'

With these words, the Earl of Warwick supposedly killed his horse with his sword, thereby claiming he would share the fate of the common soldier on foot, rather than having the benefit of fleeing if faced with defeat. Warwick's theatrical gesture comes from the pen of Edward Hall, crediting the Kingmaker with averting a major disaster in the Yorkist ranks immediately before or, depending on which source you read, after, the little-known battle of Ferrybridge.[1]

Ferrybridge (or *Feurbirga* according to George Neville) was a major strategic crossing point over the River Aire that the Yorkists and Lancastrians could not fail to ignore. However, the battle fought there was somewhat of a dilemma for writers because most failed to appreciate the local geography or the sequence of events so far north. In fact, some far-removed contemporaries could not differentiate between the two battles of Ferrybridge and Towton, unaware even that they must have occurred on consecutive days given the logistics involved in moving large armies and supplies over rivers and medieval roads in winter. The outcome of this confusion is that the more prominent and thus more bloody battle of Towton has overshadowed the 'skirmish' at Ferrybridge, an oversight that I hope to remedy here using the available sources and local knowledge.

In discussing the facts first, we learn that no sooner had the Yorkists reached Pontefract Castle than Edward despatched a small force under the command of John Radcliffe, Lord Fitzwalter, to hold the crossing over the River Aire. George Neville, in his letter to Coppini, the pro-Yorkist Papal Legate, wrote:

> And at length on Palm Sunday, near a town called *Feurbirga*, about sixteen miles from York, our enemies were routed and broken to pieces. Our adversaries had broken the bridge, which was our way across, and were strongly posted on the other side so that our men could only cross by a narrow way which they had made themselves after the bridge was broken. But our men forced a way by the sword, and many were slain on both sides.[2]

William Gregory recorded that the battle took place on 28 March 'Palm Sunday eve' and that 'Lord Fitzwalter was killed at Ferrybridge, and many with him were slain and drowned. The Earl of Warwick was 'hurt in the leg with an arrow'[3] we are told, and in *Hearne's Fragment* the chronicler states that it was Edward's 'foreprickers' (scouts) who were attacked at Ferrybridge, resulting in 'a great skirmish' in which Fitzwalter was slain.[4] However, George Neville's confusing dates and Gregory's 'Palm Sunday eve' place doubt and an almost end-of-the-day stamp on events. Therefore, more evidence is needed to place the battle more precisely in time.

As previously stated, the Yorkists arrived at Pontefract Castle on 27 March, and obviously, given the size of the Yorkist army, it needed time to reach Saxton enabling the Yorkists to fight on the 29th. From the evidence above, it seems that the Lancastrians destroyed the bridge at Ferrybridge on or before the 27th, so we may assume the battle there occurred on 28 March 1461.

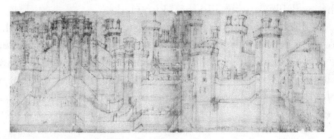

Pontefract Castle, the Yorkist headquarters before the battle of Ferrybridge, from a drawing made in the mid-sixteenth century.

According to Gregory, the Yorkists, discovering this delaying tactic, sent their 'foreprickers' out to rebuild a temporary crossing, as the road from Pontefract to Sherburn-in-Elmet and Tadcaster was the more direct line of march for Edward's army to York. Fitzwalter, according to the evidence, commanded this force, which promptly set to work either to build a pontoon across the river or, more likely, to straddle the destroyed bridge with planks of wood so the Yorkists could cross the next day. This reconstruction was 'the narrow way' that, according to George Neville, the Yorkists made themselves after the bridge was broken.

Edward Hall, writing some seventy years later, gives a unique though uncorroborated account of what happened to Fitzwalter's men once they had rebuilt this makeshift bridge over the Aire. He also makes an interesting comparison between two of the young Lancastrian nobles, which later may have been the reason behind a more baffling event:

Let no man think or yet imagine, that either the council of King Henry, or his vigilant queen, either neglected nor forgot to know or search what their enemies did, but that they prepared to their power all the men they either could persuade

or allure to their purpose to take their part. And thus, thinking themselves furnished, committed the governance of the
army to the Duke of Somerset, the Earl of Northumberland
and the Lord Clifford, as men desiring to revenge the death of
their fathers slain at the first battle of St Albans. These noble
captains, leaving King Henry, his wife and son for their safe-
guard in the City of York, passed the River Wharfe, with all
their power, intending to prohibit King Edward to pass over
the River Aire, and for the more expedition and exploit of
their purpose, after many comparisons were made between
the Earl of Northumberland and the Lord Clifford, both
being lusty in youth and of frank courage, the Lord Clifford
determined with his light horsemen, to make an assault on
those that kept the passage of Ferrybridge, and so departed
from the great army on the Saturday before Palm Sunday, and
early before his enemies were awake, got the bridge, and slew
the keepers of the same, and all such as would withstand him.
The Lord Fitzwalter, hearing the noise, suddenly rose out of
his bed, and unarmed, with a poleaxe in his hand, thinking
that it had been an affray amongst his men, came down to
appease the same, but before he could say a word, or knew
what the matter was, he was slain, and with him the Bastard
of Salisbury, brother to the Earl of Warwick, a valiant young
gentleman, and of great audacity.[5]

Lords Clifford, Northumberland and Somerset had much to
prove in the Towton campaign. As previously discussed, all
their fathers had been systematically executed when the Duke
of York's forces assaulted St Albans in 1455. Clifford, however,
was probably the most malicious of the Lancastrian vengeful
angels. He is reputed to have vowed, as some other nobles had,
to kill all the Duke of York's family for murdering his father,
and to this end, he commanded an elite body of armed men
(his personal retainers), some who also had scores to settle
with the House of York. These men were called The Flower

of Craven, and were mainly recruited from a district where border war was part of everyday life and chivalry was set aside.

On 28 March, Lord Clifford's force of cavalry, possibly five hundred spears, surprised and captured Ferrybridge and killed its keepers in an early morning raid on a Yorkist force that had not taken adequate precautions against attack. The overall Lancastrian plan seems to have been, first, to weaken the Yorkists by forcing them into a battle over an extremely difficult and defensible obstacle, and second, to let them come up against the main Lancastrian army at Towton in a further battle that would put the already bloodied and exhausted Yorkists at a grave supply, as well as numerical, disadvantage.

This sound tactical plan worked well in part, but not before the expected encounter across the River Aire, in which many were killed on both sides. When Warwick received news that the bridge had been captured and Fitzwalter slain, he was, by all accounts, fearful of the consequences. According to Edward Hall:

When the Earl of Warwick was informed of this feat [Clifford's attack], he like a man desperate, mounted on his hackney and came blowing to King Edward saying, 'Sir I pray God have mercy on their souls, which at the beginning of your enterprise hath lost their lives, and because I see no success of the world, I remit the vengeance and punishment to God our creator and redeemer', and with that he alighted down and slew his horse with his sword, saying, 'Let him fly that will, for surely I will tarry with him that will tarry with me,' and he kissed the cross hilt of his sword.[6]

According to this last statement, Warwick must have been thinking that the whole Yorkist army would flee at any moment. However, the truth is that we must either regard the above incident as a typical, but clever, Warwick ploy to try to restore his credibility, lately damaged at the second battle of St Albans; or alternatively, agree that the whole story is a figment of Edward Hall's vivid imagination. The fact is that the Yorkists immediately advanced towards the bridge to dispute it, and, according to George Neville, a 'great fight' ensued.

Site of the battle of Ferrybridge taken from Brotherton Marsh on the north bank of the River Aire. (Author)

Jean de Waurin, in his *Recueil des Chroniques d'Engleterre*, fails to mention Fitzwalter's name in association with the Ferrybridge action, but he wrote an interesting unconfirmed military viewpoint of the battle, although the nobles mentioned, plus some dates, distances and timings, are suspect. According to Waurin, after receiving the news at Nottingham that Ferrybridge had been occupied by the Duke of Somerset and Earl Rivers (then Lord Scales) on 27 March, King Edward advanced to within 2 miles of the enemy:

> And as soon as they had made camp, the Duke of Suffolk [John de la Pole] sent a small company to find out the strength of the enemy, but they went so far forward that a guard saw them and

raised the alarm. The small party was in so much danger of being routed that the Earl of March had to send reinforcements for his reconnaissance troops. They managed to push the enemy back to the bridge, where they formed a defensive line. When the Earl of March heard about this, he ordered all his council and troops to move closer to the enemy, and after he had made a new camp, he went to see the situation with his commanders. After studying the position of his enemies, the courageous and pious Earl of March declared it was necessary to gain the passage rapidly as they would not be able to press their advantage further otherwise. Therefore, the order was given to attack the bridge which the enemy had fortified, and it so happened the battle lasted from midday to six o'clock in the evening and there died more than 3,000 men on both sides.[7]

The last historical evidence we need to examine before we make any assumptions about the battle over the River Aire is the crucial factor in *Edward Hall's Chronicle* regarding the reason for Lord Clifford's hasty withdrawal from Ferrybridge. This action, which effectively cleared the Lancastrians from their position, was attributed to a flanking attack by the Yorkists commanded by Edward's veteran commander Lord Fauconberg.

After Warwick had allegedly killed his horse before the Yorkist army, Hall says King Edward bolstered morale with words of encouragement. In a speech to his troops, he gave his men leave to depart but promised that great rewards would be bestowed on those who stayed. He also added a further incentive that soldiers would be paid double wages for killing deserters:

> After this proclamation ended, the Lord Fauconberg, Sir Walter Blount and Robert Horne with the foreward, passed the river at Castleford three miles from Ferrybridge, intending to have environed and enclosed Lord Clifford and his company, but they [The Flower of Craven] being thereof advertised, departed in great haste towards King Henry's army.[8]

Ralph Neville and his children, including Lord Fauconberg, from the *Neville Book of Hours*.

Therefore, the Tudor chronicler reveals it was a Fauconberg flank march, and not the killing of horses or the courage of King Edward, that caused Clifford and his men to panic and flee from the bridge. Proof, if any proof is needed, that the

Yorkists used up massive resources and incurred many casualties trying to take it.

But what is the truth behind the heroic speeches and symbolic horse killing on that bitterly cold March day over the icy waters of the River Aire? Chronicles say very little. But if we take away the inconsistencies of time, dates, names and chivalric deeds and instead apply other historical local evidence, we can see the battle of Ferrybridge in a new light. In fact, we may conclude that Clifford and his men almost succeeded in destroying the Yorkist will to combat even before it had chance to advance to Towton.

Our first piece of factual evidence is solid. If King Edward arrived in the vicinity of Pontefract on 27 March, knowing that the bridge across the River Aire was destroyed, it would have been imperative for him to send out a force to rebuild the crossing without delay. Avoiding a delay was, as always, central to a campaign's success, especially with the ever-increasing danger of dwindling supplies and deserting troops. Secondly, if the bridge was intact, this would have prompted the Yorkists to occupy it, in this instance to guard it for Edward's army to cross over once they had been refreshed.

However, according to George Neville, the Yorkists had little to protect in the way of a bridge at Ferrybridge, which indicates that the Lancastrians had already broken it down and that the Yorkists set about constructing a 'narrow way' to get across. It is very doubtful that the Yorkists made this makeshift bridge in the face of the enemy on 28 March. Therefore, Neville's description of events to Coppini points to a Yorkist force under Fitzwalter building a temporary crossing before Clifford and his retainers arrived on the scene. As discussed earlier, bridge-breaking was a common measure to slow an enemy's advance. It would be unreasonable to suggest that the Lancastrians failed to destroy the crossing at Ferrybridge when they marched back to Yorkshire after the second battle of St Albans a few weeks earlier.

The bridge that had been destroyed by the Lancastrians 'beforehand' must have been quite substantial and was not, in 1461, as the name might suggest, a ferry at all. However, there is evidence that as early as 1070, there existed a temporary ferry over the River Aire. The Brotherton paved landing was still visible when C. Forrest wrote his *History of Knottingley* in 1871. There is also mention that William I crossed that way against the Northumbrians, later destroying the ferry in the process.[9] In 1340, 1356, 1359 and 1362, grants of pontage (bridge repairs) were issued, and barrs had been built on a static bridge for tolls to be taken. A chapel was also built here in the fourteenth century, proving that increased medieval traffic had made Ferrybridge a vital crossing on the road to York. As for the Lancastrians in 1461, they did well to sabotage the bridge to hold up the Yorkist march and put their next plan into operation.

In the early hours of Saturday 28 March, Lord Clifford's force made short work of Fitzwalter's 'engineers' who were apparently asleep at their posts. In the brief skirmish that followed, most of the Yorkists were killed, recalls Edward Hall. But *Hearne's Fragment* mentions 'foreprickers' and Waurin refers to a 'small company' who got too close to the enemy, which may substantiate Hall's claims.

However, when the Earl of Warwick was informed of this setback, probably by a survivor, he reported to Edward, who moved the whole Yorkist army forward to regain the bridge from Clifford. This action prompted the main battle of Ferrybridge, not the Fitzwalter skirmish as some historians have previously claimed. Clifford, according to Waurin, had by now further fortified the narrow crossing, and not only was the bridge a difficult objective to assault, but also the land on the north bank of the Aire was easily defended if the Lancastrians were forced into retreating to Towton.

In 1644 a similar action took place over the same ground when Colonel Sands and his Parliamentarians held the then rebuilt bridge and the road beyond for a considerable amount of time. Brotherton Marsh on the north bank of the Aire was then, and up to the first Ordnance Survey, subject to flooding, the only causeway being the road from the bridge past Brotherton village nearby. Sir Henry Slingsby, a Royalist soldier, remarked that they 'had to fight for ground to fight upon' until, through gaps and disadvantage, they drove the Parliamentarians from their position.[10]

According to this evidence, in 1461, the Yorkists probably had the same problems in the marshes against the Lancastrians. They certainly incurred heavy casualties trying to dislodge Clifford's men, and many were drowned on both sides. The Earl of Warwick was shot in the leg by a chance arrow, according to William Gregory, in what may have been one of many vain sallies across the 'narrow way.' However, in all accounts, there were high casualties in a battle in which the larger force was typically held up by the smaller only while the manpower or tactical advantage lasted.

According to *Benet's Chronicle*, Edward fought on foot at Ferrybridge and Warwick was injured, proving that desperate measures had to be employed against Lord Clifford's men strongly posted on the north bank of the makeshift bridge.[11] It was, according to sources, a tough fight until, finally, the Yorkists decided that only one option was left open to them if they wished to continue north. Not wanting two disasters on the same day, according to Hall, King Edward called for Fauconberg, Blount and Horne with the vaward to threaten Clifford's flank via Castleford. Informed of this, or after fighting their way out of the Yorkist flank attack, Clifford wisely decided to settle on a job well done. Thinking it wise to tackle Edward another day, he gave the order to mount and the remnants of the Flower of Craven galloped back up the road to Towton, with Fauconberg's men in hot pursuit.

The Death of Lord Clifford

If we suppose that these events occurred during the morning of 28 March (the attack on the Lancastrians beginning at first light after the Fitzwalter skirmish in the early hours), then this scenario allows for the various assaults on Ferrybridge, the Fauconberg flank march via Castleford 3 miles away and a simultaneous retreat by Clifford followed by the Yorkist vaward up the Towton road before nightfall. Following the fast-flowing Aire, a mounted force could have completed the flank march following the loop of the river in under an hour if pressed. However, neither Clifford nor his men ever reached the Lancastrian camp at Towton, as Fauconberg's mounted contingent, always at their heels, cut them off and destroyed them, almost to a man, about 2 miles short of their objective.

Hall's Chronicle is the only one with information on this episode, and, to make matters worse, contemporaries were predictably either indecisive about the location of Clifford's death or included his name among the long lists of Lancastrian casualties the following day. But the Flower of Craven's near annihilation is more important than might be at first assumed, as now the Duke of Somerset was deprived of one of his most valued leaders. Hall gives brief details of Butcher Clifford's last moments when he and his men:

> met with some that they looked not for and were trapped before they were aware. For the Lord Clifford, either from heat or pain, put off his gorget [armoured neck protection], was suddenly hit by an arrow, as some say without a head, and was stricken in the throat, and incontinent rendered up his spirit. And the Earl of Westmorland's brother [John Neville] and all his company were slain, at a place called Dintingdale, not far from Towton.[12]

Troops being pursued and hunted down as depicted in the *Beauchamp Pageant Roll*.

Dintingdale is a shallow valley that crosses the Ferrybridge to Tadcaster road below the high plateau where the massive Lancastrian army was encamped. Earlier I mentioned Hall's possible comparisons between some Lancastrian nobles – namely Lord Clifford and the Earl of Northumberland. Could this clash of personalities have been the reason why Clifford was not reinforced as dusk was falling on 28 March? Clearly, it seems that he was not offered any help whatsoever from his Lancastrian friends on the plateau. Therefore, was there, in fact, dissension in the Lancastrian ranks after all, with leading magnates jockeying for position in the face of the enemy? It is hard to believe that Lancastrian scouts would not have been deployed to warn the Duke of Somerset of a Yorkist approach, but where were they when one of the more valuable Lancastrian commanders was being ambushed and killed at Dintingdale, only 2 miles away?

Various reasons could account for this baffling event, such as a surprise attack in the dark on Clifford by the Yorkist mounted archers, who were by this time well up the road from Ferrybridge. Visibility may have been impaired, and we know that the weather was bitterly cold, with snow dictating the battle the next day. So, could the Lancastrians view Dintingdale from their camp at Towton? A walk south on the battlefield today offers no sight of the valley in question until the triangulation point is reached beside the hawthorn tree at 168ft. If the Lancastrians were encamped in and around Towton on the 28 March, rather than on the plateau, *Hall's Chronicle* may hold the truth about Clifford's last moments when he and his men 'met with some that they looked not for and were trapped before they were aware.'

The simple fact is the Lancastrians may not have seen the Dintingdale skirmish at all. Or knowing of Clifford's predicament, they wisely decided not to sally out into what might have been the whole oncoming Yorkist army, thereby quitting the high ground for the sake of a few hundred men. However, what does come out of this discussion is that the Lancastrian army must have been encamped in the village of Towton on 28 March not to see this skirmish. Scourers may have reported back to Somerset and Northumberland of Clifford's entrapment; they may even have attempted to help their comrades in vain. But whatever the scenario, through history's half-light, it is apparent that Somerset and his advisers kept their ground, and another member of the

Clifford family joined the mounting death toll of the Wars of the Roses.

In most chronicles of the period, as opposed to later histories (including Shakespeare), John, Lord Clifford of Skipton, was not portrayed any differently to others of his class. His actions before Towton failed to move contemporaries to blacken his name. A glance at the man's life and character cannot fail to make apparent the appropriateness of the various derogatory sobriquets he was given later, and we may wonder at his reputation and state of mind when faced with the shock of his father's death at St Albans in 1455. Historians say he never hesitated when committing any act, however cruel, if it assisted in carrying out his plans. We are told a sanguinary fierceness and barbarity marked him out from other nobles, and this was derived from his murder of the 'under-age' Earl of Rutland after the battle of Wakefield and the judicial killing of his father, York, in the same fight, but how true is this?

Edward Hall, in his history, is chiefly responsible for Clifford's character assassination, and later writers followed his example with stories of their own. Therefore, it is perhaps worth pausing for a moment to reiterate the motives of Hall, given that his grandfather had been slain at the battle of Wakefield with the Duke of York. Writing in the Tudor period, it seems several aspects of Clifford's life caught Hall's attention, and we may wonder why there was such a need to dramatise events that were becoming so commonplace on Wars of the Roses battlefields? After all, Hall's grandfather warned the Duke of York not to sally out from Sandal Castle. When York was killed, his son, Rutland, was helped to escape from the field, but when Clifford caught up with him, it is said, Rutland:

> knelt on his knees imploring mercy and desiring grace, both with holding up his hands and making dolorous countenance, for his speech had gone with fear. But the Lord Clifford marked him and said, 'by God's blood, thy father slew mine,

and so will I do thee and all they kin,' and with that he stuck the earl to the heart with his dagger and bade his chaplain bear the earl's mother and brother word what he had done and said. Yet this cruel Clifford and deadly blood-supper not content with this homicide, or child-killing, came to the place where the dead corpse of the Duke of York lay, and caused his head to be stricken off, and set on it a crown of paper, and so fixed it to a pole, and presented it to the queen.[13]

The scene has all the hallmarks of drama and revenge, not only on Clifford's part but also Hall's, who may have embellished the story in memory of his dead grandfather. Therefore, we may wonder if the way Rutland was killed is an accurate representation of what happened. Given that later writers and dramatists also related this event verbatim, and that near contemporaries of the battle of Wakefield are silent about the details of Rutland and York's death, it is likely there is at least one alternative scenario. Aside from Shakespeare, who copied from Hall and Holinshed, the simple fact could be that Clifford, inflamed with revenge, was in the right place at the right time. According to most sources, he did not kill the Duke of York, but he certainly was no different from other nobles who had suffered family bereavement in the wars. Chivalry may have been his watchword. However, the accepted form of granting mercy and exacting ransom from prisoners was well and truly dead in England by this time and Hall took full advantage of this by blackening the Clifford name.

After the skirmish at Dintingdale, Lord Clifford's body was allegedly tumbled into a mass grave pit, but this must have been a much later event considering Fauconberg's advance guard soon occupied the area, and graves were probably the last thing on their minds. However, it his hardly surprising that Clifford's last resting place is not well documented as even his son Henry was tarnished with his father's 'blood-supping' reputation in his early years:

> Thus end had he [John Clifford], which slew the young earl
> of Rutland, kneeling on his knees; whose young son Henry
> Clifford was brought up with a shepherd, in poor habit and
> dissimulate behaviour ever in fear to publish his lineage
> or degree.[14]

As discussed, Rutland was seventeen when he died at Wakefield, but we can be sure many men fought in the Wars of the Roses that were of this fighting age, including Rutland's elder brother Edward, aged nineteen, who knew war was a dangerous pastime. Given that these men had been brought up to warfare and violence, we may be shocked by their behaviour today. Still, we know from most sources that lords relished battle following purist codes of chivalry or a leaning towards more basic instincts of aristocratic greed, revenge or ambition. However, the life of Henry Clifford, the so-called 'Shepherd Lord', was far removed from the battlefield his father knew so well. He grew up incognito in Yorkshire and seldom went to court, only managing to reclaim his father's estates after a change of dynasty: a fact that likely caused Lord John Clifford's memory, and his last resting place near Towton, to quickly disappear into local legend.

Hall may have exaggerated Clifford's fearsome reputation, but according to Jean de Waurin, the Yorkists, seeing the Lancastrians in flight, 'took the [Ferry] bridge, and all the army went over it the same night'[15] During the advance, Yorkist bodies may have been cleared from the field, although, apart from Lord Fitzwalter, it is doubtful that burials would have been carried out on a large scale given the bad weather, the marshy ground and King Edward's urgency to come to grips with the enemy.

The antiquarian C. Forrest, in describing Brotherton Marsh near Ferrybridge, mentions that 'Human skeletons, ancient armour and other relics of civil warfare have been frequently found there, and should the marsh ever be under the plough,

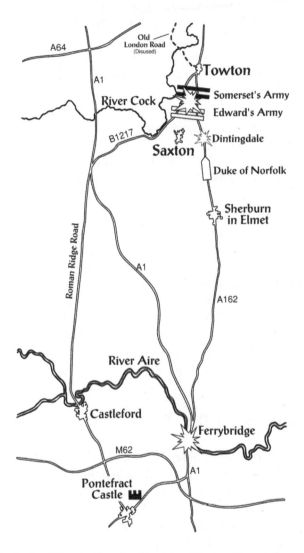

The battle of Ferrybridge, the skirmish at Dintingdale and the march to Towton. (Author)

many more such relics will certainly be turned up.'[16] However, Forrest was not certain whether the artefacts found in the area were from the 1644 or 1461 engagements. Noting *Archaeologia*, he singled out an interesting passage that speculates about the last resting place of at least one of the Yorkist lords near the battlefield. It reads:

> There was found in digging a grave in Brotherton churchyard, 21 May 1781, a chalice, very much mutilated, and its lid, a spur and parts of armour. These most probably belonged to one of the lords slain at Ferrybridge before the battle of Towton, on Saturday 28 March 1461. It was usual to inter the lords who fell in this contest near the place where they were slain, and it is probable that the chalice, spur and armour might belong to Lord Fitzwalter.[17]

Forrest's theory about these archaeological finds is that two ancient graves, one of a warrior, and the other of an ecclesiastic, were invaded by the 1781 grave when it was dug and mistaken for one. Therefore, the story and the legend has been perpetuated, but unfortunately cannot be proven since no remains survive to date them.

The March to the Battlefield

On the eve of Palm Sunday 1461, Edward's army struggled over Ferrybridge with the added burden on their minds that the whole Lancastrian army was waiting for them somewhere up the north road.

It is not clear whether John Mowbray, Duke of Norfolk, had at last arrived at Pontefract by this time, but judging by events the next day, there still seemed to be a worrying delay. Some authorities deduce that Mowbray was sick at Pontefract and sent his troops over the bridge after being strengthened on 29 March to arrive at Towton in the late afternoon of Palm Sunday. However, it is likely Norfolk was always a day's march behind the main Yorkist army and had difficulties on the road. Norfolk's men could have been dragging guns with them, slowing the pace, as it is hard to believe that Edward had not secured some artillery from the Tower of London for his campaign. Being the rearward of the army, Norfolk's lateness may have called for drastic measures like the eventual abandonment of their guns in favour of speed, as there is no archaeological evidence to date of any artillery, other than handguns, being used at the battle of Towton. Ferrybridge would also have been an excellent place to use such weapons had they been available. Alternatively, the duke may have had trouble mustering recruits, and if he was ill and awaiting recovery (he died later in the year on 6 November), this could have also caused problems on the march. Extending this theory further, if Norfolk was at Towton on Palm Sunday and seriously ill, it is unlikely that he took any part in the battle; a sick man would never have survived such a strength-sapping ordeal, especially encased in armour.

After the battle of Ferrybridge, the vaward, mainward and rearward of Edward's army were dangerously separated. After crossing the River Aire at Castleford, Fauconberg with the vaward may have advanced up the Roman road to Hook Moor, below Aberford, and veered right towards the abandoned medieval village of Lead, and Saxton beyond. But it is more likely that, because he was ordered to attack Lord Clifford in the flank at Ferrybridge, Lord Fauconberg chased the Flower of Craven up the Tadcaster road where some of them, presumably the mounted archers, closed in on Clifford later in the day. According to the evidence, Edward pressed on after Fauconberg and advanced on Sherburn-in-Elmet, the next main town on the road north. It is likely he camped here awaiting his army to concentrate, and if we must make a judgement on the condition of his men, there is no doubt that many soldiers were exhausted by the day's events according to chronicles.

There is high ground above Saxton to the southeast, bordering Dintingdale and the northwest towards Lead. Therefore, it is possible that some of the Yorkist vaward, after their skirmish with Clifford, occupied this ridge and the main village of Saxton. Jean de Waurin tells us of the plight of the Yorkists, not forgetting the Lancastrians, on that cold Palm Sunday eve as Edward's strung-out forces struggled to link up with each other. 'It was so cold with snow and ice', he recalled from those who were there, 'that it was pitiful to see men and horses suffer, especially as they were badly fed.'[18]

St Mary's Church near the deserted medieval village of Lead. (Author)

Some men must have died of exposure in such conditions as billets and tents are not mentioned. The Yorkist baggage was almost certainly still on the road carrying these basic requirements, especially food, which, judging by the above extract, was in short supply in Edward's army. Indeed, the Yorkist wagons may not have even crossed Ferrybridge. Prime billets would have been taken by the nobles, as the villagers in the area would probably have been long gone – perhaps some of them had already been recruited by the Lancastrians. But all things considered, young Edward, with a seriously undernourished force-marched army under his command, must have wondered about his earlier decision to be judged by God in battle, now that the main event was approaching. Short of his religious beliefs, his thirst for revenge and the prize of the crown of England, Edward must have been a rare individual indeed if he did not experience some doubts about the imminent fight for the throne. Being without the Duke of Norfolk's men must have weighed heavily on his mind, but it is difficult to imagine what could have been done differently to bring about a meeting with his East Anglian allies. Edward had been drawn on unpredictably by the Lancastrians ever since setting foot in Yorkshire. After being harassed by them at Ferrybridge, he again pushed on without Norfolk, possibly leaving word of his departure at Pontefract or, more likely, sending word to the duke himself to meet him the following day somewhere up the Tadcaster road.

The Yorkist vaward and the main Lancastrian army would have been close to each other across what would later become Towton battlefield. Before dawn, several isolated skirmishes may have occurred, as *Hearne's Fragment* spuriously records that some fighting occurred during the night. However, it is doubtful that the two main armies fought at four o'clock in the afternoon until the following morning, or as he described, for ten hours. Large-scale medieval battles were seldom fought in the dark, by the light of fires or torches, as the chronicle would have us believe.[19] Also, the unwieldy size of Edward's army could not cope with a running battle overnight, especially after a full-scale engagement at Ferrybridge and a forced march of over 9 miles in wintry conditions.

Of the two armies, the Yorkists must have been badly mauled by the day's events. Some soldiers would have been tired from marching, others would have been nursing wounds from Ferrybridge, and, even if still fit, they would not have relished the thought of fighting the next day with injuries. Most soldiers would have been wrapped in cloaks huddled around fires, cursing the Lancastrians for their present predicament. Only the chivalrous, such as Edward and the lords under his command, would have thought of religious observance through prayer as their solace. The unbloodied and raw recruits in both armies were likely apprehensive and fearful. Some of these men may have deserted under cover of darkness while others remained steadfast, telling stories about their fights with the French, feats of arms and loot. All, except the nobles, would have preferred not to fight a battle at all unless they were very remarkable men, and most wished only to fulfil their obligation to their captain or lord and receive their pay with as little blood spilling as possible.

The Lancastrians, tented and secure in and around Towton, had already hit the Yorkists hard at the cost of Lord Clifford's life, and their commanders must have felt very confident of victory the next day, if still suffering, like the Yorkists, from the effects of the miserable Yorkshire weather. At the risk of making the obvious comparison of the night before the battle of Agincourt, in this understandably parallel situation of the forced marched, unfed, bedraggled underdog versus the overconfident, rested, and fresh enemy, are there perhaps any greater comparisons to be made, given the evidence, that may have affected the battle the next day?

In the main, the Lancastrians were comfortable, yet very unfortunate to have so many peers of the realm in their ranks. The overall feeling in some chronicles is that the Lancastrian army lacked unity. This unity, when all else failed, was the common bond that affected morale, and in the Lancastrian's case, this aim may have been threatened by more than a dozen overmighty

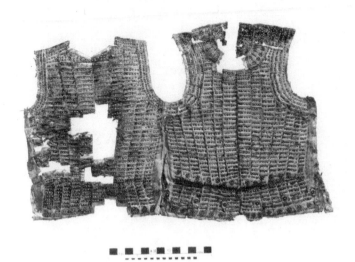

A surviving example of a fifteenth-century brigandine. (Royal Armouries)

subjects and their affinities competing for the honours that might come with victory. Useful amalgamations of various contingents under one command may not have been possible under these circumstances. Some titled individuals, like Somerset and Northumberland, would have been itching for revenge at the expense of level-headed tactics. And all this would have been compounded by the thought of their king safely ensconced in York and not present to lead them into battle.

Two massive armies were now poised for a great test of skill and resilience, never to be equalled on such a large scale on British soil in the medieval era, and in which almost half of its participants would perish for one King of England or the other. As sentries were buffeted by the freezing early morning wind and masses of men were given absolution for their sins, one can only wonder at each soldier's resolve to enter the violent abyss of battle.

Five

Bloody Meadows

There can be little doubt where the battle of Towton took place, as all the historical sources, local legends and archaeology point to the same general area. We are also lucky in the evidence of battlefield gravesites, which are, given the unusually large casualties, as far as we know to date, quite extensive in the proximities of both Towton and Saxton parishes. Other historically linked areas of the battlefield are also marked very precisely on the first Ordnance Survey maps. But as for less well-marked sites, more explanation is needed because the locality and the battle need to be evaluated together, given the incomplete documentary evidence concerning this harrowing and bloody encounter.

Medieval England was primarily an agricultural country, though, in later times, harsh climatic regions turned to mainly pastoral farming and rural crafts. Consequently, tradespeople in these areas relied on selling their goods in return for corn and supplies from the more productive parts of the country. Agricultural yields were low, which in turn brought hardship and, in some instances, famine. In the 1300s, bubonic plague ravaged the country on several occasions and remained endemic throughout the fifteenth century. However, small family farms that came through these challenging times found themselves in a stronger position when the rapidly expanding population of the earlier Middle Ages was drastically cut, and marginal land such as woods, moors, and marshes, which had previously been occupied, reverted to waste. Therefore, enterprising farmers who acquired these regions became owners of vast tracts of land, and they ditched and hedged bigger fields, which soon became commonplace on the English landscape.

Towton battlefield stands on the magnesium limestone belt of North Yorkshire, and as such, we can expect the area to have been extremely fertile, consequently bringing about an early start to the above type of field system. Most portions of the battlefield were probably open pasture in 1461, but there is evidence that the fields of both Towton and Saxton parishes were extending quite some way from the villages in this period. John Leland, who visited Yorkshire in about 1540, recorded in his *Itinerary* that places near the battlefield such as Aberford and Tadcaster were 'good high plain, corn ground' and 'corn ground and some wood',[1] which clearly indicates a trend in this locality by the Tudor period. Leland also described Towton and Saxton fields as extending from the villages, judging by his route along the River Cock past the deserted medieval hamlet of Lead. Therefore, we cannot assume that this part of Yorkshire was a barren wilderness at the time of the battle nor overrun with forest. Instead, the exposed battlefield plateau must have been chiefly pasture with pockets of cultivation and areas of partly cleared woodland bordering the site. Ridge and furrow field systems, together with ancient hedgerows and forests, have been identified on the battlefield by English Heritage to support this theory.

Towton, almost due north of Saxton, was a small insignificant village on the road to Tadcaster in 1461, although there is evidence that there was a manor house here in the reign of Richard II. The old London road from Ferrybridge and

Sherburn-in-Elmet ran through the village and turned left to ascend, then precipitously descend the northernmost edge of the battlefield plateau towards what today is a wooden bridge, but in 1461 this may have been a ford over the River Cock. The crossing known locally as the legendary Bridge of Bodies, due to the clogging up of the site by Lancastrian dead in the rout from the battlefield, is set in a valley. However, as will be seen later, it is more likely that there were several such human 'bridges' along the river after the battle, which would account for similar descriptions along its length.

In 1847 *The Field of The Battle of Towton* by Richard Brooke was read before the Society of Antiquaries in London. And concerning the absence of a bridge over the River Cock in 1461, Brooke cited Giovanni Biondi's work, which tends to confirm the existence of a ford. Translated from Italian in 1641, it contains information that, after the battle of Towton:

> those who remained alive [the Lancastrians], took the road to the bridge at Tadcaster, but being unable to reach it, and believing a small river called Cock to be fordable, the greater part were drowned therein. It is constantly affirmed that those who survived, passed over, treading on the dead bodies of the sufferers, and the water of this stream, and of the River Wharfe, into which it empties itself, were coloured in a manner to appear as pure blood.[2]

As indicated in this passage, the River Cock flows northwards towards Tadcaster and meets the River Wharfe, but upstream, south of the Bridge of Bodies, it snakes along the western edge of the battlefield, past Cocksford, another possible local crossing place, Renshaw Wood and Castle Hill Wood to the southwest. The river bulges menacingly into the battlefield plateau between these latter two landmarks and borders the slopes of Towton Dale and the legendary field known as Bloody Meadow. All this area was, and remains, bordered to the east by gently rising water-meadows. However, in the west, steep slopes rise to 150ft in almost as many paces and eventually climb onto the battlefield itself. All along the river it is the same story until, after circumnavigating Castle Hill and three ancient tumuli, the river flows past St Mary's church at Lead in the much flatter surroundings near The Crooked Billet public house.

The 'Bridge of Bodies' over the River Cock. (Author)

As described earlier, some of the Yorkist vaward commanders may have secured prime billets on the night of 28 March, but in 1461 there was little cover for the thousands of men and horses that accompanied them. Parallel to Saxton and to the west of it, the deserted medieval village of Lead, once owned by the Tyas and Scargill families, could have been the location of a Neville camp before the battle, possibly even the camp of the Earl of Warwick's ragged staff troops (hence *crooked billet*). Leland, in his *Itinerary*, mentioned that while travelling past

Lead to Towton, some buildings were still in existence then despite the ravages of plague in the previous century:

> Then by much turning to Lead, a hamlet, where Scargill had a fair manor place of timber. Cock Beck after crookith by Saxton and Towton village fields, and goith into Wharfe river a mile beneath Tadcaster.[3]

However, there is no proof of the suggestion that there was an inn at Lead in 1461, especially on the B1217 Hook Moor to Towton road, which was not a well-worn route from Watling Street in those days. To cast further doubt on this suggestion, we must also consider that, in the fifteenth century, towns and cities usually had inns rather than isolated northern trackways passing through deserted medieval villages.

Therefore, it is more likely that the hamlet of Lead with its small chapel was not a significant feature in the battle, but the down slope towards it marks quite precisely the western perimeter of the battlefield using the River Cock as a sinister landmark of an area to be avoided at all costs. Tactically speaking, the river was the most significant feature of the Towton story. It was the main artery of the battlefield that caused a brutal drama to unfold all along its tortuous course. Once breached by bridges of bodies water may have flooded the meadows below the plateau, but is there any evidence to confirm that the river was more dangerous prior to Palm Sunday? None of the chroniclers of the battle mention flooded rivers either at Towton or Tadcaster.[4] Therefore, it appears that to make the drownings that occurred there during the Lancastrian rout appear more horrifying, antiquarians may have exaggerated the numbers to agree with the chronicles. Also, a fast-flowing river so deep and in spate would have hindered the Lancastrians and their baggage wagons as they crossed the River Cock to encamp and eventually fight at Towton – unless by coincidence the river flooded immediately after they crossed? Let us also remember that this was the only line of communication open to the Lancastrian army, and to have knowingly had such a treacherous obstacle at their backs would have been decidedly foolish by any military standards of the day. Holding the River Wharfe at Tadcaster would have been a much better plan under the circumstances rather than crossing the River Cock to find there could be no retreat if they were defeated in battle.

At the beginning of Chapter One, I quoted George Neville in his letter to Coppini, which clearly states that the Lancastrians broke down the bridge at Tadcaster after they crossed it. But this statement is difficult to justify unless the Lancastrians were so confident of victory that they threw caution to the wind and resolved to go back and rebuild another bridge at Tadcaster to assist their triumphant entry into York. They may, of course, have been worried about deserters in the army and used the rivers Wharfe and Cock as natural barriers against such behaviour. But this is extremely unlikely given that such precautions never occurred in similar situations in the Wars of the Roses. Where armies had a river at their backs, every attempt was made to keep bridges intact. As explained earlier, during a retreat, bridges were better destroyed, and it is more logical that the Lancastrian fugitives from Towton may have sabotaged the bridge over the Wharfe to protect themselves and the royal family in their retreat.

Today the River Cock is only a small beck lazily running into the much larger Wharfe. However, in 1461 the Cock must have been a veritable death trap without the exaggerations of Victorian romanticism. Steep-sided and, in parts, extremely deep today, it is narrower than it would have been in 1461 because of gradual infill over the years. But in some parts, the river is more of a deep trench, and this may have been the nature of its geology in the medieval period. The unfortunate soldiers rushing in panic headlong down its vertical sides into the freezing water must have thought this was the worst possible obstacle to encounter in their bid to stay alive. However, in saying this, the River Wharfe was the more formidable barrier of the two, and as will be seen later, it played a major role in the battle when the Lancastrians fled en masse from the field.

Today the eastern edge of the battlefield is bordered by the Tadcaster to Ferrybridge turnpike road, which for our purposes runs from Towton village south, again following the contours of the battlefield plateau, past Saxton Grange to Dintingdale, Scarthingwell and eventually to Barkston Ash. This turnpike is the continuation of the old London road through Towton from The Bridge of Bodies (marked on Thomas Jeffries' map of 1771) and it was the main highway to Ferrybridge in 1461. Other local trackways were available to travellers, but claims suggesting that the main road from Barkston Ash turned left to Saxton and then followed Cotchers Lane over the battlefield plateau to meet the present B1217 to Towton can be discounted. Given that the London road was the more direct route north and the crossings over the River Cock, Jeffries' map shows quite clearly that minor roads existed through Dintingdale and Barkston to Saxton and Lead as they served a purpose to link the villages. But the current A162 road (with a small deviation at Towton towards Stutton) was undoubtedly the main road to Tadcaster and York in the medieval era.

To the east of the Tadcaster to Ferrybridge turnpike the battlefield plateau descends precipitously like that in the west. But beyond this the land is mainly flat with springs and water-meadows, which in 1461 was probably extensive marshland. Tactically speaking, this low-lying land, like the meadows in the west, would have been yet another obstacle to avoid as both armies moved into position on the battlefield plateau. Dintingdale is south of this, and as mentioned earlier, it is marked on most maps of the area. However, pinpointing this elusive 'valley' is problematic only because Lord Clifford was probably killed there. We know Dintingdale existed when Edward Hall wrote his chronicle in the 1500s, as he alone explains what happened to Clifford on the eve of Palm Sunday. Therefore, the epicentre of medieval Dintingdale may have been the junction of the Saxton road and the turnpike, or, as its name suggests, the whole valley stretching from Scarthingwell to Saxton.

At the southernmost edge of Dintingdale at Barkston Ash there is a derelict stone cross plinth, commonly called The Leper Pot and we may be forgiven for thinking this landmark is not connected with the battle. However, a photograph taken in 1912 disproves this theory as the plinth once supported an upright cross situated in the still visible hollowed-out block of limestone. Moreover, the medieval cross on the photograph is the same that now tops the battlefield memorial beside the B1217, therefore the two must be connected in some way. Could the original cross at Barkston have marked the site of Clifford's death in 1461? Maybe this would account for the Lancastrians not seeing The Flower of Craven's skirmish with the Yorkists from their camp? Further support for the existence of 'Lord Clifford's Cross' at Barkston Ash is that The Leper Pot tradition is rather weak. In my view, even given that Tadcaster had a colony of lepers at one time, it is extremely unlikely that they would have travelled such a distance (through Towton village) to receive food for money out of a hollowed-out stone slab. Therefore, did the cross have another purpose?[5]

As mentioned earlier, stories of a possible grave pit containing the bodies of Lord Clifford, John Neville and others of their contingent near the present-day Dintingdale were recorded in 1835. An amateur excavation was carried out in the vicinity, and a trench was dug close to the turnpike road and quarry. In it were found bones supposed to have been the remains of Lord Clifford, although how the antiquarians could have identified his body remains a mystery. However, despite these claims, the Dintingdale grave is evidence of a burial pit of some kind near the main battlefield.[6] It is doubtful that

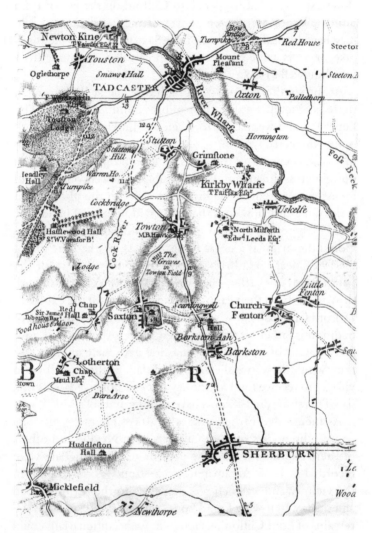

Thomas Jeffries' hand-drawn map of Towton and Saxton made during the 1730s.

bodies were carried very far from where they fell, and this fact is confirmed by the position and exhumation of many other mass grave pits found in the vicinity.

To complete the topographic 'anatomy' of Towton, the southern edge of the battlefield is famous for the most tangible, visual and time-evoking relic of the battlefield story. The battered and mysterious tomb of Lord Dacre bears silent witness to the fact that the battle of Towton was about death at its most basic level. However, not only is this noble interred in Saxton village beside the church All Saints, but also with him are hundreds more soldiers of a lesser degree. The trench graves recorded here in most topographic accounts and letters must hold literally thousands of bones, and these are said to have been located on the north side of the parish church running east to west where remains have been continually unearthed over the centuries.

'The Leper Pot' at Barkston Ash. The alternative site of Lord Clifford's death on 28 March 1461? (Author)

Visible as regular undulations in the ground, the Saxton graves represent the burial mounds of those bodies that found consecrated ground in contrast to the more unfortunate who were left on the field of battle. John Leland recorded the existence of graves here first, and in his *Itinerary* he wrote that 'In the churchyard were many of the bones of men that were killed at Palmsunday Field buried'.[7] One of Leland's contemporaries in the local Hungate family added to the fellowship of death when he 'gathered a great number of the bones from the fields and caused them to be buried in Saxton churchyard'.[8] The Hungates were lords of the manor at Saxton and the shallow graves on the battlefield, of which more later, may have prompted this venerable man to re-inter some exposed bones of Yorkists and Lancastrians alike when the plough was used to extend Saxton village fields in the late fifteenth century. Some of these remains are said to have been unearthed in the churchyard during the 1840s, lying about 4ft below the surface, and the bones exposed were thought to have been 'either young, or in the prime of life, because the skulls were remarkable for their soundness and excellence of teeth'.[9] These excavations, however, were possibly the original Yorkist trench graves on the north side of Saxton Church and not the Hungate haphazard collection of bones, which may have been stumbled across by grave-diggers over the years.

In his *Itinerary* Leland also suggests that John Neville (mistaken by him for the Earl of Westmorland) was buried within Saxton Church by the fathers he interviewed in the village during his travels. Similarly, Lord Clifford, as Neville's kinsman and partner in death at Dintingdale, is also thought to be buried there along with his Lancastrian ally Lord Dacre, which makes sense if the local gentry were allowed to bury them soon after the battle. Someone obviously took time to make sure that at least some of the Lancastrians, like Lord Dacre, had decent burials, and indeed were recorded by lasting memorials, in contrast to the Yorkist unlettered dead of which no names, memorials or records survive.

To explain this further, this part of Yorkshire was Lancastrian country in the Wars of the Roses. Therefore, we can assume that some men loyal to King Henry were most certainly interred in Saxton churchyard. Some of their rough-hewn stone gravestones may have been used to extend the church, and even the bells in the tower of All Saints are old enough to commemorate a Lancastrian loss rather than a Yorkist victory. Despite their age, these date from the late medieval period and still function perfectly well in their original housing. The donor of one of them, William Sallay, who died in 1492, had an inscription cast on his that speaks volumes of a lost cause kept alive by the faithful. The inscription reads:

Willeimus Sallay armiger de Saxton me fecit fieri Sancta Margarita ora pro nobis. [William Sallay Lord of Saxton caused me to be made, St Margaret pray for us.][10]

Lord Dacre's tomb in Saxton churchyard. (Author)

Given this interest in the battle, either William Sallay or the Hungates, both consecutive lords of the manor of Saxton during the period, must have been partly connected with Lord Dacre's tomb due to their Lancastrian sympathies, the locality, and because the re-burial of bones from the battle-field soon became their ultimate responsibility in the reign of Richard III. As will be explained in another chapter, these re-burials are recorded in official royal documents. Therefore, it is extremely unlikely that the Yorkist regime would have taken time to bury and commemorate such traitors as Lords Dacre, Neville and Clifford who were, along with their allies, attained by Edward IV in 1461.

The Anatomy of the Battlefield

Towton battlefield, is a partially protected heritage site, and lies in the confines of the triangle of roads and features so far described. The actual fighting took place on a natural plateau bordered by varying degrees of slopes and gullies, and it was here, between Saxton and Towton, that thousands of men fought, died, and were buried in unconsecrated ground. There is no doubt of this, as, first, the battle site is corroborated by inherent military probability, or put simply, that the features investigated so far, such as rivers, villages and marshland, provide a totally unsuitable terrain for fighting a large-scale medieval battle. Space is the crucial factor here, and this became a vital prerequisite and, eventually, a major concern to both armies when the main trial of strength was so delicately balanced above Saxton that the battle could have swung either way. Second, unlike some other medieval conflicts, the battlefield is marked quite precisely by other well-documented features such as grave pits, bloody mead-ows and consistent legends and traditions. And third, the archaeology and the wealth of artefacts unearthed on the plateau describes quite precisely where the action, or several actions, took place.

In the principal areas of conflict, the battle zone is 100ft above the surrounding land (150ft above sea level in some places) and, in general, consists of the high ground bisected east to west by a low valley known as Towton Dale to the west and North Acres to the east. On the western side of this hollow depression in the land, Towton Dale funnels steeply into the River Cock valley below, in which Bloody Meadow shares its steep descent. Bloody Meadow contained five grave pits that John Leland saw when he visited the site in the Tudor period. He related these mounds in his *Itinerary* to the removal of bones and their reinterment in consecrated ground by Richard III and the Hungates in 1483. The full passage reads:

> In the churchyard were many of the bones of men that were killed at Palmsunday Field buried. They lay afore in 5 pits yet appearing half a mile by north in Saxton fields.[11]

These five mounds were still visible fifty years before Richard Whittaker published his account of Towton in *Leodis and Elmete* in 1816. In his book, Whittaker stated that he saw little trace of the grave pits then, which is surprising because some accounts of a later date contradict this statement. In the Field of the White and Red Rose, also alluded to as Bloody Meadow, Richard Brooke, who visited the battlefield between 1848 and 1856, claims that:

> The large meadow is remarkable for producing rich rank grass and also for three or four extensive irregularly shaped patches of very small wild dwarf rose bushes, which I was told, were both red and white.[12]

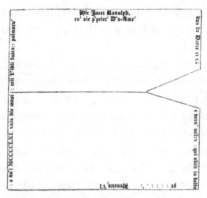

Or read at length, and with the defects supplied :

ᚼic jacet Ranulphus Dominus de Dacre et Greystocke berus miles qui obiit in bello pro rege suo ᚼenrico Sexto Anno MCCCCLXI.—Vicessimo die mensis Marcii bidⁱlt. Dominica palmarum cujus anime propicietur Deus—Amen.

In this reading I have been greatly assisted by the following copy of the inscription, which I have retrieved from Hopkinson's MSS. as it was partly read, and partly guessed at, by a transcriber about the time of Charles I.

ᚼic jacet Ranulphus Dⁿˢ. de Dacre et Greystocke, heros, miles strenuus qui obiit in bello pro rege suo ᚼenrico sexto Anno MCCCCLXI. videlicet Dominica palmarum cujus anime y̌pitietur Deus Amen.

A transcription of the engraving around Lord Dacre's tomb, taken from Whittaker's *Leodis and Elmete*.

These patches of the Towton Rose (*rosa spinosissima*), are now almost an extinct plant species in the area. They were located on the left-hand side of the B1217 road to Towton as it begins to descend into the shallow valley below the battlefield plateau. They are, in my view, evidence of disturbed ground cover on probably four of the five original gravesites described by Leland in 1540, and we may conclude that the roses were extensive and visible enough to be recorded by antiquarians in the mid-nineteenth century. Therefore, the roses (as markers) cannot be dismissed out of hand, and the plants may have once marked a traditional site, probably where battlefield graves used to be.

Part of the large area known as Bloody Meadow. (Author)

Bloody Meadow was to become the bloodiest of the bloody meadows on Towton battlefield. However, given the resulting carnage, it is more than likely that this whole valley at the western end of the plateau was by the end of the conflict so littered with corpses that it is perhaps irrelevant to mark one meadow as being more horrifying than another. More important is the persistent fact that this forward slope may have been the best place to bury the dead because some, if not all, of the battlefield is even today situated on limestone, which in parts is only just below the surface. However, it is apparent from Richard III's proclamation to the Hungates that the Towton graves were initially dug in shallow ground because human remains were continually rising to the surface after the battle.

Evidence of more burials existed in the middle of the battlefield looking north towards Towton, on the opposite ridge, and at a site clearly indicated on Thomas Jeffries' map and known locally as The Graves. According to the Harleian Manuscript MS 795, there were:

> Certain deep trenches overgrown with bushes and briers containing 19 yards in breadth and 32 yards in length in Towton field, a bowshot on the left hand in the way betwixt Saxton and Towton, half a mile short of Towton.[13]

According to some sources, this was a raised enclosure, the borders of which were still visible on maps in the 1730s. However, the plough has been here too over the centuries and levelled the land so that nothing remains of these once extensive trench graves today except a few human bones that tractors and archaeologists still unearth accidentally.

This tract of land beside The Graves extends a considerable distance west to the B1217 road and east to the Tadcaster to Ferrybridge turnpike, and it has always been called North Acres. It was somewhere in these fields that Lord Dacre was supposed to have been killed at the height of the battle of Towton. Legend has it, writes Glover in his visitation, that 'the Lord of Dacres was slain in North Acres'[14] by an archer sat in a bur tree who shot him after the unfortunate noble had unclasped his helmet to drink a cup of wine. The tree, featured on the first Ordnance Survey maps, is precisely marked almost opposite The Graves in what once was the parish boundary, 250yd from the B1217 on the right-hand side of the road to Towton. Several overgrown bur elder tree stumps are still visible in this high bank, which may once have been an ancient hedgerow. These stumps are situated at the base of the plateau. However, even though nothing remains today of the 'actual' Dacre bur tree, the tradition picked up by Glover in 1585 pinpoints the battle zone precisely and perpetuates an interesting legend that may hold an element of truth.

At the eastern end of North Acres, the depression in the land dips sharply to the Tadcaster to Ferrybridge road, Saxton

Grange and the flatlands beyond. This descent does not fall away as quickly as Towton Dale to the west, but, at the hawthorn tree and the triangulation point above North Acres, the terrain does become perilously steep, like that in the west. At over 150ft above sea level, the hawthorn tree vantage point is a commanding position, and there is no better point to view the battlefield and the surrounding countryside. It must also have been a similar vantage point in 1461 and one to occupy if possible once the battle of Towton was underway. However, on the corresponding ridge across the depression was also a very commanding position, which in parts is almost as elevated although less so today due to constant ploughing over the centuries.

On this site, where the battle cross now stands, the land is also approximately 150ft high and offers just as good a vantage point looking south as the hawthorn tree does north. There is a theory that this 'Battle Cross Ridge', containing The Graves, was in 1461 more extended towards the turnpike road and Saxton Grange, and, due to the levelling effects of the plough, Towton Dale and North Acres combined were originally more of a valley and not like the hollow depression that exists today. This ridge is where the Lancastrians deployed for battle, and it takes little imagination to visualise multiple ranks of men at arms and archers assembling in the fields awaiting the Yorkists and confident of victory.

The battle of Towton memorial cross, namely the carved section at the top of the more modern obelisk, is medieval, but as explained earlier, its history is uncertain because various stories have been attributed to it over the years, all of which are unfounded. One antiquarian's book (W. Wheater, *History of Sherburn and Cawood*) has the battered stone cross sketched in a hedge bottom captioned 'Lord Dacre's Cross'. Other theories are that the cross could have been part of Lord Clifford's memorial linked with The Leper Pot legend at Barkston Ash. My theory, which is not unique, is that originally the cross may have come from the unfinished chapel commissioned by Richard III at Towton 'In token of prayer' and for the souls of 'the men slain at Palmsunday Field'.[15]

The Towton Battlefield Cross marking the site where thousands perished in the snow on Palm Sunday 1461. (Author)

This chantry chapel was situated on rising ground to the north of Towton Hall, where many more grave pits are to be found, as one might expect. Again, it comes as no surprise to learn that some of these trenches have been excavated by the curious, and sadly not well recorded for posterity. Before Francis Drake published his *Eboracum* in 1736, he and two others went to see a grave opened, which may have been near Towton Hall. Among vast quantities of bones, they found some arrow piles, broken swords and five groat pieces of Henries IV, V and VI. These were laid together, close to a thigh bone, which made them conjecture that there had not been time to strip the bodies before they were tossed into the pit.[16] However, given the confusing events after the battle, and the next day, the assumption that looters missed the coins is also a reasonable theory since only small burial parties could have been organised to dig the vast number of graves needed for the Towton dead. The clearing-up operation must have also been hampered by bad weather because, according to George Neville, the dead were left in the fields for several days without burial.

Chapel Hill and Towton Hall, which have been subjected to archaeological work in recent years chiefly to find the location of the battlefield chapel begun by Richard III. *(Author)*

Hundreds, perhaps thousands, were buried near the unfinished chapel in Towton, the full extent of which came to light when the cellars of Towton Hall were extended to meet a solid wall of human skeletons in the late 1700s. Excavations conducted by Bradford University and West Yorkshire

Archaeology Service in July 1996 also uncovered a substantial burial pit which was thoroughly investigated and recorded. Therefore, it is not surprising that this area of Towton village was selected to raise a chapel to the dead, and perhaps the battle cross originally marked the site of these graves or was part of the chapel itself. Richard III, who commissioned the chantry, would have known, but unfortunately he was to join the Wars of the Roses' dead on Bosworth Field in 1485. Thus, the chapel was never finished, fell into ruin, and in time disappeared completely.

Bordering the battlefield's western edge along its length, except for the valleys of Towton Dale and Bloody Meadow, are wooded areas. Renshaw Wood, extending northwards from Towton Dale along the course of the River Cock and the battlefield plateau, spreads further than the Bridge of Bodies, while to the west of Bloody Meadow, Castle Hill Wood covers a bluff overlooking a curve in the River Cock. In 1461 these two woods must have extended a lot further eastwards onto the battlefield but judging by the site, and confirmed by the areas we have investigated already, not so far as to have caused severe positional problems for the two armies. Indeed, there must have been a great many trees on the battlefield at the time, probably windswept and bent due to the terrain's exposed outlook, and like the surviving hawthorn tree above North Acres.

The all-important point to remember here about the battle site, aside from its bordering features, is the width available to both armies on the plateau and, because of it, the effect on the masses of men thrown into combat. At this stage of the battlefield anatomy, it is sufficient to say that, of the two elevations split by the depression, the southern ridge was, and is more so today, the larger width, extending some 1,500yd. But of this, only 1,000yd faces the parallel northern ridge, leading us to assume that at some point during the battle, this area, containing Bloody Meadow, the Field of the White and Red

Rose, Towton Dale, the 'Dacre' bur tree and North Acres, was only one of the main killing fields of Towton battlefield. I say 'only one' simply because, as will soon become apparent, we can confidently say that the depression was not the only area of fighting, nor deaths for that matter, because there was ample space for manoeuvring and retreat for both armies on the plateau once hand-to-hand fighting began in earnest.

Taking this point further, and using gravesites to map the battlefield more precisely, we must also consider the three tumuli (once thought to be graves) at the base of a steep descent to the southeast of Castle Hill Wood. This meadow has not been under the plough, and in October 1993, I, together with the Towton Battlefield Society and archaeologist Andrew Green, carried out preliminary excavations on two of the three mounds to determine precisely what they were. However, no human remains or artefacts from the battle were found here. Evidence of burning was detected, and therefore the age, purpose and relevance of the tumuli are not directly relatable to the battle. Indeed, the mounds may be Bronze Age kilns, proving habitation in the Castle Wood area in pre-history.[17]

As mentioned earlier, gravesites are important in identifying the general area of the battle, but a more critical point to remember about the movements of the armies on the day is the yardage available from the battlefield depression to the edge of the southern plateau. By recognising this, along with the topographic and chronicled evidence of the battlefield, we may conclude that Towton was fought in a very circumscribed area of just over half a square mile, not including the rout, which according to the Bishop of Exeter was mercilessly followed up to twelve times this distance towards Tadcaster and York.

By studying the chronicles and attainder documents, we can further pinpoint the site by stating that Edward Hall wrote 'both hosts approached each other in a plain field between the villages of Towton and Saxton'.[18] Second, John Leland's *Itinerary* recorded that 'This field was as much fought in Saxton parish as in Towton, yet it beareth the name of Towton'.[19] And third, in eking out the bad blood of the then rebel Lancastrians, King Edward stated in his official attainder document that the Lancastrians traitorously rebelled against his person 'on Sunday commonly called Palm Sunday, the 29th day of March in a field between the towns of Sherburn-in-Elmet and Tadcaster' and in 'Saxtonfield and Towtonfield'.[20]

Prelude to the Battle

More concerning the manoeuvres before Towton, the chronicle written by Jean de Waurin (1394–1474) provides some interesting, though unsupported, evidence that could be linked to the importance of the two towns of Sherburn-in-Elmet and Tadcaster rather than the villages of Towton and Saxton. Substantiating the Burgundian chronicler's claims is the key point here but considering the timing of the actions at Ferrybridge and Towton, plus the logistical necessities of Edward's army on the march, we may be able to draw some new conclusions following Waurin's unusual prelude to the battle.

After spending a bitterly cold night somewhere across the River Aire after the tough battle at Ferrybridge, the exhausted and strung-out Yorkist army was brought news of the Lancastrian position by its scouts early on Palm Sunday morning, the day of the battle of Towton:

When the Earl of March [Edward IV] and his lords were told that King Henry was nearby in the fields they rejoiced, for they wished for nothing more but to fight him. The earl called for his captains and told them to put their men in formation and to take their positions before the enemy came too close. And so it was he organised his battles, and he sent some of his men to look around the area because they were only four miles from the forces of King Henry. They did not go very far before they spotted the reconnaissance party from the enemy, and they quickly returned to the Earl of March to tell him that they had seen large numbers of men at arms in the fields and the banners of King Henry. They told him how the enemy was moving and their position, and when the earl was warned of this he went to his cavalry, which he had positioned on the wing, and said to them, 'My children, I pray today that we shall be good and loyal to each other because we are fighting for a good cause!' After they had all echoed this thought a messenger came to tell the earl that the vaward troops of the king had started to move forward and the earl went back to place himself behind his banners.[21]

According to Waurin, the Lancastrians were already well advanced early on Palm Sunday morning and 'in the fields' when the Yorkists, 4 miles distant, broke camp – a clear indication that both armies were marching on the day of the battle not camped at Saxton or Towton. However, given the battlefield plateau position, a chance encounter is misleading. The battle was almost certainly a set-piece action, given the size of the armies and because of the amount of reconnaissance that was going on. Part of the Yorkist vaward was, after all, very close to the Lancastrian host due to its skirmish with Lord Clifford late the previous day. Therefore, it is likely that Lord Fauconberg sent word back to Edward during the morning of 29 March that the enemy was advancing.

Existing theories about the battle of Towton are that the two armies were lined up against each other on Palm Sunday morning. However, if we follow Waurin's account, it is apparent that reconnoitring and movement of the two armies was still going on. Therefore, the above piece of unique evidence could lead us to consider a credible alternative that most historians have not fully grasped about Towton.

Edward IV's bill of attainder maintains that the main towns of Tadcaster and Sherburn-in-Elmet were far more critical staging posts than the two hamlets of Towton and Saxton on the road north. Therefore, if the Yorkists were encamped at Sherburn-in-Elmet (4 miles from Towton) soon after the battle of Ferrybridge and the Lancastrians were similarly camped at Tadcaster en-route to Towton it seems likely that this may have been remembered and worthy of recording by Waurin. The two towns would have provided far superior foraging and command positions for both armies the night before the battle, plus the fact that the Yorkist army must have been exhausted and widely dispersed or strung out on the road.

If we accept this logistical need, and the time of day, we must in turn rethink existing theories that the entire Yorkist army was encamped at Saxton and Lead before the battle – in fact it may have been only Fauconberg's vaward that was stationary. According to Waurin the Yorkist mainward of Edward's army was still marching up the Ferrybridge to Tadcaster road on the morning of 29 March to link up with their vaward and the same may have been true of the Lancastrian army. It has always been a mystery how the separated Yorkist vaward and mainward arrived together at Saxton and Lead the night before the battle, considering the previous day's actions. Therefore, if the reader accepts Waurin's account as plausible, considering all the above evidence, here is one new theory about the battle of Towton to consider.

Waurin's account of the battle may be fanciful in parts, but he was a soldier and had witnessed the battle of Agincourt in 1415 from the French side. He also had a strong interest in English affairs and visited London in 1467, meeting leading nobles such as Lord Rivers, brother-in-law to Edward IV. He may have even met the king himself, explaining his Yorkist bias and interest in Towton, although this cannot be substantiated. Waurin may have met with many veterans and nobles whose evidence was more chivalric than factual, but it is certain that some of his strategic observations are unique and cannot be found elsewhere.

More information about the predominance of Towton village over Saxton regarding the battle's name is supplied in *Hearne's Fragment* (one of three fifteenth-century chronicles printed by Thomas Hearne in 1719) and Polydore Vergil's *History of England*. These two sources have the Yorkists advancing on Towton and not Saxton, but, considering the accepted Lancastrian presence in this area, it is perhaps not surprising considering that Towton was on the main road north and Saxton was situated on a local trackway. However, the name of Towton has stuck with the battle, even though the action was mostly fought in Saxton parish. Before this, contemporary documents of the period referred to the battle of 'Palmsunday Field', 'York Field', 'the battle of Cockbridge' or even 'the battle of Sherburn'. Such are the problems of topography in this period and a lesson not to take the words contained in sources literally as contradictions, in most cases, abound.

The actual battle of Towton is not, however, in my opinion, about contradictions, but instead about alternatives for the reader to analyse and consider. Obviously, no one can be absolutely certain what happened in the snow south of Towton village in 1461. Documentary evidence is sadly lacking, so-called reliable chronicles fall short of detail, and eyewitness accounts (like that of William Gregory at the second battle of St Albans) are non-existent. So, how can anyone judge what unfolded in the bloody meadows of Towton battlefield without good, detailed evidence? In this situation, our only way forward is to support the undeniable facts with what John Keegan called the 'mechanics of battle' and employ a multi-disciplined approach to reach a conclusion. We must start at the beginning with the contemporary or near contemporary evidence, apply the tactical effects of weapons and armour, sift through the archaeological evidence, and yes, even consider the legends that have been passed down to us over the centuries. But above all, we must apply logic, apply an appreciation of the medieval mindset and consider the 'anatomy of the battle' in detail. More importantly, we must apply what we have learned so far about the wars between York and Lancaster, the attitude of kings, nobles, retainers and levies to warfare in general, and take note of the physical and mental drain on the human body in such a horrific and violent situation. Then we may at least come close to what happened between Saxton and Towton and marvel at what many historians have called the Pharsalia of England.[22]

Six

Palmsunday Field

The northern party made them strong with spear and shield,
On Palmsunday after none they met us in the field,
Within an hour they were right fayne to flee, and eke to yield,
Twenty-seven thousand The Rose killed in the field,
Blessed be the time, that ever God spread that flower.[1]

The *Rose of Rouen* contains one of the many disputed casualty
figures used to describe the horror of the battle of Towton.
Indeed, all the chroniclers and historians of the battle provide their readers with unbelievable figures, both in numbers
of participants and the enormous death tolls incurred there
due to the apparent length and ferocity of the conflict. Not
surprisingly, these estimates have long been the subject of
much debate, causing more recent theories of smaller sized
armies and consequently proportionally lower casualties to be
accepted as the truth.

This daunting mathematical dilemma, whether approximately 10,000 or 100,000 soldiers took part in the battle of
Towton and if 3,000 or 38,000 of these men were left dead
on the field is, to say the least, a great problem to resolve with

The battlefield of Towton, looking from the Lancastrian position towards the Yorkist line. The hawthorn tree is on the left and Castle Hill Wood is situated on the far right. (Author)

logical thinking. But to judge truth from pure exaggeration in the chronicles and letters of the time is an even more frustrating task. In concluding armies of biblical proportions, chroniclers, in their often moralistic and monastic way, abhorred bloodshed yet elevated their king to greater heights of power if mass killing suited national politics. In giving the plague-like death tolls, writers undoubtedly aimed to please their benefactors, and in George Neville's case, he mourns the loss of English lives while taking the opportunity to sympathise with the Papal Legate Coppini in support of his popular crusade against 'the enemies of the Christian name'.[2] In short, each chronicler makes the numbers work for political reasons. Historians all inherently tend to do the same, no matter how tough the competition.

So how many men faced each other across the fields beneath the banners and standards of their captains at Towton? Was it the more usual period armies of approximately 5,000 to 10,000 men, or perhaps ten times this number, defying all logic and rationality?

Besides such musters of men undertaken, for instance, at Bridport using commissions of array, the only reliable recorded benchmark we can use to assess how many soldiers a king and his loyal nobility could muster in England during the Wars

of the Roses is the army that Edward IV took on his blood-less (and well documented) expedition to France in 1475. An army of almost 12,000 men was raised on this occasion – a similar figure, as it happens, to King Henry's southern counties muster in 1457, of which Bridport was a part. Regionally, though, records show that leading nobles could each raise average retinues of 2,000 to 3,000 men from their domains and did so on numerous occasions during the wars. Bills of sale still exist for payment of cloth to make livery jackets and badges for their men, and at the other end of the social scale, a Westmorland squire such as Walter Strickland, who contracted with the Earl of Salisbury in 1452, could also muster a respectable force of 300 armed men, comprised of archers and billmen. Therefore, if we apply the above evidence to the large number of peers in the Lancastrian army at Towton and the lesser proportion of magnates in the Yorkist force, then the claims of chroniclers like Edward Hall must be considered wildly exaggerated. Hall gives an exact figure of 48,640 for the Yorkist army at Towton, using the 'pay roll' as his source of information. He computes the Lancastrian army at 60,000. However, each noble could not possibly have raised such a vast army in the fifteenth century, and many in the army were paid who did not fight, such as secretaries, royal servants, councillors and camp followers. We also know that casualties occurred at Ferrybridge, and the weather conditions were frightful, leading to more fatalities on the road north, not to mention desertions. So, the apparent authority of Hall is questionable, not to mention where his elusive payroll is today.

Greater figures than Hall's can be discounted, while armies of less than 12,000 men insults both the structure of Livery and Maintenance and commissions of array in England, not forgetting that foreign mercenaries, Scottish and Welsh troops, were also present in the two armies at Towton. The critical point to remember here is that a great effort was made to muster all able-bodied men in the country for the battle through all recruitment methods possible. After all, the war was by this stage at its height. It was a civil conflict, a battle between north and south in some respects, and king against king, in which everyone had some sort of stake in the outcome.

A.H. Burne, in his *Battlefields of England*, had an interesting theory about the combatants at Towton, which warrants attention purely because it represents a best estimate per head of population. Burne, a man with military experience, confidently states that:

> No one knows what the population [of England] was in 1461. *The Historical Geography of England before 1800* computes it as 4,688,000 about a century later. So, if we accept a conservative estimate of 3 and a half million in 1461, with a fighting age of 15 to 40, we get something in the neighbourhood of 500,000 potential soldiers. If we allow that 75,000 took part in the battle [of Towton], that comes to 15% of the potential soldiers available.[3]

Burne's fifteen per cent computation led him to believe that the Yorkists fielded 36,000 men and the Lancastrians, being better supplied with peers, amassed 40,000, the largest amount of manpower ever assembled for a pitched battle on British soil. However, these sorts of figures have been challenged in respect of the low fighting age of fifteen, for instance, and the estimated population at the time – and I am no exception.

To counter the first problem, let us not forget that the potential King of England, Edward IV, was only eighteen himself when he fought at Towton and, for all his youthful years, he commanded, took an active part in the battle, and towered over his subjects at 6ft 3in tall. As Burne reminds us, Harry Hotspur commanded a successful assault on Berwick at the age of thirteen, so it is not unreasonable to suggest, indeed it is more than likely to expect younger men than Edward IV on both sides at Towton. The endurance and fitness of such soldiers must have been a vital prerequisite to an efficient fighting force in the medieval slogging match that most battles became in the end. Most of these troops would have been well versed in arms, especially the warbow, from an early age. Violence was a part of everyday life, and therefore the reason for using their potential is self-evident. At the other end of the social scale, older fighting men were present at the battle. The veteran captain Lord Fauconberg was aged sixty at Towton. Some nobles were in their mid-fifties, while others averaging forty years old were found in the Towton graves making Burne's total of potential soldiers even greater.[4] Also, the population of England was a lot less in 1461 (possibly 2.2 million), and the wars must have already depleted the potential number of soldiers, not only in casualties inflicted but also in the inability of the nobles to raise such large contingents time and time again. As explained earlier, it is not surprising that this whole subject of numbers at Towton is a quagmire of supposition.

However, it would be wrong of me to disregard the issue and not to make a judgement myself, based on averages of men raised by the nobles for other campaigns in the Wars of the Roses, available frontages, the duration of the battle, and, to verify the resulting figure, the all-important casualty figures inflicted on the day. Hopefully, by assessing the above factors throughout this chapter, the resulting calculations may prove that what an army 'looked like' in numbers, and how many casualties there 'appeared' to be after a battle, differed greatly from reality. It is perhaps not surprising that chroniclers and modern historians' figures vary when describing such large bodies of men, as even witnesses of Towton must have had great difficulty quantifying the massive armies facing them and those left dead afterwards.

If the leading peers in both armies could raise an average of 2,000 to 3,000 men and the lords an average of 300 to 500 men, then we should, with the help of Edward IV's attainder and a list of proven combatants, be able to calculate the 'average' Lancastrian strength with some degree of accuracy. The royal army had in their ranks five peers of the realm, eight lords and an impressive array of knights, who may have mustered up to 20,000 men, according to the averages above. These were the retinues that formed the foundation stone of the army. Add to this the town militias who were recruited through commissions of array, such as the City of York, which sent 1,000 men to Towton, the use of foreign mercenaries and Scots, accounting for another 5,000 more, and we may come to an informed decision that a Lancastrian army of 25,000 took the field at Towton.

Edward's army of the Marches, recently engaged at Mortimers Cross, and the Earl of Warwick's remnants from the second battle of St Albans must have numbered at least 15,000 at the start of the campaign when fully mustered in London with the southern shires. As will be remembered, there were at least 8,000 men in Edward's army alone when it occupied the capital at the end of February, and this was before Warwick and Norfolk began to recruit troops elsewhere in England. When fully mustered, the new king's army may have been even larger before leaving London, given that the southern counties could, and did on several occasions, muster far greater armies with the help of propaganda. However, the Yorkist march, the bad weather and the battle of Ferrybridge must have claimed lives. So, if we say that Edward, Warwick and Fauconberg's contingents once united at the beginning of the battle of Towton amounted to 20,000 men, with the Duke of Norfolk still on the road with 3,000 additional troops, we cannot be far away from the truth, given that the Lancastrians were superior to the Yorkists in strength on the day. Let us not forget that almost all the nobility of England was assembled for Towton, in contrast to the usual Wars of the Roses armies fielding relatively small turnouts of nobles, which when mustered probably amounted to around 5,000 men – a figure that may have formed only one of the usual three main divisions or 'battles' at Towton.

In accepting the above calculations, can we support these figures with the horrifying death tolls given in the chronicles and, in turn, draw some new conclusions about the numbers of men engaged in combat? Some sources give casualty figures of well over 30,000 men, and one can accept that this figure may be accurate for losses on the field, drownings in the two rivers at Towton and Tadcaster and deaths from wounds in the aftermath. However, it is questionable whether more than twenty-five per cent of the total combatants were killed on the battlefield. The rout is another problem if the dead were spread over an area 6 miles long by 3 miles 4 furlongs wide.

In the letter read by William Paston in Chapter One, Edward IV informed his mother, Cicely Neville, the Duchess of York, that 20,000 Lancastrians were killed at Towton, and, judging by the heralds' estimates, 8,000 Yorkists.[5] The Milanese merchant Pigello Portinaro also received news from London that 20,000 Lancastrians and 8,000 Yorkists were killed, corroborating the above and confirming approximate figures by Abbot John Whethamstede, Polydore Vergil, the *Rose of Rouen* and the bishops of Salisbury and Exeter. Therefore, a death toll of between 20,000 and 28,000 from one original contemporary source, possibly one of those discussed in Chapter One, seems to be a reasonable approximation, of which figure the Lancastrians had the more significant loss of life. The rout at the battle of Towton undoubtedly claimed many more lives as the blood-letting continued to York. But the problems of accounting for these lives with any accuracy are not practical.

Instead, I am inclined to believe that approximately 10,000 men may have been killed on both sides on the actual battlefield of Towton, 5,000 more Lancastrians in the immediate rout across the plateau to the River Cock and even more in the general pursuit to Tadcaster where further drownings and killing occurred in the River Wharfe. More soldiers were obviously injured in battle and consequently, in the medieval era, died from infected wounds after the event. But even my approximations regarding casualties are horrifying to comprehend and need no further exaggeration, given that these figures refer to deaths before mechanised warfare.

The hawthorn tree, where the two armies first saw each other. (Author)

As a matter of interest, since it is a common misunderstanding by some, Edward Hall's exact figure of 36,766 for the dead at Towton is not only based on deaths 'on the field'. Instead, it represents the casualties on both sides over a four-day period, inclusive of Towton, the battle of Ferrybridge, the skirmish at Dintingdale and the protracted overland pursuit to York. It is evident to anyone who has considered medieval conflicts deeply, even discarding the larger casualty figures of Hall and accepting the lower estimates of deaths on the field and in the rout of, say, between 20,000 and 28,000, that the battle of Towton is Britain's bloodiest pitched battle.

So much for calculations, which play a part in understanding the battle's large format. For a commander such as the Duke of Somerset or Edward IV, it is more likely that their visual appreciation of the troops opposing them would have been far different, and they certainly would not have been counting numbers of men with their fingers. An impression of strength would have been far more valuable to them and their chief captains, coupled with an understanding of which nobles were present on the field, pinpointed by their heraldic banners and standards.

In my view, it is a hazardous and fruitless enterprise for anyone to quote figures on medieval battlefields with any accuracy, and, in studying the battle of Towton, playing around with noughts only complicates the issue.

The Yorkist Advance

Whichever theory we accept concerning the approach march of both armies to the battlefield, at some point, one army would occupy a better position than the other, either by chance or by design. If according to Jean de Waurin, the main Yorkist army marched to Saxton from Sherburn-in-Elmet on the morning of 29 March, it would have had to ascend the plateau to meet the Lancastrians in the same way as if it were camped around Saxton, Lead and Dintingdale the previous night. However, according to Edward Hall, both forces were out of sight of each other during the final movements onto the battlefield and 'when each party perceived each other, they made a great shout, and at the same instant time there fell snyt [sleet] or snow'[6] – a statement that proves that the Yorkist army was at a disadvantage and that the Lancastrians occupied a prepared position.

The lie of the land holds the clue to this statement by Hall, who places the Yorkist advance in battle formation onto the plateau, totally concealed by its southern edge, until reaching its highest point where shouts of defiance came from both armies when they saw each other. These few lines by the Tudor chronicler also further disprove the theories of a Lancastrian position on the southern ridge overlooking Saxton and Dintingdale because, if the Duke of Somerset had formed his army here, it would have been in full view of the Yorkists most of the morning. Equally, the theories of a Lancastrian position between the hawthorn tree and Castle Hill Wood can be discounted, considering that part of the Lancastrian battle line, namely its right flank, would have had its back to the steep slopes of Bloody Meadow and the River Cock valley, an unenviable tactical position for any army to occupy given the steep descents of the plateau.

Before the armies moved into position, absolution of sins would have been given by the various priests in the army, the church playing a crucial part in preparation for battle. This process may have been hurried for some knights and commoners, especially on such an uncertain Palm Sunday morning. However, neither army seemed one bit concerned about fighting and possibly dying on such a holy day – quite the reverse in fact. Vengeance, bloodlust, orders of no quarter, the killing of traitors and the resignation to kill or be killed echoed in the ranks. Edward's boast of no quarter is typical under the circumstances and comparable to similar feelings of those who had lost their fathers or sons in the wars on the Lancastrian side. For some, the imminent battle was the zenith of a quest for revenge that had been exposed like an open wound ever since the first battle of St Albans in 1455. Executions of such nobles as Somerset and Northumberland had caused their sons to pledge oaths of vengeance. Likewise, for young Edward, not only against the killers of his father and brother at Wakefield but also because a chance now presented itself to cut a clear path to the throne as an extra incentive. In this frame of mind, Edward must have regretted King Henry's absence on the battlefield because, unlike his father, the Duke of York, it is doubtful whether he would have given the anointed king such fair treatment. Later in 1471, he ordered Henry murdered in the Tower of London after the battle of Tewkesbury. Who knows what would have happened to the royal family after the battle of Towton?

Depending on whether you were Yorkist or Lancastrian, there were also traitors to punish. Sir Andrew Trollope and Lord Grey of Ruthin, to name but two, had already changed sides in the conflict, and it would not be the end of this behaviour in the wars. In Trollope's case, we can have some sympathy for his predicament in that, because of his loyalty to King Henry in 1459, he had not only become the perpetrator of the Yorkist defeat at Ludford Bridge, and thus an enemy to Edward's regime, but also, he was now a dangerous military brain in the service of the Lancastrians. As such, a price of £100 had been placed on his head and the heads of some other named men in the forthcoming battle.

Certainly, by midday (9 o'clock according to Edward Hall), the two massive armies were in sight of each other, and most probably it was the Lancastrians, considering their presence on the plateau first, who had the best opportunity to choose the ground and consolidate their position on it. Lord Clifford's sacrificial abandonment may have been the cost of concealing

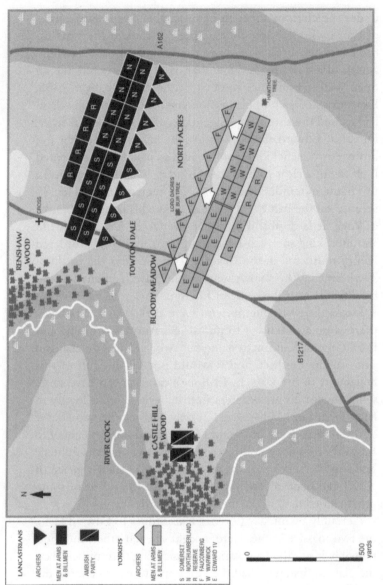

The initial positions of the armies and the advance of Lord Fauconberg's archers. (Author)

this prepared plan of action – prepared in so much as Sir Andrew Trollope and the Duke of Somerset may have formulated a plan to trick the Yorkists, such as an ambush like that at the battle of Wakefield. Given the Lancastrian track record since Trollope joined their ranks, it is unreasonable to suggest that the Master Porter of Calais would not have deliberately swayed his overmighty young benefactor into preparing a position on the battlefield plateau with his keen tactical eye.

It would have undoubtedly taken some time for the two armies to get into formation between Towton and Saxton, and trumpets, drums and shouts from captains, muffled by the strengthening wind, would have formed the men into contingents and 'battles'. Although most soldiers who had horses would have dismounted by this time, especially the archers, the darting of horsemen to deliver messages, and round up stragglers, would still have been apparent. The large baggage camps behind both armies would have been bustling with activity earlier on, as horses were tethered, weapons supplied and what little food and drink the army had with it were distributed to the men. But now, as the armies faced each other in deadly preparation, only the extinguished fires, smoking between the wagons, and the guards around the perimeter would have been visible.

Both Yorkist and Lancastrian commanders would have consulted yet again with God before the final moves were underway. It is recorded that, before the battle of Agincourt, Henry V heard mass three times and took communion, as did most of his followers. This observance was a vital part of a Christian king or chivalrous knight's routine before battle, especially when, in his eyes, the power of God was far greater than the power of man in such matters of uncertainty. However, of greater and more down-to-earth tactical importance were the orders from the commander-in-chief to his captains, as, even with God on their side, military science was well established in English armies, and proven tactics walked hand in hand with religious observance.

English archers in action as depicted in the contemporary *Beauchamp Pageant Roll*. The thickness of their longbows bears out the fact that this was an immensely powerful weapon.

English captains took the art of war very seriously, and they organised men into companies and contingents that formed the usual three 'wards' or 'battles' of the era. The two variations of the battle formation were, by the fifteenth century, in line abreast or in line astern, and split 'vaward' or vanguard to the right or in front (foreward) of the army, 'mainward' or middleguard in the centre and 'rearward' or rearguard to the left or taking up a position at the back of the column. Other variations existed when space was unavailable, but this was generally the organisation of medieval English armies, even on their march to encounter the enemy.

At this point, the vaward would arrive on the battlefield first to cover the advance of the two remaining wards, as Fauconberg's archers would have done the night before the battle, it being well supplied with bows and, more often than not, much enlarged to give battle first if needed. Even this tactic was not, however, cast in stone, and on several occasions in the Wars of the Roses, battles formed up opposite each other purely out of choice or by mistake as at the battle of Barnet ten years later.

Of the three main arms of bows, bills and men at arms, it is uncertain whether archers alternated with knots of men at arms and bills at Towton, like the formation adopted by the English at Agincourt, or if bows fronted the battles with the other soldiers filling in behind. I am inclined to believe the latter because of the events surrounding the opening stages of the battle, and I further suggest that the Yorkist vaward was wholly comprised of archers in separate contingents under their captains massed together in formation with one overall commander. Probably 10,000 men strong, and given the lie of the land, compacted into a ten-man-deep chequerboard formation, this arrangement would have given each archer not only room to reload his bow but also the ability to view his target slightly better. The second of the army's battles astern, because of the space available, would have comprised the heavy infantry of knights, men at arms, billmen and mercenary companies, who would inevitably have to sustain the brunt of the fighting when the warbow had done its deadly work. Edward and Warwick undoubtedly commanded this Yorkist division. The rearward would, in Towton's case, have been a reserve made up of all arms contingents, and it would have contained some mounted troops to sweep the rear of the army, plugging gaps and, more importantly, dissuading deserters with their fifteen-foot lances. These horsemen were called 'prickers' for several good reasons, as their name might suggest, when not everyone in an army was willing to fight.[7]

The Yorkist advance onto the battlefield would have taken time to complete unless Fauconberg's vaward was in position first. Therefore, it is important that we also look at the possibility of a Yorkist arrival on the plateau first because this theory could further disprove the claims of some historians that the opening battle lines were placed somewhere other than across Towton Dale and North Acres.

English jack, *c.* 1580. (Royal Armouries)

If the Yorkists occupied the southern ridge first, between the Tadcaster to Ferrybridge road and Bloody Meadow, taking the hawthorn tree as a command position, then the Lancastrians would have had no alternative but to advance to conform as much as possible with their enemy's frontage. As was usual in the Wars of the Roses, the vawards implemented this manoeuvre to begin the archery duel, which often decided who would be disadvantaged. Polydore Vergil told of an interesting development in the Lancastrian camp on the morning of the battle of Towton:

> And it came to pass by mean of the soldiers, who, as their manner is, like not upon lingering, that very self-same day, by daybreak in the morning, after he [Henry VI] had with many words exhorted every man to do his duty, he was forced to sound the alarm. His adversaries were there as ready as he.[8]

We could deduce from this passage that the Lancastrians were caught unawares, especially if, according to Jean de Waurin, Edward marched to the battlefield during the early morning of 29 March. But more than this, if the Lancastrians were slow to move their army forward, then, forgetting de Waurin's comments, this would account for the better position of the Yorkist army and the cramped conforming alignment of the Duke of Somerset's forces across Towton Dale and North Acres. Trying to deploy the massive army under his command on the northern ridge must have been a headache for the young duke, especially with other unruly nobles vying to be the first into the fray.

In my opinion, however, Somerset's army was in position on the plateau first, as this was by far the main objective of the Lancastrian command all along. In occupying the Battle Cross Ridge, the Yorkists were disadvantaged by a similar space problem, which may not be immediately apparent. The reasoning behind this is that the greater space available to the Yorkists on the southern ridge would have been wasted when conforming to the Lancastrian battle line. It would have been pointless for the Yorkists to spread their army any further towards Castle Hill Wood where their archers, overlooking the area of the River Cock, would have had nothing to shoot at.

Therefore, the Lancastrians straddled between Renshaw Wood and the steep banks of the River Cock to their right and the Ferrybridge road marshes to their left occupied a strong position. If their archers also planted sharpened wooden stakes before them, as was usual practice in medieval battles, the slope before them, possibly slightly steeper in 1461, would have presented Edward IV with a difficult frontal assault, that is providing the Lancastrian bowmen won the archery duel and made the Yorkists advance first.

The wait for contingents to take their positions during the advance may have been protracted. It was likely approaching midday before both armies were in position, and much heavy drinking on both sides might have quelled fear and numbed senses, especially among the Yorkist soldiers, who would have become drunk very quickly due to their empty stomachs. John Keegan, in his book *The Face of Battle*, has this to say about the battle of Agincourt:

> The English who were on short rations presumably had less to drink than the French, but there was drinking in the ranks on both sides during the period of waiting, and it is quite possible that many soldiers in both armies went into the mêlée less than sober, if not indeed fighting drunk. The prospect of battle, excepting the first battle of a war or a green unit's first blooding, seems always to alarm men's anxieties, however young and vigorous they may be, rather than excite their anticipation. Hence the drinking which seems an inseparable part both of preparation for battle and of combat itself. Alcohol, as we know, depresses the self-protective reflexes and so induces the appearance and feeling of courage.[9]

Much has been said and written about the heraldic pomp and extravagance of armies assembling for a battle such as Towton. However, the truth about the appearance of the common soldiers and the medieval knights on the battlefield must have been far removed from Arthurian legend. In the first place, the shivering recruits waiting for action may still have been wrapped in additional clothing, such as cloaks, and their once-resplendent livery jackets, now ingrained with grime and mud from the march, must have made identification far from easy. Their weapons, however, would have been in good order – the inspections by captains would have made sure of this – and the trusty warbow would have been well looked after, being bagged when not in use and meticulously honed by its owner, like all the best missile weapons, in readiness of attack.

Armour, especially the noble's expensive 'harness', was looked after and cleaned by pages, but most of the Yorkist men at arms had been encased in plate for some time in anticipation of battle, and because of this rusting around joints and rivets may have been apparent due to the bad weather. However, as the nobles rode along the ranks of these cheering bedraggled, bawdy and unkempt troops, they alone must have represented a lavish vision of medieval splendour to their men. That sight at least must have boosted morale, especially if the man looked up to was a potential King of England.

Tens of thousands of Englishmen and their allies in deep, grey-steeled phalanxes, spiked with lethal blades of destruction and pent-up bows of Spanish yew, now faced each other in grim resolve to await their orders. Beneath stiff banners treated with buckram, to set them permanently 'on the fly', eagle eyes strained to see their enemies' first movements through the driving snow. It was to be the Yorkists who would take the initiative first, and with this step, they unleashed the biggest exchange of arrows in recorded medieval history.

The Archery Duel

After the Hundred Years War, everyone in Northern Europe knew the potential of the English warbow, especially the

French, who had fallen victim to its killing power on several occasions. Because of this power, by the Wars of the Roses at least, horses and men became even better armoured with designer plates, shaped and curved to deflect the cloth-yard arrow with its bodkin-shaped head. Many other types of head and weights of arrow were used for different purposes in battle. Still, with a 100–120lb draw weight and an effective range of up to 220–300yd, the common warbow was devastating enough with these specifications, if shot quickly and by the right number of men, to wreak havoc in even the best-protected ranks of men. At long range, this was precisely the result of prolonged shooting. At closer range, the warbow was more lethal, easily penetrating plate armour, if the trajectory of an arrow was approximately ninety degrees to the surface, and skewering anything else in its path, through flesh and bone up to the goose feathers at its end.

Lord Fauconberg's archers advance at the beginning of the battle of Towton. (Author)

However, the real strength of the medieval archer was his rate of fire, estimated at between ten and fifteen arrows a minute. Only by law-enforced practice at the butts from an early age was this achieved, and, as Bishop Latimer recorded, this was by his day a time-honoured tradition to which all the Towton archers owed their great skill:

> In my time, my father was diligent to teach me to shoot, as other fathers were with their children. He taught me how to draw, how to lay my body to the bow, not to draw with the arms as other nations do, but with the strength of the body. I had my bows brought to me, according to my age, and as I increased so my bows were made bigger, for men shall never shoot well unless they are brought up to it.[10]

The archery duel at the battle of Towton was particularly and uniquely one-sided, unlike some other engagements in the Wars of the Roses when the warbow's effectiveness was invariably cancelled out because of each side's knowledge and use of the weapon. However, one of the Towton chroniclers is more certain about this phase of the battle than any other. Edward Hall gave the details of who was in command of the Yorkist archers, what effect the weather conditions had on both sides, and what the Lancastrians suffered when the clattering arrow storm reached its target:

> The Lord Fauconberg, which led the forward of King Edward's battle being a man of great policy and of much experience in martial feats caused every archer under his standard to shoot one flight and then made them stand still. The northern men, feeling the shoot, but by reason of the snow, not perfectly viewing the distance between them and their enemies [the snow and wind was driving into the Lancastrian faces from the south] like hardy men shot their sheaf arrows as fast as they might, but all their shot was lost and their labour in vain for they came not near the southern men by 40 tailor's yards. When their shot was almost spent the Lord Fauconberg marched forward with his archers, who not only shot their own sheaves, but also gathered the arrows of their enemies

and let a great part of them fly against their own masters, and another part they let stand on the ground which sore annoyed the legs of the owners when battle was joined.[11]

Polydore Vergil confirmed the obvious fact that 'the archers began the battle, but when their arrows were spent, the matter was dealt by hand strokes'.[12] Whatever transpired when the Yorkist archers advanced after their first flight of arrows and delivered more similar barrages at the Lancastrians, it was annoying enough to force the issue. In fact, the arrow storm must have been so devastating in the ranks of the lesser armoured men fronting Somerset's army that, at this range, possibly 300yd across Towton Dale and North Acres, the tendency must have been for some of the Lancastrians to fall back. In the chronicles of Jean Froissart, some Genoese crossbowmen were at a similar disadvantage at the battle of Crécy when:

> The English archers took one pace forward and poured out their arrows on them so thickly and evenly that they fell like snow. When they felt these arrows piercing their arms, their heads and their faces, the Genoese, who had never met such archers before, were thrown into confusion. Many cut their own bowstrings, and some threw down their crossbows and began to fall back.[13]

The bitterly cold driving snow and wind must have seemed insignificant to the Lancastrian archers, as wave after wave of hissing arrow shafts clattered and thudded into their ranks on the Battle Cross Ridge. The falling missiles would have impeded their own shooting drastically and many archers and footmen were likely pierced so thickly with arrows that they looked like 'hedgehogs with quills', according to an earlier chronicler's observation of Scottish troops under similar circumstances. If the '40 tailor's yards' (60yd) shortfall of arrows is to be believed, then, at maximum range, the wind must have been either so strong to slow the Lancastrian response, or Lancastrian captains miscalculated the distance to the Yorkist lines due to poor visibility. Whatever the problem, the opening 'fire fight' at Towton went against the Lancastrians and the usual archery duel rapidly developed into a one-sided turkey shoot favouring the Yorkists.

Bodkin arrowhead found on the battlefield. (Simon Richardson)

The incessant orders of 'notch, stretch, loose' or 'knock, draw, loose' by the Yorkist vaward captains must have unleashed intermittent showers of arrow shafts by contingents, rather than a complete one volley burst at the enemy. However, it had the desired effect as each storm of arrows punished the Lancastrian position with tons of wood-propelled shrapnel. In reply, the Lancastrian strike would have been a lot more erratic due to their increasing casualties and disarray. In a few minutes their ranks went mad with confusion and blood. There was no way out, other than wait for the Yorkist quivers to empty.

Lord Fauconberg had judged the following southeasterly wind well, but one must say it was pure luck that it carried the Yorkist arrows with ease to their target. However, considering that arrows climbed to a height of about a 100ft in some instances, and had to achieve from this a very narrow zone of impact to have the desired effect, the skill, especially in the weather conditions at Towton, is awe inspiring. The wind and driving snow were certainly disadvantageous for the Lancastrians as, contrary to their prepared plans, and because of their mounting casualties, they had no alternative but to advance first and give up their defensive position on the ridge.

The Lancastrian Advance

Stepping over the bodies of their fallen comrades and possibly half a million fallen arrows, a large, unwieldy mass of full and partially steel-clad men at arms and billmen began to trudge forward. Helmets and visors were adjusted into position, weapons were drawn or clutched in tighter grips, and the nobles dismounted from their warhorses to lead their retainers and household men into battle. This act of dismounting was 'the English manner'[14], as described by Philip de Commynes, and, apart from being a good morale boost for their men, it was hazardous. Once battle was joined and weapons started to fly, the chance of being surrounded with no escape became an awful reality. Some prominent nobles were killed in the Wars of the Roses by conforming to this typically English fashion, which resembles the exposure and sacrifice of officers in wars of the nineteenth and twentieth centuries rather than to that of the medieval battlefield knight.

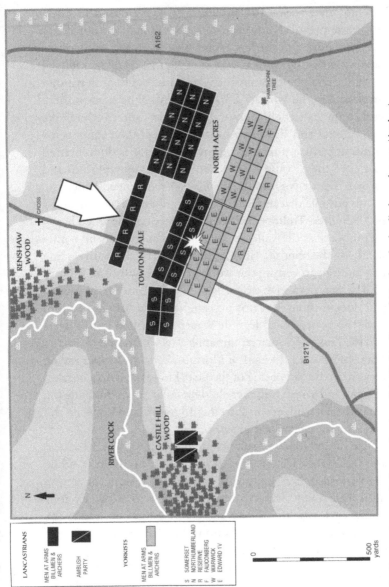

The Lancastrian attack, the overlapping of the Yorkist line and Northumberland's slow advance. (Author)

One other reason for this levelling of the classes in battle was more practical, however, and as the knight on horseback became more and more a target for the archer, and consequently at the mercy of serious injuries that could be inflicted by falling and being trampled by his horse, the English manner dictated that the knight's horse should only be used to carry him to the battlefield. Senior commanders such as the Duke of Somerset and Edward IV may have kept their mounts for communication purposes at Towton. But it is documented that even they would have dismounted for long periods and thrown themselves into the conflict when the need arose.

It is possible that the Earl of Northumberland, accompanied by Sir Andrew Trollope, led the first wave of dismounted heavy infantry across the valley to engage the enemy sitting confidently on the opposite ridge, as this part of the Lancastrian line may have been getting the worst of the arrow storm. Edward Hall depicts both men as commanding the Lancastrian vaward and 'seeing their shot not prevail, hastened forward to join with their enemies'.[15] Jean de Waurin described Lord Rivers and the Duke of Somerset initiating a two-battle attack on the Yorkist line, with the Earl of Northumberland slowly moving forward on the other side of the field. However, with a blizzard of snow and arrows still mercilessly raining down on them, the Lancastrians trudged on into the no man's land between the two armies despite their losses.

The vaward followed suit behind the mainward in the attack, and the Duke of Exeter's reserve brought up the rear, while the Yorkist archers kept up the incessant loosing of arrows until their supply was exhausted. Two sheaves of twenty-four arrows each would not have lasted a long time, even with the retrieval of Lancastrian shafts from the fields in front of them and the possibility of replenishment by runners from the baggage carts behind the lines. However, many of the Lancastrians, even well-armoured men at arms, would have been killed or wounded in the assault as the trusty warbow did its deadly work. Finding gaps in their continuously moving metal plates, especially at the joints, the steel-tipped arrow shafts would have had no trouble in puncturing the chainmail and leather beyond. It must have been a deadly advance because not all the Lancastrians were so well armoured. Being mustered together as a contingent, a structure of well-armoured gentry accompanied by their similarly armed retainers would have been leading others with only partial armour-plate, padded jacks, brigandines and the like, covered by thin livery coats. These types of lesser armoured troops would have been fair game for the warbow's close-quarter accuracy as the Lancastrian drums beat the advance.

When Somerset's army started to climb the Yorkist ridge, some isolated skirmishes would have occurred. But a lull in the shooting may have been evident, and only at short range would the cracking and malfunctioning of some handguns, because of the foul weather, have been heard. Jean de Waurin gave a rare description of one of the Lancastrian attacking battles from the Yorkist viewpoint above Bloody Meadow and North Acres:

At that moment [Edward IV] saw the army of the Earl of Northumberland coming for battle carrying the banner of King Henry. [He] rode his horse along his army where all the nobles were and told them how they had wanted to make him their king, and he reminded them that they were seeing the next heir to the throne which had been usurped by the Lancasters a long time ago. He suffered his troops and knights to help him now to recover his inheritance, and they all assured him of their desire to help, and he said that if any wished not to fight, they should go their own way. But all of them hearing this good request by the young earl, who was already thinking like a king, shouted in unison that they would follow him until death if necessary. Hearing this support, the earl thanked them, jumped from his horse and told them, sword in hand,

that on this day he would live or die with them to give them
courage. Then he came in front of his banners and waited for
the enemy which was marching forward with great noise and
shouting 'King Henry!'[16]

Propaganda aside, the steady advance of cheering Lancastrians
towards the Yorkist lines must have been a sight to snap even a
veteran's nerves. And it was probably at this moment that the
order was given for the Yorkist archers to fall back through the
ranks so that heavier troops and men at arms could get to the
front in time for the next phase of the battle.

However, this seemingly straightforward manoeuvre could
not have been easy under the circumstances. It is foolish to
think that lines of troops, especially a 1,000yd in length, could
have moved on the battlefield with Napoleonic precision,
or all at once for that matter. Some confusion, indeed, great
panic, must have occurred when the order was given to retire,
and in pushing through and round their own advancing mainward, men may have been irreverently jostled to the ground.
Archers may have been caught up in the Lancastrian advance,
as the chronicles suggest that Fauconberg's vaward was stepped
forward in front of the Yorkist main body. Even if we accept the
alternative three-battle formation in line abreast, this ordered
act of exchanging ranks must have occurred at some point
during the Lancastrian attack, as a collision with practically
defenceless men on this scale would have been catastrophic for
the Yorkist army.

Apart from enduring the grim ordeal of their advance and
the mounting casualties incurred because of it, the Lancastrians,
in moving to the attack at the same time, probably found more
room to deploy their compacted ranks across the battlefield,
especially on their right flank. Also, as Somerset's mainward
assaulted the southern ridge, it became apparent that now the
Yorkists must suffer what they must have been dreading all
along – the full weight of greater Lancastrian numbers against

them. The real battle of Towton would be fought on the southern plateau, the most exposed tract of land in the area.

The Main Battle

> Soon we shall see fields littered with quarters of helmets, and shields, and swords, and saddles, and men split through the trunk right to the belt. I tell you I have no such joy as when I hear the shout, 'on! on!' from both sides, and the neighing of riderless horses and the groans of 'help me! help me!' When I see both great and small fall into ditches and on the grass and see the dead transfixed by spear shafts, I rejoice. When he is in the thick of it, let no man of birth think of anything but the splitting of heads and arms, for a dead man is worth more than a live prisoner. Barons put in pawn your castles and farms and towns, but never give up war![17]

In the above passage, Bertrand de Born graphically tells us about his own attitude towards the 'joys' of battle, which probably comes very close to what most knights, and especially the nobles, must have believed and justified to others of similar status during the medieval period. The apocalyptic quest for destruction, the abandonment of others, merciless killing and the joy because of it, instinctive bloodlust to do more of the same, and the detachment and unconcern for the dead and dying are all apparent in the above passage. The perpetrator of such deeds is joyous in war, especially when facing the lower classes ranged like ninepins against him. He seems numb to suffering and rides in blood. Total abandonment to random violence is his code of honour, and we can be sure this state of mind was apparent at the battle of Towton.

To understand this, it is necessary to grasp what a knight expected to do once hand-to-hand fighting began on the medieval battlefield. And by the Wars of the Roses, we may be confident that his *raison d'être* had changed. Whereas in the Hundred Years War with France the gentry might have followed the codes of chivalry and granted mercy to their prisoners, this practice had been largely erased by the battle of Towton. Civil war meant that there was no ransom, and this can be proven by the muffled silence in the chronicles. Executions were far more likely to occur in defeat and it seems the upper class were willing to risk this to avenge their enemies or gain advancement.

Conversely, the lower classes must have felt very different about the whole affair, and their concept of killing on this scale must have been a far more basic case of survival through all means possible, which ultimately could include running away if the opportunity arose. As the Lancastrian army eventually came within 50yd of the Yorkist battle line, these recruits must have felt the same pangs of fright and gut-churning unease that any duty-bound soldier must endure in warfare. Most would have held all outward signs of this back from their comrades, hurling abuse at the enemy and taking part in various forms of bravado to cover up their apprehension about the inevitable clash of arms. Veterans and the knightly class would have known the desperate situation all too well, and what to avoid in combat, based on their past experiences. However, for all men in the front line, the rush of adrenaline was probably enough to sway the advancing ranks of steel against each other like a wave, pre-empting orders from commanders, and apparent enough to cause Edward and Warwick, commanding the Yorkist mainward, to initiate a charge at the Lancastrians to avoid disarray.

Slipping and sliding towards each other, the two front ranks probably clashed upslope on the southern plateau of the battlefield. Filling out and finding more width as they advanced, the Lancastrians pushed into Bloody Meadow up the steep gradient, incurring heavy casualties. Along the ebb and flow of front lines, various weapons would have been at work, beating down on their enemies' defences with deafening repetition and attempting forward and backward movements in the

A contemporary manuscript depicting the heaps of slain commonplace on medieval battlefields.

limited space available. Some weapons may not even have been used or caused any damage because of the closely compacted masses of men, and, in the push and shove from the rear, many soldiers must have been caught under the metallic stampede and simply crushed to death by friends or enemies without landing a blow. Eyewitnesses to this type of death vouch for how commonplace it was on the battlefields of the fifteenth century. Edward, Duke of York, at Agincourt was probably either killed by this kind of suffocation under falling masses of men or he had a heart attack in much the same situation.

By mid-afternoon, the two remaining Lancastrian battles would have joined the fray, but in so doing would have caused more problems in their own front line. This effect of perpetually advancing ranks of men eager to be at the enemy or pushed and shoved into the fray, unaware of the situation to their front, would have contributed dramatically to casualties on both sides. The first heaps of dead recorded by the chroniclers

The heraldic battle standard of the Earl of Warwick from the *Rous Roll*.
Banners and standards depicting single livery badges were also used in this
period to minimise confusion in battle.

may have been formed in this first assault, as Yorkists and
Lancastrians stumbled back and forth on the snow-covered
and arrow-strewn slopes, causing domino effects in the rear
ranks of their unscathed and oblivious troops.

As the third stage of the battle progressed, 'so great was the
slaughter', according to Polydore Vergil, 'that the very dead

carcasses hindered those that fought.'[18] And because of this, gaps and areas of dead ground would have appeared between the two armies, clogged with barriers of corpses and fallen weapons. In such an event, the tendency would have been for troops either to clamber over the top of such an unsteady platform to get at the enemy or to find a way around the obstacle in the hope of gaining a better foothold somewhere else. Thus, pockets of fighting would have developed along the battle line, making shoring up the front ranks an ongoing problem for the captains. Once exploited, these gaps could immediately be turned to advantage if the ground was won or left unguarded, and nobles supported by their retainers would have disputed these narrow defiles on foot, in large fighting groups under their battle banner working as a team. In the bloody hand-to-hand fighting that would have followed, the aim was for the retainers to cut a swathe through the enemy and forge a route for the noble to advance his banner. Thus, a rallying point could be established, and the rest of their men followed suit. However, movements such as this must have been far from straightforward or technical under battle conditions, and, apart from heraldic banners or standards hovering above the metallic stampede, troop recognition would have been impossible as the battle wore on.

As the orders in the chain of command became more and more garbled, some troops must have been confused about whether they were landing blows on the enemy or, accidentally, on their comrades. In payment for livery jackets, the Nottingham chamberlain's accounts recorded that red cloth was purchased 'for soldier's jackets and white fustian to make letters, and for the cutting out and threading on the letters'.[19] However, red jackets were a common uniform colour in the Wars of the Roses, and as for the recognition letters of their company, who would care in the heat of battle? The only way to minimise mistakes in such a confused mêlée was to fight in close order as a team; thus, the battlegroup was managed as a fighting unit, and morale could be instilled more efficiently either by words or personal feats in arms by leading captains. If this formation was achieved in such an attack, escalades could be defended and rallying points established for rest and reorganisation.

Polydore Vergil, describing the battle of Bosworth, had this to say about the martial attributes of Henry Tudor's chief vaward commander during the battle:

> In the meantime, the Earl of Oxford, fearing lest his men in fighting might be environed of the multitude, commanded in every rank that no soldiers should go above ten feet from the standards; which charge being known, when all men had throng thick together, they stayed a while from fighting, their adversaries were afraid, supposing some fraud, and so they all forbore the fight a certain space and that verily did many with right goodwill, who rather coveted the king [Richard III] dead than alive, and therefore fought faintly. Then the Earl of Oxford in one part, and others in another part, with bands of men close one to another, gave fresh charge upon the enemy, and in array triangle [a wedge formation] vehemently renewed the conflict.[20]

It is apparent from this account that the Earl of Oxford, seeing a problematic situation developing, rallied his men, confused his Yorkist enemies and reorganised his contingents into a strong battle formation, which later crushed Richard III's vaward under the Duke of Norfolk. Actions such as this by commanders would have been commonplace in the Wars of the Roses and of major importance when the recognition of troops was difficult or, as at Towton, when numbers were exceptionally large and confusing. The mistaken identity of some soldiers returning to the fighting in thick fog, only to be shot at by their own men at the battle of Barnet, illustrates what could happen if contingents lost contact and the threatening aspects of treachery came into play.

As time passed between Towton and Saxton, and the bleak morning turned into an even more miserable afternoon of blood, sleet and snow, both front lines continued with their grim task like thousands of foundry workers hard at work. For knights and their men at arms, displacing and puncturing riveted metal plates and their contents within was the only way to kill their enemies. One way in which a weapon such as the poleaxe or battle mace could crush an opponent's limbs or skull was by repeated pounding at one part of the metal defences until the resulting depression caused injury or rendered that part of the armour useless. When this was achieved, guards would inevitably come down as previously moving joints seized, and the vulnerable knight would be despatched, probably by groups of soldiers, through vulnerable gaps in the armour such as the armpit, the groin and the visor, with weapons specifically designed for that purpose.

As the battle became a one-to-one mêlée, a lightly armoured soldier like the archer also came into his own, using sword, buckler and small side-arms such as daggers, axes, and mauls to defend himself. By carrying less weight and working in groups with these weapons, nimble and bowless archers could quite easily catch men at arms and knights encased in armour at a disadvantage, singling them out to be killed if they became vulnerable. The billman, carrying his trusty weapon, and others with similar shafted weapons such as the glaive, may have found that space was cramped in the early stages of the battle. He, like those who used the pike, which was not common in England at this time, needed enough room to wield the weapon, but as more space eventually opened, the bill may have become more effective, it being particularly useful for both hooking an opponent to the ground and then thrusting the spike forward, thereby utilising all three classic attacking movements in one weapon.

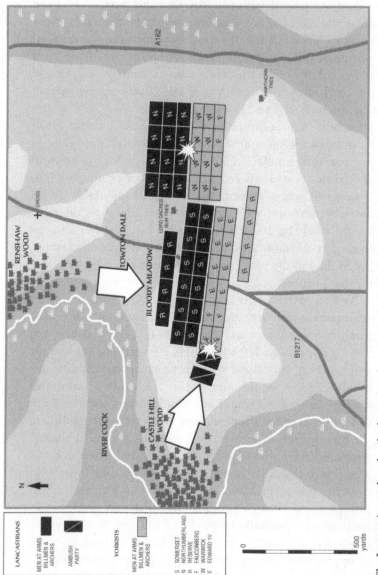

The Lancastrian push and ambush, causing the swing in the battle lines. (Author)

Distress and fatigue inevitably overcame many men and whole contingents, and as this phase of the battle wore on, the tendency would have been either simply to break off and try to retire or to be killed by a fresher or more experienced enemy. Because orders of no quarter were quite specific at Towton and the ferocity more intense than usual, this cry of alarm was a sign to any commander that fresh reserves or, in some instances, the king himself was needed to increase morale. Philip de Commynes stated that Edward IV won nine battles, 'all of which were fought on foot',[21] so there is no reason to doubt that he dismounted at crucial stages of Towton, his greatest triumph, to lead his men into the thick of the fighting. Naturally, we would expect no less from all the nobles of both sides, including the Earl of Warwick, who may have been in great danger, possibly limping across the field because of the arrow wound sustained at Ferrybridge the previous day.

It may have been at this point in the battle, as the Lancastrians brought their greater numbers to bear, that the Yorkists were slowly pushed back, step by step, across their own opening position on the southern plateau. Gradually, both armies moved towards Saxton, leaving thousands of dead and wounded behind them on the slopes of the shallow depression, especially in Bloody Meadow and on the Lancastrian ridge, where their ranks had fallen foul of the opening archery duel with Lord Fauconberg.

But was this sudden Lancastrian advance merely the effect of additional men overlapping the Yorkist left flank as they found more room to manoeuvre? Or was there a more serious cause for the backtracking? Surely the extra Lancastrian manpower appearing up the slopes of Bloody Meadow was not so overwhelming as to have a lasting effect on the Yorkist battle line? However, both these reversals in fortunes and a further serious setback seem to have caused a serious problem on Edward's exposed left flank. In addition to the overlapping effects of the main Lancastrian attack, a degree of panic seems to have occurred in Yorkist ranks. Indeed, according to one chronicler, it caused not a widespread retreat by Edward's already exhausted troops, but a gradual pivoting angle to form in both armies.

Despite the great trial of strength on other parts of the field, various sources indicate that this incident on Edward's left had a significant effect on the battle. Indirectly it dictated what happened at Towton from then on, and it caused a counter issue to occur in the Lancastrian army in the closing stages of the conflict.

As the leaden sky yielded yet more snow on York and Lancaster, and both sides fought as if 'they were at the gates of Paradise', there was a thunder of hooves, and a clash of steel as horsemen appeared from nowhere and plunged into the Yorkist left from the outskirts of Castle Hill Wood.

The Lancastrian Ambush

This sound prearranged plan of the Lancastrian high command has often been hinted at but has never been supported by much evidence, apart from the musings of military probability. Analysing this flank attack without substantial contemporary evidence, it is easy to discard the event as pure fiction. Therefore, I will try to shed more light on it considering that, first, a previous battle of the wars might highlight this tactic was contemplated, second, that actual chronicled evidence may indicate a severe setback occurred once the Yorkists were fully committed and, third, that other evidence may prove that the Yorkists were cautious of such a tactic happening again later in the wars.

To address the ambush theory fully, it is necessary to accept that the Lancastrian army was in position first on the Battle Cross Ridge and that a mounted detachment of 'spears' was sent to occupy Castle Hill Wood. This detachment was most probably located on the outskirts of the wood because even today the area is unsuitable for cavalry inside. Consequently, when the battle of Towton was fought, it must have been similarly impassable, if not a much more enlarged feature. If a prearranged order was given for the spears to attack when the enemy was fully committed, then the Lancastrian horsemen may have chosen to charge the Yorkists no later than when their army was beginning to push forward up onto the southern plateau. Surprise would have been the key to success, which would have been helped considerably by the effects of the falling snow and poor visibility on both sides.

The steep slopes southwest of Castle Hill Wood, where part of the Yorkist battle line may have come to grief. *(Author)*

Once hit by such a shock tactic, part of the Yorkist line would almost certainly have buckled under the pressure and now attacked on two fronts inevitably fallen back, taking the immediate ranks with it. In a smaller army, this assault by mounted men on unprepared, dismounted infantry would have been enough to sway the battle in favour of the Lancastrians and perhaps sufficient to cause panic and a Yorkist defeat. However, because of the huge numbers of men engaged at Towton and the distance of other troops from the problem, the Yorkists held onto their position.

As stated earlier, Richard Beauchamp, Bishop of Salisbury, received information that 'the result of the battle remained doubtful the whole of the day' and, 'at a moment when those present affirm that almost all our followers despaired of it, so great was the power and impetus of the enemy,'[22] King Edward, according to the bishop, stepped into the breach on foot to steady his men.

So significant was the despair of the Yorkists that, in my opinion, this caused both contending battle lines to change alignment, and the Yorkist left flank, engaged by Lancastrian cavalry, was at this point pushed down the southwest slope of the battlefield plateau, leaving the right flank still in the grip of bitter fighting in North Acres. If this scenario is correct, Yorkist casualties would have mounted in the vicinity. Indeed, these men may have been chased from the field, fleeing towards Lead and the banks of the River Cock. Further support for the Lancastrian ambush theory is available if we consider Jean de Waurin's chronicle regarding the opening stages of the battle. We can also pin down the basic concept of a Yorkist disaster and the apparent cause for concern when Waurin indicates that some of Edward's cavalry routed unexpectedly on a wing. Behind his banners at this time, Edward saw this rout, and his anger underlines the seriousness of what happened after the event in a story that is far from typical – especially from a chronicler who was pro-Yorkist. Waurin, an experienced soldier, who had probably gleaned his evidence from the Woodvilles, tells us:

> when Lord Rivers, his son [Anthony Woodville] and six or seven thousand Welshmen led by Andrew Trollope, following the Duke of Somerset himself with seven thousand men,

charged [Edward's] cavalry they fled and were chased for about eleven miles. It seemed that Lord Rivers' troops had won a great victory because they thought that the Earl of Northumberland had charged on the other side of the field, but unfortunately, he had not done so, and this became his tragic hour for he died that day. During this catastrophe, many of the Earl of March's soldiers died, and when he learned the truth of what had happened to his cavalry, he was very sad as well as very annoyed.[23]

During this period, it is to be noted that cavalry or 'spears' was a general term for an infantryman or man at arms that was either mounted or dismounted. However, here we see from an experienced commentator, who may have spoken to Anthony Woodville after the battle, that at least a serious reversal occurred on this side of the battlefield during the fighting.

Apart from the ambush being a sound tactical plan to use an available terrain feature to achieve surprise, and two similar accounts to support this, there is also compelling proof ten years later of Edward's fear of a similar ambush ploy at Tewkesbury. However, this time, with the hindsight of Towton, the king took immediate action before the battle began. *The History of the Arrivall of Edward IV in England* provides the details of this:

Here it is to be remembered that when the king [Edward] had come to the field before he attacked, he considered that upon the right hand of the field was a park, with many trees. He, thinking to provide a remedy in case his said enemies had laid any ambush of horsemen in that wood, he chose out of his troops 200 spears and set them in a group together about a quarter of a mile from the battlefield, charging them to keep a close watch on that part of the wood and do what was necessary if the need should arise.[24]

Even if this was an isolated surprise attack in the Wars of the Roses, we cannot get away from the fact that this tactic was well known and highly likely to occur by the time of the battle of Tewkesbury in 1471. Could Edward's reconnaissance of the wooded park have been sparked by the memory of a similar situation, which caused a problem for the Yorkists at the battle of Towton?

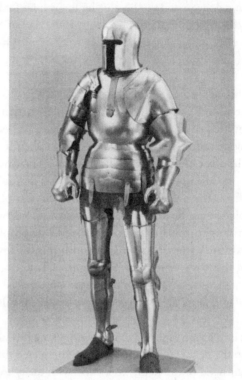

Fifteenth-century Italian armour, *c*. 1450. (Royal Armouries)

It is easy to accept Edward's precautionary move at Tewkesbury, knowing that the folly of exposing a flank to an unreconnoitred feature such as Castle Hill Wood could spell military disaster. However, considering that open battle was generally more simplistic in the medieval period, we can only highlight that a successful ambush was far more serious in 1461 than it was later in warfare. In fact, it had already been so disastrous in the Wars of the Roses that it had swept away a rash move without proper precautions by Edward's father, the Duke of York, at the battle of Wakefield in 1460. I believe this is what the Duke of Somerset and Sir Andrew Trollope intended to do at the battle of Towton as the Yorkists exposed their flank to Castle Hill Wood, hence the Lancastrians initial position on the Battle Cross Ridge rather than on the southern part of the plateau, where the woods and the ambush of 'spears' could not possibly have worked so well.

The main plan would have been to draw the Yorkists on across North Acres and Towton Dale for what would then have been a surprise attack at the rear of the Yorkist army. It would undoubtedly have been a crippling blow for Edward IV. However, because of the abandonment of their position, the Lancastrian detachment settled for the Yorkist flank, which admittedly caused disarray and localised panic, but posed no irreversible problems for Edward's commanders given the numbers of men, the exhaustion on both sides, and the deep ranks of the largely unaware armies.

However, another major event at Towton may also point to why the Yorkists could hold on and temporarily retrieve the developing situation on their flank. This was because of another weakness, but this time in the Lancastrian army, as highlighted by Jean de Waurin in the passage above.

It seems that, as the Lancastrian army advanced, the Earl of Northumberland's battle was slow to engage the enemy and, because of this, was pushed back into North Acres by the Yorkists counterbalancing the effects of the ambush on their flank. If this setback occurred, the Yorkists may have gained some ground, and thus the armies may have pivoted even more severely, extending diagonally from North Acres to the very edge of the southern plateau southwest of Castle Hill Wood. It is also possible when the Lancastrian left retreated, that, according to Waurin, the Earl of Northumberland was struck down and, being severely wounded, was dragged to the rear.

The Yorkists Give Ground

At least three chroniclers agree about the persistent snowstorm during the battle of Towton. *Hearne's Fragment* maintains that 'all the while it snew',[25] and the Croyland chronicler has it that 'the snow covered the whole surface of the Earth'[26] after the battle. Edward Hall verifies the wintry conditions during the opening manoeuvres on the field and the one-sided archery duel. So, given this dreadful weather, coupled with the length of the battle, we can imagine that conditions on Palmsunday Field were deplorable by the late afternoon. Even if the snow showers were intermittent, after three to four hours' fighting, there must have been a substantial covering shrouding dead bodies and debris littering the battlefield. However, stained red with the blood of the dead, the dying and the fighting wounded, the ground must have been far from pleasing to the eye. In fact, the snow would have changed colour due to churned up blood on the surface and gradually turned to mud and slush with the effect of thousands of men continually moving over half-buried corpses. The carnage shocked most contemporaries, and we can be sure the results of smashed and butchered human remains would have been more apparent than usual. But even this did not cause a slackening in the resolve to kill, and the slaughter continued amid the incessant cries of agony and butchery.

The armoured knight encased in his sallet helmet, straining to see through narrow eye slits, and sweating from the heat and pain caused by, among other things, chafing neck armour, cannot have fought for long in these conditions without rest. If he did not rest, he was prone to exhaustion and dehydration, both of which could lead to death as reflexes became slower and blows from the soldier's blind side rendered him partially stunned or unconscious. Once down on the ground, the enemy would have inflicted fatal injuries, so it is obvious that such men at Towton did not fight for hours under these conditions (ten hours, according to some chroniclers) or without some form of respite.

Soldiers and entire contingents had to leave the front line for rest at some stage, under challenging and confused circumstances, or instead be killed by the enemy and then irreverently stepped over by their comrades. When rest was possible, however (and the nobles were proficient at doing this because of their protective household men), the first requirement was liquid. Off would come the helmet and possibly the bevor (armoured neck protection), and the unprotected knight was immediately vulnerable, especially to archers. Lord Dacre of Gilsland may have done just this at the battle of Towton, and while drinking a cup of wine was shot in the neck or head by an arrow in North Acres. The 'lad' in a bur, or elderberry tree, remains a legend if indeed he existed at all. Tabards bearing the heraldic achievements of a lord or noble were not always worn in a battle over armour. Therefore, the archer's recognition of Dacre, especially in the confusion of battle, is open to question, and a stray or ricocheting arrow is a more likely explanation for Dacre's death.

A lord's demise would undoubtedly have affected his troops' morale, but how this manifested itself is hard to comprehend. Some of Dacre's men may understandably have looked over their collective shoulders if they were not fighting or otherwise occupied. But for many, the bond of retainer may have compelled them to fight on because their name, as well as that of their overlord, would be part of an attainder document issued by the winning side if they were to lose the battle and live. The laws of attainder required complete submission of land and titles in addition to the penalty of death for treason. So, this threat, more than any other, may have been the compulsion that in the end made many men fight on, as either dead or alive they were subject to the bad blood forfeit that accompanied their defeat.

However, in such a soul-searching situation, the local militiamen or levies were kept closely in check by their captains as they could disappear into the background with ease after a battle and reappear without such an obligatory weight on their shoulders. As such, these poor wretches were invariably made

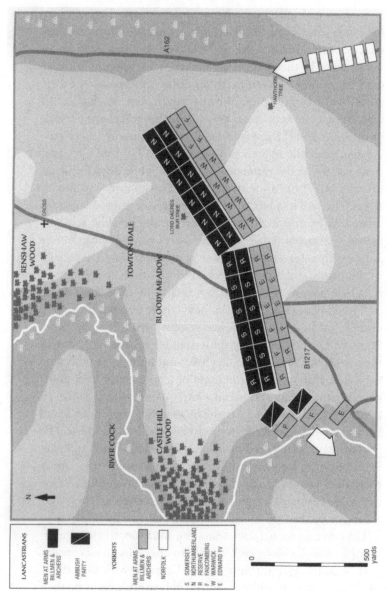

The ambush party's success. Both sides employ their reserves. The Duke of Norfolk's arrival. (Author)

the fifteenth-century 'cannon fodder' of the Wars of the Roses, and it is certain that more of these ordinary levies were buried on Palmsunday Field than their overlords or paymasters.

For both sides, it seemed the battle would never end. There was no way out, and, by this time, the human conveyor belt of troops arriving at the front line must have included the reserves of the Duke of Exeter's Lancastrians and his counterparts on the Yorkist side, Lords Wenlock and Dinham. At this time, as dismay crept into Yorkist hearts, it seemed the Lancastrians would carry the day. Edward and his commanders, Warwick and Fauconberg, must have wondered if the Duke of Norfolk would ever arrive on the field, and asked themselves not only would he be true to his word, but, if Norfolk did arrive, would it be only in time to witness a Yorkist defeat? Edward's messengers probably reported back Mowbray's position at regular intervals throughout the battle, but now, according to the chronicles, desperation was the order of the day, and time was rapidly running out for the Rose of Rouen. The Yorkist army was being pushed back in a large unwieldy mass, closer and closer to the downslope of Saxton, Dintingdale and Lead. Once reached, the terrain would undoubtedly have done its worst and thrown back the struggling and battle-worn troops, signalling disaster for the Yorkists after an unbelievable five hours of fighting. But, it seemed, all was not lost.

In all the chronicles recording King Edward IV's achievements, the stirring propaganda of his fighting ability comes flooding vividly across the centuries, similar in some respects to Henry V at his most glorious hour. Yet less is spoken, or indeed publicised, about the Yorkist warrior, who was more at home in battle than anywhere else. Later in his reign, Edward became a philanderer and womaniser, tortured by his inactivity, and like an athlete who has outgrown his usefulness, he sought other habits to fulfil his passion for war. However, at Towton, he was a young man and by all accounts a giant of powerful proportions, so most chronicles affirm that it was Edward's attributes alone as a warrior knight that spurred his men on at this most desperate hour. George Neville recorded in his letter to Coppini:

> I prefer you should learn from others than myself how manfully our King, the Duke of Norfolk, and my brother and uncle bore themselves in this battle, first fighting like common soldiers, then commanding, encouraging and rallying their squadrons like the greatest captains.[27]

Pushing into the weakest part of the battle line on foot with the 'Black Bull of Clarence' carried by his standard-bearer, Ralph Vestynden, Edward, with his household men, would have endeavoured to stabilise the ever-thinning line with reserves and rested troops. The twelve-foot-long battle flag of the new king's ancestors would have served as a marker for all to see and the line to rally behind. Thus, a breach in the line would have been temporarily closed and morale boosted by the king's intervention on such a fundamental level. This passage in the *Arrivall* concerning the battle of Barnet vividly describes Edward and his fighting unit in action and illustrates the king's strength of courage and character at the maximum point of danger:

> With the faithful, well-beloved and mighty assistance of his fellowship, that in great number dissevered not from his person, and were well assured unto him as to them was possible, he manly, vigorously and valiantly assailed them, in the midst and strongest of their battle. Where with great violence, he beat and bore down afore him all that stood in his way and then he turned to the range, first on one hand, and then on the other hand, in length, and so beat and bore them down, so that nothing might stand in the sight of him and the well-assured fellowship that attended truly upon him.[28]

Stirring Yorkist propaganda this might have been, but the facts concerning King Edward's exposure to danger must be appreciated in that those who knew him maintained that, by fighting on foot in all his battles, he not only encouraged others to greater personal prowess but also caused a greater oneness and unity in his army. In this battle-hardened frame of mind and with his strength of character, rather than his later stagnation, King Edward, in my opinion, was far better equipped both mentally and physically as a commander of men than any fighting monarch of England, including Henry V.

At the battle of Towton, however, the future king's army may have been almost beaten by the late afternoon, and, for all his strength of character, the battle was being lost. The Lancastrians' priority, sensing this advantage, must have been an even firmer determination to kill the usurper and quickly end the ordeal by flinging all their remaining reserves into the groaning mass of bodies for the final push. It is more than likely that, in this last-ditch attempt to end the battle quickly, all the nobles on both sides were fighting on foot. And judging by the forward push from their original camp, the Lancastrians were by now quite some way from their tethered horses. In fact, the Lancastrian nobles were in great danger as, like the Yorkists, each of their dwindling contingent's strength was eroded, and they edged closer and closer to their churning front ranks of clashing weapons, blood, and butchery.

Norfolk's Flank Attack

Why, with such an apparent advantage in the closing stages of the fight on the plateau, did the Lancastrian battle line suddenly break after winning so much ground and causing so much uncertainty, damage and despair in the Yorkist army? The answer is in the last phase of the battle of Towton and the sudden effects of the Duke of Norfolk's men finally entering the strung-out mêlée on the Lancastrian left flank.

However, as we shall see, the battle did not end quickly even after this, although the Lancastrians lost a significant number of men in the initial panic. Edward Hall, who gave the fullest account of Towton, was unsure why the Yorkists turned the tide and, like most of his fellow chroniclers, attributed the Lancastrian rout to the outcome of Edward IV's great skill as a fighter rather than a reinforcement by the Duke of Norfolk. Only the anonymous author of *Hearne's Fragment* mentions the duke by name and records that 'about the noon the aforesaid Duke of Norfolk with a fresh band of good men of war came to the aid of the newly elected King Edward',[29] and this was the same chronicler who recalled the dubious night battle of Towton alluded to earlier. However, to substantiate the above claim of a Yorkist reinforcement, Polydore Vergil states:

> Thus did the fight continue more than ten hours in equal balance, when at last King Henry [in this case the Duke of Somerset] espied the forces of his foes increase, and his own somewhat yield, whom when by new exhortation he had compelled to press on more earnestly, he with a few horsemen removing a little out of that place, expected the event of the fight, but behold, suddenly his soldiers gave the back, which when he saw this he fled also.[30]

To this reinforcement we must also add the telling effects of the unusually long duration of the battle. In the confusion, it must have been apparent as the fighting continued that the scales had become so delicately balanced that either side could claim victory given a slight advantage. Clearly, the Yorkists would not have held on much longer if something immediately telling had not occurred to turn the tide of the battle, and, indeed, bolster the retreating ranks of their hard-pressed army. Already such men as Robert Horne, Lord Scrope and Sir Richard Jenney had been struck down and dragged out of the mêlée to the rear by their loyal retainers, suffering from severe wounds.

The Kentish captain and Sir Richard were eventually to die on the field, but even this may not have been enough to make their exhausted contingents panic, provided the rest of the line did not crumble because of another major catastrophe. As for the effects of the flank attack on ordinary soldiers, there could be little or no help, and, in terms of affecting morale, this cannot have been an issue if the battle now resembled a free for all. As the Lancastrians continued their push, Yorkist victims of their army's retreat were now quite literally behind enemy lines and, as such, were soon finished off by the enemy bringing up the rear, killing and looting bodies as they went.

Taking the Yorkist reinforcement as the most plausible reason for the Lancastrian defeat, can we make any assumptions about where it was used to such good effect and what then happened to the Lancastrians because of it? From the Duke of Norfolk's point of view, as he approached the battlefield up the Ferrybridge road, the whole affair must have looked very confusing as the southern rim of the plateau came into sight. The main Yorkist army must at this time still have been holding the Lancastrian line from North Acres to the southwest edge of the plateau because pushed any further back they would have encountered the downslope and broke ranks immediately. Therefore, apart from isolated details of movement on the ridge itself, the duke (or possibly his chief captains) may have chosen to continue, now admittedly with some urgency, up the road, sending out couriers to make contact with King Edward. It is very doubtful that Norfolk (if he was present in person) could have seen the hard-pressed left flank of the Yorkist army struggling badly on the other side of the battlefield or was able to make out a battle at all from the Ferrybridge road position, or even from the high ground of Windmill Hill to his left. Therefore, it is more likely, because of this confusion and urgency to come to grips with the enemy, that Norfolk's force-marched contingents 'found' their Yorkist allies as they manoeuvred around the right of the southern plateau. Here they probably picked their way up the snow-covered slopes and quickly engaged the enemy with their stunned but grateful comrades, oblivious to what was going on.

If a judgement must be made on what happened to the Lancastrian army at Towton, I suggest that it began in North Acres, where the Yorkist right flank was probably the strongest. As the White Lion standard of the Duke of Norfolk was seen by the Lancastrians, the sight of fresh troops arriving on the field must have immediately panicked their already battle-fatigued soldiers and thrown their formation into confusion. Worse still, the Yorkist ranks on this flank were soon considerably extended as more and more men overlapped the enemy front. Some may have come up behind the Lancastrians causing greater panic, but all would have been thrown back and wondered where the fresh reserves were coming from.

'The Earl of Northumberland's signet ring', found on the battlefield of Towton and now in the British Museum.

Suddenly a trickle of Lancastrian fugitives sped to the rear in panic. With the fainthearted in flight, it was now up to the battle-hardened veterans to stave off defeat on that side of the field. However, this was not possible due to the overwhelming Yorkist numbers and the effects of an already long, hard battle. One man after another looked to his neighbour for support as backs turned, only to be struck down from behind, making panic and retreat inevitable for whole contingents. This was probably the worst position any man of courage could encounter. While supported and facing front with his weapons towards the enemy, any soldier was still a formidable obstacle for his enemy to overcome. But in hand-to-hand combat, the greatest physical and psychological asset to the opposition was for his opponent to lose heart. Indeed, more casualties were inflicted by this attempt to break off than any other single event in medieval battle. The problem was no different at Towton as the first cracks in the Lancastrian battle line rang the death knell of defeat. As Edward Hall recalled in his chronicle:

> This battle was sore fought, for hope of life was set aside on every part and the taking of prisoners was proclaimed as a great offence by reason whereof every man determined either to conquer or to die in the field.[31]

Norfolk's body punch to the Duke of Somerset's army must have looked like a great rolling wave of panic across the battle-field, as more and more contingents suffered from this increasing pressure on their left flank. However, soon even the strongest part of the Lancastrian army, which had pushed the Yorkists back initially, turned in horror to witness their men fleeing in disorder across the body-strewn plateau. In short, Norfolk's men had hit the Lancastrians hard and consequently the battle lines swung even more diagonally across the plateau, now almost at right angles to their opening positions on the field.

Even at the Lancastrian strong point on their right flank, some men would have lost heart and struggled to flee, while the jubilant Yorkists rallied and renewed their attack. As a result, the compacted ranks suddenly opened, and huge yawning gaps appeared as knots of levies and militiamen attempted to retreat or were temporarily pushed back into the fight by their leaders' poleaxes. Here battle standards wavered and fell in the snow, and under those that remained, some nobles and their loyal retainers may have fought on against the odds as sections of their front line disappeared to the rear. However, even this was a temporary escape as packs of Yorkist horsemen encircled to cut off their retreat. Once outnumbered, the nobles would have been targeted and bludgeoned to the ground by every man who was not fighting or exhausted. Their pursuers plundered Lancastrian bodies at will, and no doubt mutilation occurred in some instances.

This military habit by medieval soldiers, which is supported by the injuries on some of the bodies found in the 1996 grave, would have added to more confusion and wholesale pillaging by the Yorkist army. Therefore, some contingents may not have pursued the enemy immediately, as many Lancastrian rings, purses, weapons and armour were cut from their dying bodies by more than eager Yorkists looking for valuables. Certainly, the motivation and indeed the strength after such a long ordeal must have been sadly lacking for an immediate pursuit on foot, and because of this, the Lancastrians may have been able to rally and form pockets of resistance along their ever-thinning line.

Breathing heavily into the cold air and unbuckling their helmets for one last attempt to stop a complete massacre, armour may have been discarded as the brief pause in the fighting warned them of the possible consequences of running with such equipment to encumber their flight.

As the clusters of Lancastrian resistance braced themselves for yet another enemy charge, some of the more alert among them may have seen hundreds of mounted men armed with spears filling the gaps in the Yorkist line where they expected to see infantry. Beneath the tattered remnants of the once-resplendent Lancastrian banners, it was not long before a tumult of desperate cries echoed in Towton and Saxton fields. Previous orders of no quarter were suddenly re-affirmed

The steep slopes from the battlefield plateau into the River Cock valley where many Lancastrians perished. (Author)

in every Yorkist and Lancastrian mind, and the panic in Somerset's army confirmed this when men threw down their weapons and ran.

The Rout and Pursuit

Philip de Commynes wrote in his memoirs after visiting the English court that:

> King Edward told me that in all the battles which he had won, as soon as he had gained victory, he mounted his horse and shouted to his men that they must spare the common soldiers and kill the lords, of which none or few escaped.[32]

And it is certain, according to at least two sources, that this unchivalrous and uniquely targeted cull of the aristocracy was carried out at the battle of Towton after the initial trial of strength was over. When the Lancastrians eventually broke ranks, more out of practical necessity than tradition, Yorkist horses were brought forward from behind the lines to be readied for the expected pursuit. The contemporary Croyland chronicler took up the story in his usual apocalyptic style:

> For their ranks being now broken and scattered in flight, the king's army eagerly pursued them, and cutting down the fugitives with their swords, just like so many sheep for the slaughter, made immense havoc among them for a distance of ten miles as far as the city of York. [King] Edward, however, with part of his men as conqueror, remained upon the field of battle, and awaited the rest of his army, which had gone in various directions in pursuit of the enemy.[33]

As the Yorkist cavalry sprang forward, they set upon the fleeing Lancastrians in an unprecedented massacre that carried on to the banks of the River Cock and beyond. However, as mentioned by Commynes, the main targets were obviously the Lancastrian nobles, especially those with prices on their heads, such as Sir Andrew Trollope, and those hunted by blood feud or land-hungry enemies. With such a great opportunity as this in his grasp, King Edward must have been fully determined to further his cause and ensure that every effort was made to sweep what was left of Lancastrian resistance away from his throne. To this end, all the Yorkists were ordered to aim for the nobility, not only for the spoils of war, admittedly one of the reasons why men took up arms in the first place, but also for the rewards that could be gained from killing their domestic and local enemies with royal consent.

The obvious place for the Lancastrian army to flee was back in the direction from which they had marched a few days earlier, but this involved first crossing the River Cock, then the larger River Wharfe at Tadcaster. Also, now that the battle lines had been altered, their route was being further dictated by their Yorkist pursuers towards the precipitous sloping western edge of the plateau, which became the Lancastrian fugitives' first obstacle to overcome in their bid to stay alive.

It is almost impossible to descend any of the western edges of Towton battlefield without breaking into a run. It is even more difficult in wet or snowy weather to keep a sure footing or defy the effects of gravity before encountering the fast-flowing River Cock below. It follows then that this also happened to the Duke of Somerset's panic-stricken and broken army when, running at breakneck speed, they encountered the snow-covered edges of the plateau and the river beyond. Some armoured gentry may never have recovered from the hundred-foot drop as they were irreverently pushed over the precipice by Yorkist spears, their heavy spinning bodies taking others with them on their journey to the bottom. Some Lancastrians may have sought cover and refuge in Renshaw Wood and therefore made good their escape under its cover to the fords across the river, only to find their route cut off by Yorkists who were already making short work of many of their comrades crowding into the valley.

By far the worst place encountered by the Lancastrian routing army must have been the 'funnel' of Towton Dale and, for a second time in only a few hours, Bloody Meadow. Here, where the descent is not as steep, the Yorkist horsemen must have inflicted many casualties. Because of the valley's easy access, the crowding here must have been beyond belief, and, unlike most of the steeper slopes of the western edge of the battlefield, this area was more suitable for cavalry action up to the banks of the river. In fact, this is probably how the Yorkist pursuers entered the valley of the River Cock following the rout to strike all along its course in a massacre of Lancastrian fugitives trying to cross its icy waters. It is doubtful that the Yorkists would have attempted to drive their horses down any of the steep snow-covered slopes of the plateau. Therefore, they probably fanned out from Towton Dale, hounding the Lancastrians as they went.

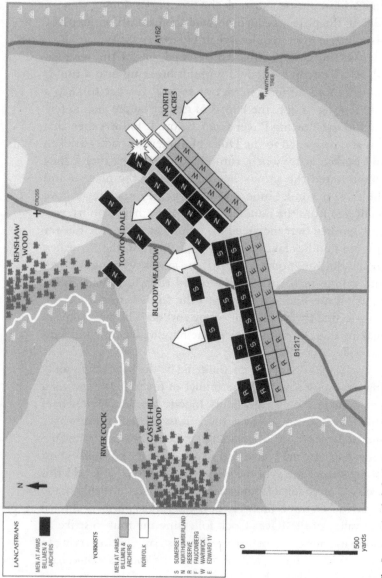

The Lancastrian left flank is turned. (Author)

The Yorkists pursuing the Lancastrians over the River Cock at the battle of Towton. (R. Caton Woodville)

The River Cock. (Author)

Finally, many of these confused fugitives were herded towards the easy access points to the River Cock, their only line of retreat, and along with their comrades, they were attempting to cross there in their thousands. Here the legendary bridges of bodies were built up as, one after another, each Lancastrian tried to wade across the deep gully that formed the riverbed, only to be slowed by the sponge-like effects of water seeping into their clothing. Such protective overgarments as padded jacks and brigandines, studded with metal fastenings, would have caused their owners great problems once soaked with water, and the effect of heavy armour in this situation is obvious. Many of the unfortunate fugitives must have been drowned by panic in the push and shove to reach the opposite bank, also not forgetting that the Yorkists were killing many and relentlessly hounding their speed of retreat in the process to make matters worse. Edward Hall gives his lasting impression of the rout from the battlefield when the Lancastrians:

> like men amazed, fled towards Tadcaster bridge to save themselves, but in the mean way there was a little brook called Cock, not very broad but of great deepness, in the which, what for haste of escaping, and what for fear of followers, a great number were drent and drowned, in so much that the common people there affirm that men alive passed the river upon the dead carcasses, and that the great river of Wharfe, which is the great sewer of the brook, and of all the water coming from Towton, was coloured with blood.[34]

By late afternoon the whole scene of death and destruction by water and steel must have been horrific. As the rout moved across the blood-soaked banks of the River Cock, the fortunate Lancastrians who had made good their escape earlier, and the ones who had managed to cross the river over the bodies of the fallen, raced for Tadcaster across open country to the bridge there. However, the same manner of death awaited the Lancastrians here, we are told, as one misfortune after another caused Towton's casualty list to increase as men drowned trying to cross the River Wharfe or were speared to death near its bridge and in the streets of Tadcaster.

The rout was utter and complete, leaving Lancastrians dead and dying for miles. However, the battlefield itself must have been a far worse place to behold with such sights as human dams choked with dead bodies and more isolated bodies littering the slopes from the battlefield. On the plateau itself, there would have been a great expanse of scattered corpses and thick tangled heaps of dead in Towton Dale, Bloody Meadow and the battlefield in general. Telltale snow-covered mounds of the fighting earlier in the day would have also been apparent. The whole battlefield in the areas of greatest slaughter must have been soaked in blood, on which Yorkist soldiers now began stripping the dead of their valuables, quickly killing any Lancastrians who were still alive in the process.

Executions, according to some accounts, occurred at this time (see Chapter Eight) and the mutilation of bodies may have occurred prior to a hasty burial in mass graves. The heralds and scribes from both sides would have been hard at work, trying to number and record the dead and making notes of the aristocracy using their coats of arms and badges to distinguish who they were. These men would also later have organised the burial parties to begin the laborious task ahead once some normality returned to the area. According to the Croyland chronicler, it is recorded that King Edward remained on Towton battlefield with most of his army while some of his force pursued the Lancastrians to the gates of York, and this is hardly surprising considering the great trial of strength that both sides had endured during the day. Edward created many Yorkist knights after the battle, and it is most likely some of these men were dubbed on the field. While waiting nervously in line to congratulate their new Yorkist monarch may have been a delegation of Lancastrian heralds begging him to grant God's mercy on the dead, to let them bury their bodies in consecrated ground despite rebelling against him.

Finally, as Palm Sunday ended and darkness enveloped the plateau, the lists of the dead would have been brought to the king. This time the victorious Yorkists occupied the village of Towton, having undoubtedly secured much-needed supplies from the abandoned Lancastrian camp. Here surgeons would have been hard at work too, stitching and cauterising wounds with primitive instruments in less than adequate conditions. However, this would not have been enough to save most men's lives, as infection would, in the end, claim many wounded in the days to come. For the dying left on the field, such a grim form of extinction is hard to contemplate, or indeed attempt to visualise without any amount of human compassion for the sufferers. Exposure would eventually have claimed them all as most weakly called for help into the darkness until the extreme drop in temperature during the early hours finally brought their suffering to an end.

Towton was a great fellowship of death and an even greater tragedy to visualise by modern standards. But amid these scenes of destruction and confusion, it became increasingly apparent that an even greater uncertainty threatened the Yorkist regime as night closed in. King Edward must have wondered what he had achieved, who had managed to escape the field and whether the haphazard lists of Lancastrian dead were, in fact, correct or complete. He knew he had won a great battle and that the enemy was utterly routed. But as he bent in silent vigil that night to thank God for his victory and his life, many of his captains' words of congratulation must have fallen on hollow ground as the names of such nobles as Somerset, Northumberland, Exeter, Devon and Wiltshire, his mortal enemies, rose yet again to threaten his throne, as none of their dead bodies had been found in the blood-soaked snow of Palmsunday Field.

Seven

Nowe ys Thus

What happened to the Lancastrian peerage during and after the bloody rout from Towton? At what point did the more prominent nobles decide to quit the field, and how did some of them manage to escape back to York so quickly?

Apart from the erroneous lists of dead given by chroniclers, who recorded the casualties in the whole Towton campaign, a few scraps of evidence emerge that enable us to piece together the main Lancastrian leaders' whereabouts after the battle. For instance, *Gregory's Chronicle* maintains that:

> The Earl of Devon was sick [in York], and could not get away, and was taken and beheaded. And the Earl of Wiltshire was taken and brought unto Newcastle to the king. And there his head was smote off and sent unto London to be set upon London Bridge.[1]

Wiltshire's capture at Cockermouth in Cumberland is clearly a later event. The Yorkists caught up with him after pursuing the Lancastrian fugitives further north, while King Henry, his queen, and the Prince of Wales managed to make a quick escape from York to Berwick (then garrisoned by the Scots) where they contemplated their next move.

As previously mentioned, the Earl of Wiltshire was quite an expert at extracting himself from battles. Earlier in the Wars of the Roses at the first battle of St Albans, according to William Gregory 'this said James [Butler] set the king's banner against a house end and fought manly with the heels, for he was afraid of losing his beauty, for he was named the fairest knight of this land'.[2] Therefore, it is probable that the earl was the first to extract himself from the mêlée at Towton. But this time, he was not alone. The dukes of Somerset and Exeter, Lord Roos and others must have been similarly calling for their horses when the Lancastrian flank was turned in North Acres. It is doubtful any would have escaped the Yorkist cavalry if they had delayed their flight later than this, as, encumbered by armour, they would have been cut down like the rest of their men in the general rout from the battlefield.

According to the *Brut Chronicle*, after hearing news of their defeat at Towton, the Lancastrian royal family fled from York at midnight accompanied by the Duke of Somerset, Lord Roos and others. King Edward arrived in the city with his army the next day (Monday 30 March), and it was here that the sick Earl of Devon and three others were promptly executed, according to Edward Hall. Their heads replaced the decomposing skulls of the Yorkist nobles executed after the battle of Wakefield three months earlier, and the sight of the latter must have prompted King Edward to condone further atrocities in the city. Edward was certainly in a vindictive mood even though some prisoners (Lord Montagu and Lord Berners) were found alive and well. They had been captured by the Lancastrians after the second battle of St Albans and had apparently been set free as Edward's army approached Micklegate. However, we are told this gesture by York officials failed to move the king, and he immediately set about rooting out the last pockets of Lancastrian resistance in the city.

Regarding the whereabouts of other Lancastrian nobles, some authorities state that the Earl of Northumberland perished on the battlefield of Towton and was found among the dead. He was certainly wounded during the battle, according to writers, but he may have reached York with the rest of the nobility, only to die from his injuries later in the day. It is said he was buried in the church of St Denys in Walmgate, York, 'in the north choir under a large blue marble stone, which had two effigies on it and an inscription in brass around it'.[3] However, in 1736, this tomb was destroyed, and only the tradition remains, although St Denys' was the parish church of the Percy family and opposite once stood the palace of the earls of Northumberland.

The City of York was, without doubt, the Lancastrian lords' destination after Towton, not only to warn the king and queen but also to escape north into Scotland. The small contingent of gentry, their servants and some of their household men would probably have left Towton as other nobles began to fall. Lord Dacre, Lord Welles, Lord Willoughby, Lord Mauley and many other lesser knights and squires were already slain, including Sir Andrew Trollope and his brother David. The army may not even have seen Somerset and his companions escape across the ford that would soon become one of the infamous bridges of bodies over the River Cock.

En route to York at Tadcaster, the Duke of Somerset may have ordered the bridge over the River Wharfe destroyed to delay the enemy and protect King Henry, aware that, if he did not, the pursuing Yorkist cavalry would soon reach York and capture the king as he endeavoured to escape northward. As mentioned earlier, this action at Tadcaster, unfortunately, caused the last major disaster of the day as thousands of Lancastrian refugees from the battle tried to cross the River Wharfe.

It was here without doubt that the greatest drownings and killing occurred after Towton. Concerning the Lancastrian casualties in the rout, George Neville's letter to Coppini a few weeks after the battle emphasises the River Wharfe crossing as the main culprit for large-scale drownings in contrast to the River Cock, which he fails to mention. Because of these casualties, while attempting to ford such a major obstacle as the Wharfe, the death toll on Palm Sunday increased, and it points to a near massacre of all those Lancastrians who found themselves trapped on the southern bank and in Tadcaster.

Lionel, Lord Welles' alabaster tomb at Methley, West Yorkshire. (Author)

It seems to me that there was, and consequently always has been, some degree of confusion among historians surrounding the two rivers linked with the battle of Towton. In particular, the unsupported claims of the River Cock being 'in spate' on Palm Sunday have been badly misinterpreted, probably to account for the unusually high death tolls in such a small river. Admittedly the River Cock did claim many lives and ran red with blood because of the slaughter across it. Still, the Wharfe is and was then a much more formidable obstacle and consequently must have accounted for the more significant casualties compared with its smaller tributary, which was, in Edward Hall's words, only a brook in the Tudor period.

Others escaped the battle in different directions because Edward IV's attainder lists many who are not labelled as 'late' (denoting their deaths) before their titles. However, on the field, some knights and lords were eventually found dead among the common soldiery and taken away by relatives and friends, such as the Lancastrian noble Lord Welles, whose body was concealed in a sack and was buried in St Oswald's Church at Methley, West Yorkshire. A fine alabaster tomb, and an even more remarkable likeness of him in typical period armour, still exists in the Waterton chapel.

On Monday 30 March, King Edward left Towton for York with his victorious Yorkist army. But for those left behind with the responsibility of clearing the battlefield and digging graves for the slain, it was immediately apparent that an unprecedented task lay ahead, considering that the bodies covered such a large area. Therefore, we may conclude, given the inclement weather, that this operation took an extremely long time to complete and that the dead were not buried straight away as was usual, principally to prevent the spread of disease. When the Croyland chronicler recorded his estimate of casualties at Towton, he added another ten thousand to the heralds' official figures for good measure. He then provides his readers with unique evidence that the weather conditions changed after the battle. Indeed, he indicates that a thaw set in, enabling the gravediggers to complete their task and see where the bodies were located under the heaps of snow. The following passage may also show that the River Cock did flood due to this rise in temperature, but after 29 March. The Croyland chronicler maintains that:

> After distributing rewards among such as brought the bodies of the slain and gave them burial, the king hastened to enter the before named city [York]. Those who helped to inter the bodies, piled up in pits and in trenches prepared for the purpose, bear witness that eight and thirty thousand warriors fell on that day, besides those who were drowned in the river before alluded to, whose numbers we have no means of ascertaining. The blood, too, of the slain, mingling with the snow which at this time covered the whole surface of the earth, afterwards ran down in the furrows and ditches along with the melted snow, in a most shocking manner, for a distance of two or three miles.[4]

As one would expect, of the named Lancastrian dead, by far the greatest number were squires, yeomen and commoners, including men from all walks of life such as grocers, priests, merchants, clerks, grooms and gentlemen. Also mentioned in King Edward's Act of Attainder are the knights killed on Palmsunday Field. However, it is not immediately apparent whether they all perished because some of the presumed dead appear later in records of the wars to override these claims. William Gregory recorded that forty-two knights were executed after Towton in the reprisals, which, if nothing else, illustrates King Edward's ruthless bid to consolidate his throne and his unremitting attempt to destroy his enemies' will and ability to oppose him.[5]

More important, however, is that, even though many of the gentry had been killed in battle or executed after it, the Lancastrian king and the Duke of Somerset had escaped the Yorkists to breathe yet again, and no doubt planned to canvass support for their cause in the north and the continent.

Therefore, we must admit that the battle of Towton was not as decisive as some might suggest. We may agree that on the day the Yorkists thoroughly destroyed the Lancastrian northern army in the heart of their power base, causing carnage and slaughter on an unprecedented scale. But herein lies a much deeper meaning that cannot be ignored during this period. Primogeniture continued, despite the carnage, so long as sons, brothers, and the female line survived. This fact was true no matter how many titles suffered during the periodic civil wars, and was similarly apparent after Towton when the rule of a shire might prove difficult without hereditary governance.

This was the legacy of the Wars of the Roses, when, even after such a decisive victory as that of Towton, the victor could only temporarily alleviate his problems. To be sure of absolute power, the king had to destroy all opposing nobles or woo them to his cause. However, this was not always possible, which is why such important titles as Somerset, Northumberland, and even Clifford, succeeded to thrive in the period and why, in some instances, such families remained enemies unamenable to any kind of compromise.

With Lancastrian nobles on the run and their threats of reincarnation a stark reality, King Edward soon put plans into action to capture his enemies. The Bishop of Elpin stated in his letter to Coppini that the king 'sent a great number of men at arms in pursuit of the fugitives, so that not one would escape when taken'.[6] The urgency and importance of this mission are further underlined because news reached London that 20,000 of Edward's men had been sent from York to pursue the Lancastrians and that Newcastle was already besieged.

Here King Edward left the Earl of Warwick, Lord Fauconberg and Lord Montagu in command of the army. Having reached as far north as he dared without additional support, the king returned to York, where he spent Easter. *Gregory's Chronicle* ends this chapter of the Wars of the Roses and the aftermath of the battle of Towton with a fitting epilogue:

And the king tarried in the north a great while and made great inquiries of the rebellions against his father and took down his father's head from the walls of York and made all the country to be sworn unto him and his laws. And then he returned to London again and there he made eighteen knights and many lords, and then he rode to Westminster and there he was crowned the 28th day of June in the year of our Lord 1461, blessed be God of his great grace.[7]

Artefacts including spurs, buttons, rings, etc. found on the battlefield. (Simon Richardson)

The new king naturally advanced his friends and relatives after his coronation. He made his uncle, Viscount Bouchier, the Earl of Essex, Lord Fauconberg the Earl of Kent, knights, such as Hastings, Wenlock, Herbert, Devereux, Ogle and others, became lords and Edward's younger brother, George, who was later to cause him so much trouble, was created Duke of Clarence. However, of all the participants who fought at Towton and received their rewards, Edward may have overlooked the Earl of Warwick because of his already powerful status. He was consequently treated very coolly by his protégé from then on. After all, because Edward was now king, the earl was impotent as far as real kingmaking was concerned, and we may ask ourselves where he now turned to fulfil his ambitions. Warwick was certainly not elevated to a duke for all his efforts to place Edward on the throne, and for the moment, he might have been content with being superior to the Percys in the north now that the Earl of Northumberland was dead. However, his attitude was eventually to change when the Woodville family found King Edward's Achilles' heel in Elizabeth, their most eligible asset, who was to turn the king's head and, more importantly, Warwick's in the direction of the king's 'false, fleeting and perjur'd'[8] younger brother Clarence to refuel the Wars of the Roses.

As for the strong-minded king, he was to have his own way, and he secretly married Elizabeth Woodville while Warwick was away negotiating Edward's marriage elsewhere. Elizabeth became Queen of England in 1464. She was previously Elizabeth Grey, who had been married to Sir John Grey of Groby, allegedly 'slain at York field' (Towton) according to some chronicles, but actually killed at the second battle of St Albans. Elizabeth was also the daughter of Lord Rivers, who had also fought at Towton in the Duke of Somerset's army with his son, Anthony Woodville. All these Greys and Woodvilles were staunch Lancastrians, so we may wonder at King Edward's reasoning. After all, were these not his mortal enemies? Apparently not when it involved his queen. His infatuation with Elizabeth Woodville eventually helped all her family climb the social ladder at court after their Lancastrian attainders were reversed in July 1461. Such were the Wars of the Roses. The Woodvilles were later not only to cause Warwick's disaffection from the king, which would ultimately lead to his death at the battle of Barnet in 1471, but also create further problems for Richard, Duke of Gloucester, Edward's youngest brother, later Richard III, in his attempt to secure the throne for himself in the 1480s.

At the other end of the social scale, what became of the humbler soldiers of Palmsunday Field who had come through the battlefield slaughterhouse with as much fateful help as strength and fortitude in war? Many would undoubtedly fight again in the castle sieges and skirmishes in Northumberland, and perhaps, ten years later, some might have even been involved in the campaigns of 1471 with King Edward, Warwick and Queen Margaret at Barnet and Tewkesbury. Most Yorkists were greatly rewarded for their services at Towton, like Ralph Vestynden Esquire, King Edward's standard-bearer, who was given a £10 annuity for the rest of his life 'for the good, agreeable service which he did unto us'.[9]

Ordinary soldiers would undoubtedly have benefited from looting the battlefield at Towton before local scavengers plundered the area later at will. All would have secured some memento or souvenir in part payment for their ordeal, be it only weapons and additional armour. Even a pair of new boots would have been greatly prized for a soldier on the march. As for the Lancastrians after the battle, most would have disappeared into the Yorkshire landscape and later back to their homes or north to re-join King Henry's cause. Even if they remained in the immediate vicinity, it is doubtful that they would have caused Edward trouble now he was king. In fact, Edward's policy must have been quite the reverse compared to the Lancastrian nobility, of whom he had such hatred, because here in the Yorkshire area was a valuable pool of levies just waiting to be tapped by commissions of array if ever the need arose in the future.

Earl Rivers presenting a book to Edward IV. The earl fought for the Lancastrians at Towton.

However, most Lancastrians would have lost much in the way of belongings in their escape from the battlefield and later when some of them were in hiding. Thomas Denys, who fought for the Earl of Warwick at the second battle of St Albans, escaped the rout from the battlefield to write to the Paston's about his ordeal, claiming that 'There lost I £20 worth, horse, harness and money and was hurt in divers places'.[10] It is apparent that he was fortunate to be alive in that he barely escaped the field with the clothes on his back. His horse was very probably still tethered behind the lines, his armour would have been discarded for greater speed in the rout, and his money may have been used to buy a safe passage from the battle zone. Not only this but he was wounded as well. In fact, most of the letters attesting to this experience of medieval warfare are very explicit in detailing the personal loss of belongings, and in some cases, the individuals' mental and emotional state is also mentioned, reflecting, among other symptoms, remorse and trauma.

As we have explored so far, a great deal could be won or lost on a battlefield, and, in the aftermath, mothers were written to, and friends sought out for help and comfort, echoing the experiences of soldiers in similar situations in other eras. A surviving document in the National Archives tells the story of Elizabeth Normanville of Kilnwick in Yorkshire, who made her will out unsure if her two eldest sons were alive after Towton. News had not reached her even on 20 April, and it is known that Elizabeth's third son succeeded to her estates instead. John and William had probably been slain fighting for the Lancastrians in great contrast to one of Edward IV's royal clerks who made a £30 claim for compensation after 'the field at Sherburn' having lost cash and, more amazingly, a certain book.[11]

It is perhaps not surprising that many Lancastrians lost a great deal in land and money. Not to forget titles and lives if they had been attained for treason. In fact, reluctance to engage in combat ever again is alluded to in some accounts, not only because of the financial loss that might befall a soldier but also, reading between the lines, the apparent fear that could follow such a commitment to one side or the other.

To support this argument is the case of John Paston, a participant in the battle of Barnet, who was almost a complete wreck after his flight from the battlefield in 1471. In his letter home, he uses phrases like 'and I beseech you send money … I neither have meat, drink or clothes', and also that he was 'now in the greatest need that ever I was in',[12] confirming that his predicament far outweighed the danger of the battlefield in some respects and that his life had been turned upside down by fighting. In short, the tone of such letters reiterates the human experience of battle, and of its losers' aftershock in terms of nervousness of being caught, vulnerability to physical

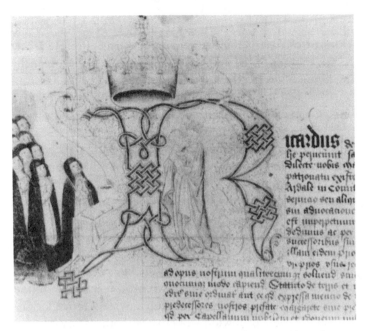

The Esholt Priory Charter was granted by Richard III in 1485 to Margaret Clifford, the widow of Lord Clifford, who was killed at Dintingdale on the eve of the battle of Towton. (Geoff Wheeler)

and mental strain and, above all, some soldiers' horror and fear of fighting may have dissuaded them from ever willingly taking up arms again.

This factor alone quite naturally makes us question the size of Wars of the Roses armies overall after Towton and, coupled with the casualty rates, furthers the possibility of lower estimates than given in the chronicles and letters of the period. However, as indicated, the battle of Towton was exceptional in that it took place at the most effective time in the wars in terms of the manpower available to both the king and his nobles and was a climax to a feud that had been raging for at least ten years.

The aftershock of Palmsunday Field on the Lancastrian side effectively scattered their power far and wide as many loyal followers fortified the great castles of Northumberland against the Yorkist regime. During a skirmish at Hedgeley Moor, another of the Percys was killed while bravely launching himself into the thickest part of the Yorkist battle line. And on 14 May 1464, the last of the main Towton refugees were hunted down by Lord Montagu, Warwick's brother, at the battle of Hexham, where the Duke of Somerset and Lords Roos and Hungerford were captured and executed within a matter of days. King Henry again made a lucky escape, but as he wandered the north in search of a safe haven, the Lancastrian cause crumbled, and their strong points fell one by one to the Yorkists. Henry was finally captured in July 1465, imprisoned in the Tower of London, and King Edward now sat on a secure throne, at least for the time being, his victory at Palmsunday Field just another memory. The next threat to the king would eventually come from within, from the man who had helped him to the throne and who had commanded with him at his most glorious hour at the battle of Towton – but that is another story.

The Legacy of a Battlefield

As often as the ploughman turns the fields,
Half buried human bones the soil still yields,
The dire remains of horrid civil strife,
A hundred thousand men bereft of life.
This quarrel claims, and Tadcaster may boast
That thirty thousand in her fields were lost.[13]

Over the years, Towton battlefield has remained very much the same as it appeared in 1461. In fact, travellers such as John Leland would have been familiar with the area today and the ground they trod in the Tudor period. Over time and centuries of agricultural ploughing, some battle relics have been found on the field, in Towton village and in the River Cock to attest to this bloody encounter. However, considering the size of the battle and the casualties inflicted, few genuine artefacts have been unearthed considering the number of years the land has been worked, and people have spent hunting for relics.

Today the land is combed meticulously by the metal detector. However, it should be argued that after medieval battles, most valuables, such as armour and weapons, were searched for and appropriated by the living as the dead were systematically stripped and buried in mass graves. The cold weather would have aided this looting considerably, and although we may wonder at the treasures waiting to be uncovered in the Towton graves, the bodies unearthed there in 1996 prove that scavengers are much the same in any era and that they stole anything of value. Therefore, preserving such graves and the reburial of remains after research seems a far more appropriate measure considering that these are, after all, war graves comparable to those set aside for the dead who fell in the modern era.

If artefacts are found, there is, of course, no guarantee that they are genuine battlefield regalia or even that they belong to the fifteenth century. In fact, some quite plausible finds over the years have surfaced at Towton that are of dubious authenticity. Some of the more famous relics have been deposited in museums and other repositories, others have been lost in time, and there are yet others that have disappeared into private collections. In about 1786, a gold ring weighing one ounce was deposited with the Society of Antiquaries in London and was then placed in the British Museum. The ring is thought to have belonged to the Earl of Northumberland due to the lion passant crest on its face, and many historians believe this may have been lost by the earl on the battlefield. The ring bears no stone, but the inscription on its face is intriguing, and the words 'Nowe ys Thus' give the impression that this was a signet of power rather than a family motto.[14] The Percy motto *Esperance en Dieu* would have been a prominent feature on the ring if it had belonged to the Northumberland family. Also, the lion was a common heraldic badge of the period. Therefore, the ring could have belonged to any number of nobles whose arms incorporated this much-used symbol during the Wars of the Roses.

Another ring, of silver and gilt with two hands conjoined, was found on the battlefield and was in possession of Richard Whittaker the author of *Leodis and Elmete* in 1816, but its whereabouts today is unknown.[15] A rowel spur of brass and gilt with an ornamental scroll pattern and an inscription on the shanks reading *en loial amour, tout mon coer* (all my heart in loyal love) was discovered in about 1792 and was given to the Society of Antiquaries.[16] The so-called Towton Dog Collar is also an interesting find (see Appendix 3) but again this artefact has been lost to a private collector and therefore cannot be authenticated or dated as belonging to the battle or the era. Among relics shown to me by metal detectorists over the years, a gold signet ring bearing the initials I.H. is one of a whole host of finds that cannot be linked with the battle, as are the various weapons, or parts of weapons that have allegedly been found on the site.

By far the most famous of these weapons is a small 'battle axe' recovered from the River Cock valley and once owned by a miller at Saxton. It was purchased from him by Colonel Grant, RA, and was preserved in his family until 1854, when it was presented to the Duke of Northumberland, and it has been on show in Alnwick Castle ever since. The axe bears a handle (although not the original), and it is thought that the head either belonged to a small hand axe used by a foot soldier or alternatively a poleaxe minus the beak used by a man at arms of the period.[17] Spearheads, daggers and other relics have surfaced occasionally on the plateau, and antiquarians have documented these as authentic. However, most relics can be made to represent almost anything if a piece is missing. In short, it is much more probable that the finder has uncovered a piece of rusted agricultural equipment rather than the arrowhead that killed Lord Dacre in North Acres.

Battle-axe found in the River Cock valley and now in Alnwick Castle, Northumberland. (Author)

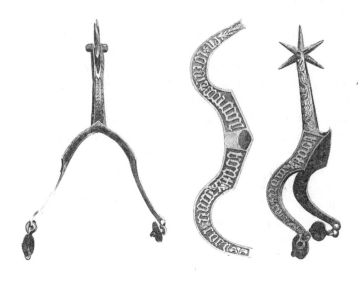

Rowel spur found on the battlefield in 1792. (Society of Antiquaries)

However, with the land being under the plough for so many years and the movement of earth contributing to the misplacement of relics, it is awe-inspiring when occasionally one can witness something special found on Palmsunday Field that brings the battle, and those who fought it, to life. Recently both graves and recorded artefacts have contributed to our understanding of where and how the battle was fought. The finds are the subject of endless debate among enthusiasts, and the incredible archaeological evidence is a powerful reminder that medieval warfare was extremely brutal and premeditated.

Thanks to many years of personal research, we can now prove where the battle was fought purely from where certain artefacts have been found. The items unearthed by Simon Richardson include small pieces of armour, belt buckles, fragments of spurs, sword pommel heads, scabbard chapes, strap ends, clothing fasteners, horse trappings, samples of chain mail, arrowheads, heraldic buttons, purse frames and coins, which are all in an incredibly good state of preservation. Plotted on a map by Richardson, these 'hotspots' confirm that the main hand-to-hand fighting at Towton was fought on the southern plateau and close to the reverse slope that falls away to Saxton village. However, the most crucial point is that the survey also proves that some areas of the battlefield are devoid of artefacts. Some relics were found in tight concentrations, including the area west of the Yorkist left flank towards Castle Hill Wood. Others found in and around Dintingdale demonstrate that the Yorkist skirmish with Clifford's men before the main conflict may have been more significant than previously thought.

But where are the tons of arrows shot in such abundance at Towton?

The short answer is perhaps an obvious one that most were retrieved from the battlefield after the event. Arrows stuck in the ground or even embedded in bodies were visual, valuable and reusable weapons that archers would have had no trouble retrieving. Unlike the mass production of musket balls, for example, in later eras and their consequential loss and damage on battlefields, arrows could be reused and would no doubt be needed for future engagements. They were harder to replenish in great quantity, and therefore it is certain that this type of missile scavenging went on at Towton after the battle as a general order from above. As previously stated, some artefacts found on the battlefield were in a good state of preservation when found. Hence ferrous and non-ferrous items had not suffered significant corrosion over time. Therefore, given that archery was used extensively at Towton, we might expect a proportionately large haul of arrowheads given that a complete clearance of the field was a physical and logistical impossibility. However, a relatively small geophysical survey conducted in Bloody Meadow and Towton Dale by Tim Sutherland was disappointing, although not altogether inconclusive. The tests affirm that the residue of such battlefield debris would have been cleared naturally by time and more intrusively by seasonal ploughing that has been evident on the battlefield since 1461.[18]

Despite this erosion of artefacts, a stockpile of arrowheads unearthed on the battlefield by Simon Richardson was analysed at the Royal Armouries in Leeds, and not surprisingly, the uniqueness of the find corroborates the types of war arrow commonly used by medieval archers. The hoard (comprising some 200 corroded piles) was meticulously X-rayed in 2004, and there seems to be no doubting their authenticity. They are obviously arrowheads from a bygone age – but to which era do they belong, and were they once attached to war arrows with an overall weight of three to four ounces as detailed by Strickland and Hardy?[19] The debate centres on an amount of brazing evident in the two-piece assembly and consequently the effectiveness of this type of head in warfare. One-piece bodkin and Type 16 dual-purpose arrowheads were used during the Wars of the Roses, and the distribution of these at Towton, according to contemporary sources, must have been on a very wide front

Two medieval armies loose a hail of arrows at each other while men at arms wait for the outcome. *(Bibliothèque Nationale)*

given the size of the armies and the damage inflicted. Were some medieval arrow makers producing two-piece arrowheads that might not be fit for purpose? Were the heads in question originally the correct weight to suit arrows shot from the great warbow with a 120-pound draw weight? Is a hoard of arrowheads what we would expect to see on a medieval battlefield as opposed to a general spread, found intermittently over time and constantly redistributed by centuries of ploughing?

Of course, it is impossible to demonstrate that all such objects were used or lost during the battle of Towton. Still, the work done by Simon Richardson and the Towton Battlefield Archaeology Project demonstrates beyond doubt that at some point in the fifteenth century the area between 'Towtonfield and Saxtonfield'[20] was subjected to increased activity far beyond normal use. What is amazing is that science, literary evidence and in some cases local tradition meet at a point worthy of further research. This point forms an essential catalyst when attempting to track down the battle and the rout from Towton. The disorganised fighting during a medieval battle was not static, and in Shakespeare's words, it ebbed and flowed in a way that cannot be plotted easily. The movement of troops was not regimented in any way once the fighting began. The opening positions may be simulated, and the effects of the archery duel at Towton assessed in part, but close combat can only ever be viewed as a confused brawl. Individuals and whole contingents may have run and returned to the fight later. The lulls in the fighting, the mounds of dead hindering movement, the personal and haphazard movements of men, along with the periods of stubborn resistance, give us cause to question and question again the truth of what occurred during such a brutal mass mêlée. Above all, we can be sure that the word 'mêlée' lived up to its definition at Towton as being a disorganised and bloody free-for-all on an immense scale.

Of the more mortal remains of the conflict, in April 1993, a human skull found on the battlefield was deposited with Tadcaster Police and underwent forensic tests at York District Hospital. It was found to be of a nineteen-year-old male, dated approximately 1461, and due to the injuries sustained to one side of the face, in particular the eye socket, it was thought that he may have died during the battlefield rout. The horrific wound is believed to have been inflicted by a heavy blow from either a poleaxe or similar shafted weapon, and the fact that the skull was found near the River Cock points to the possibility that either the soldier drowned there or that he was part of a grave dug specifically to clear the river of dead bodies. However, in stark contrast to this is the more significant distribution of bodies that workmen accidentally unearthed during the building of a modern extension at Towton Hall in 1996.

This Towton grave is, without doubt, our most tangible human link with the battle to date. Originally some sixty-one bodies occupied the pit abutting Towton Hall, although only around thirty-seven of these were analysed in detail by experts. This multi-disciplined team was headed jointly by the staff of Bradford University and West Yorkshire Archaeology Service, and due to the trauma inflicted on the skulls of all the bodies found in the grave criminal forensic methods were employed with the help of an expert from America. The tests and conclusions carried out by Shannon Novak told a fascinating if brutal story of each soldier's final moments. Massive injuries had been sustained. Repeated blows to the skull told of frenzied attacks with heavy weapons such as poleaxes and war hammers. Daggers were thrust into the back of skulls, throats were cut, and mutilation was carried out on the corpses indicating overkill. One man had been hit more than fifteen times, so great was the hate felt by his attacker.[21]

Due to the historical significance attached to the find, I was among those lucky enough to witness the Towton dead face to face, but even I was unprepared for what the science unearthed. Even though some of the cadavers had been reburied in Saxton churchyard and therefore not examined, it became immediately obvious that the victims of the grave had met their deaths while not wearing helmets. It is ironic that initially the team thought that one of the soldiers had been tossed into the grave with his hands tied behind his back, and further questions can be asked why these particular bodies were buried such a great distance from the battlefield.

Although some opinions about how the victims died were formed in 1996, and these were presented in *Blood Red Roses* (both titles translated into a book and a television documentary called *Secrets of the Dead*), it was impossible to form an opinion about the broader significance of the battle due to lack of evidence. However, at the time, I began looking for comparisons to corroborate or disprove what seems to have been, in my opinion, a massacre of unarmed individuals, some probably knights of the realm. This event forms part of the conclusions explored in the next chapter. But to put this reasoning in context, it is essential to briefly explain the details of the 1996 grave and the initial conclusions about the men who saw the events expounded in this book. What emerges tells us a great deal about ourselves as humans and explores the state of mind of those involved in the Wars of the Roses.

The bones in the 1996 grave were found packed into a trench originally excavated to take as many bodies as possible. Variously orientated 'like sardines in a can' it was clear that no religious or orthodox method of interment had been followed – the bodies were literally just dumped in the grave, and one had been turned ninety degrees indicating that space was at a premium. The original grave cut was approximately 5m × 2m. Its southern edge partially invaded the limits of Towton Hall, which in 2003 had its dining room floor removed to expose more bodies dating to the medieval period and the battle: a survival which questions the date of that part of the building and whether the grave inside was a continuation of the 1996 excavation or something else. Little in the way of artefacts were found in the original grave fill apart from a silver ring, a few copper alloy tags, a small armour attachment and a worked bone object with copper rivets. However, what is interesting is that the backfill of the grave was littered with twelfth and thirteenth-century pottery, indicating that the original manor house of Richard II probably dates to this period.

All the bodies in both graves had been stripped before interment. Osteological analysis established that their ages were between sixteen and fifty years, fitting neatly with what we would expect from commissions of array and local musters of the time. The men were generally tall (some were six-footers) and in a good state of health, although one individual was only 5ft 3in and most had suffered from a life of considerable physical hardship. Irregular bone formations in the arms and shoulders proved that some men used the warbow (or had been trained in arms from an early age). Towton 16, one of

The 1996 trench grave found at Towton containing the remains of some thirty-seven soldiers who fought at the battle. *(Bradford University)*

the thirty-seven/eight bodies examined, became the model for a facial reconstruction that appeared in *Blood Red Roses*. His injuries graphically show that some men had received wounds before Towton and were, therefore, veterans of other conflicts, possibly even the Hundred Years War. Of the twenty-seven skulls examined, a total of 113 wounds (a ratio of four to one) were found on each, raising the crucial question of why so many blows were delivered to each man in one specific area (i.e. the head) and how much time the various attackers needed to complete their gruesome task. Two individuals had received over ten head wounds each. The skull of Towton 25 had been beaten to pulp and needed complete reconstruction before the level of trauma could be recognised – a clear indication that others did not threaten the attacker while he struck. Most attacks were made from the front by right-handed assailants, but some cuts and blows to the head were delivered from behind and above while their victims were on the ground. Fifty per cent of the postcranial injuries were to the hands and arms, indicating that some men tried to defend themselves, and multiple attackers *using different weapons* were involved in the assaults.[22]

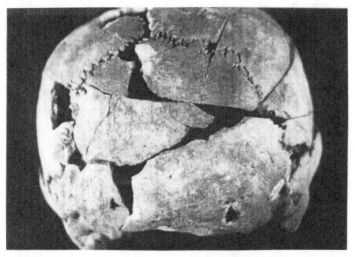

The reverse of Towton 18, showing multiple blade wounds to the back of the head and two dagger wounds to the base of the skull. *(Bradford University)*

So, was this simply battle-related trauma or something far more sinister and premeditated? The contents of the grave adjacent to Towton Hall give a chilling insight into how the soldiers died and, in my opinion, the nature of medieval warfare in general. However, since the initial excavation in 1996, I have been trying to equate this type of killing with historical precedents that might be analysed by us in the twenty-first century. The conclusions reached provide an insight into the savagery that motivated a man to fight in such battles and his apparent willingness to commit atrocities in their aftermath. The questions raised by the evidence may be contrary to what we might expect in a world of chivalry, but then again, what exactly was chivalry in the Wars of the Roses? Are the injuries in the Towton grave consistent with the psychology of the knightly code? Was there no room for ransoms or mercy in 1461? In fact, was chivalry dead by the second half of the fifteenth century?

Whatever our conclusions about those who fought at Towton, we must explore the wider context of the battle and its aftermath. How did it affect the local population? How was it commemorated? What did contemporaries really think of the mass slaughter? And why were so many men killed over a protracted timescale? What emerges is that intense feelings of self-preservation led to such savagery at Towton and that this savagery was based on an unquenchable thirst for revenge and caused by the most primal cause for war in the human psyche – the blood feud.

Eight

'O heavy times, begetting such events!'

The battle of Towton should have been the last battle of the Wars of the Roses. A decisive victory won by the Yorkists in 'enemy' territory inflicting substantial casualties ought to have been the end for Lancaster. However, the wars continued intermittently for the next twenty-six years, and therefore we may question whether the real impact of Towton was more localised and short term.

Margaret of Anjou was deprived of manpower and support after her defeat. Her broken army was forced into exile, and a bleak future was predicted for her son and hapless husband in the north of England. The physical and psychological impact of the battle was so telling on the surviving nobility that Margaret had to employ foreign mercenaries to continue the fight, and later in the wars, treacherous nobles, such as the Earl of Warwick and the Duke of Clarence, had to be coerced into their ranks to win back the throne. The writers of contemporary chronicles and letters give the impression that Towton was an epic event and that the death toll was so great that it was 'hitherto unheard of in our realm for almost a thousand years'.[1] Polydore Vergil maintained that the battle 'weakened wonderfully the force of

England, seeing those who were killed had been able, both in number and force, to have enterprised any foreign war'.[2] Later commentators thought Towton was a tragedy and warned their readers that the dangers of civil war might be just around the corner. Biased chroniclers took full advantage of the high death toll and marvelled at how completely the Lancastrian threat had been erased. In stark contrast to what had previously been endured by the northerners who had done 'harms innumerable … so that men of the shires had almost left no beasts to till their land',[3] their words must have rung true in many hearts. Given the evidence, we may take the majority's view and conclude that the battle of Towton was a decisive victory for King Edward and that the country was stabilised under his rule. So great was the slaughter among the Lancastrian nobility that the English king had become a worthy successor of Henry V and may have heralded in a new era for many. However, we would be mistaken on both counts. The Yorkist propaganda machine was well oiled by this time, and it is far more likely that Edward's triumph temporarily tamed only northern England (and Yorkshire in particular) rather than the whole kingdom.

In the years before the battle of Wakefield in 1460, the north was in a state of political and social chaos, and as K. Dockray maintains, this is crucial to our understanding of Towton and the size of the armies that fought there.[4] The feuding aspects so ingrained in some ancestral families, particularly those of Neville and Percy and Courtenay and Bonville, illustrates just how lawless some parts of England were in the 1450s. Indeed, the Neville and Percy feud is one of the reasons why the battle of Towton was fought in Yorkshire: it being the medieval training ground for aristocratic violence, rebellion, thuggery and gangsterism. Jack Cade's uprising, aristocratic feuding, and the first battle of St Albans in 1455 all prove that noble lawlessness was endemic, and violence was commonplace. The soldiers, and in most cases the commoners who took up employment with local lords, had their own issues with their neighbours, and in

November 1460, many of the Duke of York's tenants were killed by men who were slain at Towton. The Earl of Northumberland and Lords Clifford, Dacre and Neville were all marked men in battle and fair game for any Yorkist would-be assassin. Their bands of well-armed ruffians and personal henchmen had previously run riot, laid ambushes and fought pitched battles against their counterparts in a mini Wars of the Roses that threatened the crown. At Heworth Moor, Topcliffe and Stamford Bridge in the 1450s men were arrayed against each other in their thousands and blood was spilt at St Albans as a result.[5] Those who controlled central government in place of Henry VI were largely impotent against such guerrilla activity, and it was this anarchy that King Edward tried to curb on such a bloody scale at Towton and in its aftermath. In short, Edward let his victorious army execute at will in Lancastrian territory, and the killing, which we are told included the pillage and burning of villages, was seen as judicial punishment for all that had gone before.

Never again did two great medieval armies of 'innumerable warriors'[6] move against each other in England, and we can be sure that most of these warriors fought for gain rather than patriotism. Towton was a culmination of at least ten years of private feuding that had spiralled out of control with the aid of propaganda and the undercurrent 'spin' of a north–south divide. Dynastic ambition, brought about by a weak and unstable king, inflated localised disputes over land and titles. The various accounts of Towton prove that most chroniclers were out of touch with events in the north and that initial reports of the battle were conflicting. Writers and later chroniclers, who acquired their information 'from men that were there'[7] give us cause to question the casualty figures, the dispersal and position of King Edward's army before the battle, the topography of the battlefield, and the timings of certain events in the campaign. If Towton was the longest, biggest and bloodiest battle on British soil, why was there so little written about it at the time? Did those who chronicled the carnage purposely inflate the bloodletting at the behest of their king? Did the heralds, who were well known for their veracity and impartiality, lie about the death toll? Or are there unique reasons why so many men died at Towton? Do the mass graves at Towton Hall indicate that some of the Lancastrian soldiers were singled out after the battle and killed like those executed the following day in York? Was it an everyday occurrence in the Wars of the Roses to round up local enemies, known turncoats and traitors and assassinate them? The questions, of course, are myriad and controversial. However, some of the answers lie in logic and in the act of commemoration that occurred in the reign of Richard III that still retains some of its pathos and mystery today.

The Towton Chapel

The evidence for a battlefield chapel at Towton is wholly conclusive. However, the evidence leads to several questions, not least regarding the important matter of where the chapel was built and what significance its foundations had on the social, cultural and religious minds of the time.

Several years after the battle, the chapel was a focal point of commemoration for the Yorkist kings – Edward IV and his younger brother Richard III. Indeed, many efforts were made to try to finish the building work by the Tudors and endow the chapel with the materials it needed to make it flourish. But it seems that due to lack of finance and political apathy of the time, the chapel fell into a ruinous state and by the reign of Henry VIII it became an embarrassing reminder of a conflict best forgotten.

It is easy to wax lyrical about such things and assume that the Yorkists had an overriding personal urge to commemorate those men who lost their lives at Palmsunday Field. To overplay the pious nature of medieval monarchs is still a common line for some historians today. However, the reality is far more in keeping with such foundations in the fifteenth century, and

Lord Dacre's Cross, now forming part of the Towton Battlefield Cross, as depicted by Edmund Bogg in 1904. It is thought that this stone once adorned the Towton Chapel. *(Author)*

the need to advertise power and reconciliation are important keys to understanding why the Towton Chapel was conceived. In an age when piety was linked with propaganda, the reasons for its foundation are comparable to why other ecclesiastical buildings were erected on other British battlefields in the Middle Ages. No doubt the 'lytyll chapell' at Barnet was established by Edward IV primarily to heal the deep divisions in his kingdom after the recovery of his throne in 1471.[8] A much earlier church and college founded at Shrewsbury in 1408 was not only built as a memorial to the slain of 1403 but also to advertise Henry IV's ability to put down aristocratic rebellion. At St Albans, funds were made available to pay for prayers to be sung in one of the abbey chapels for the nobles who had been deliberately killed at the onset of the Wars of the Roses. While on a much grander scale, Battle Abbey near Hastings was primarily built so that the Normans, and William I could commemorate his successful invasion and victory against the Saxons in 1066. It is no accident that he founded the abbey on what is considered to be the spot where his counterpart Harold I was slain. Therefore, the founding of chapels, churches and monasteries on battlefields have double meanings.

Such memorials were magnets for pilgrims and those who wished to make a political statement, and the latter reason was undoubtedly in the mind of Richard III when he became king in 1483. He took the opportunity to commemorate the bloodiest battle of his brother's reign while at the same time celebrating the precise moment when the Yorkist dynasty was founded. The battle of Towton was also fought in Yorkshire, which was periodically Richard's adopted home and his pool of military support in times of crisis. Therefore, the existence of a chapel commemorating both Lancastrian and Yorkist losses was one way of gaining allegiance from wavering nobles when he acquired the throne. The fact that the Towton commemorative chapel was built so close to the main road from London to York also proves that Richard was out to create a win-win situation beside one of the main arteries of the kingdom.

However, contrary to popular thinking, there was an earlier chapel at Towton long before 1461. Recent research by the Richard III Society has unearthed evidence of a papal bull, dated 6 November 1467, which tells of a partially abandoned and ruinous chapel in the village that Edward IV intended to renovate so that services could be held there for the Towton dead. The original chapel was dedicated to St Mary, which is in keeping with the dedication that later became attributed to it in the late Yorkist and early Tudor period. It seems that this original manorial chapel was free-standing and had a small cemetery where some of the slain were buried after the battle. In 1472 there was even a chaplain assigned to it. But evidently, the renovation was not finished, and alms were being used to try to upgrade its status – a sad indictment of Edward's former willingness to commemorate the dead of both sides after his victory at Towton.

The next piece of evidence relating to the chapel is in the register of grants offered by the Duchy of Lancaster. The revealing passage proves that there once was an original chapel at Towton, and that Richard III was clearly interested in it. After identifying the battlefield, the great armies engaged there and that his brother had won a resounding victory over those that had rebelled against him, Richard mentions that the Towton dead:

> and a number of noblemen sprung from the family of our said brother and ourselves, and other leading men and people of this kingdom in a great multitude, the pity of it, were cut off from this human life, and their bodies were put in three pits in the said field [on the battlefield] and other nearby places completely without any Christian burial, as is well known. Wherefore we, deeply sorry that the dead should be buried in this way, in these last months have caused their bones to be exhumed and given Christian burial, partly in the parish church of Saxton in our said county of Yorkshire and its cemetery, and partly in the chapel of Towton and in its surrounding.[9]

Soon after Richard's coronation in September 1483, he decreed that £40 was to be provided for the construction of a chapel out of the revenues of the Honour of Pontefract. The details of the building work were entrusted to his 'trusty and well-beloved servants Thomas Langton and William Sallay',[10] the latter being then Lord of Saxton and who, it will be remembered, provided the bells for the parish church. The Langtons owned the limestone quarry at nearby Huddlestone, and it appears that the Multon family, kinsmen of the Dacres of Gilsland, were also involved in the chapel and its foundation.

We can be sure that this Towton Chapel (probably built on the site of the original) was made of local stone, although its actual design is unknown. In fact, there is no mention in contemporary documents where the chapel was situated, but Leland saw ruins of a 'great chapel' in about 1540, and he recorded this in his *Itinerary* of 1558 as being erected where many men slain in the battle were once buried.[11] Leland also mentions that John Multon's father had laid the first stone of the chapel in a commemoration ceremony which may have also coincided with other religious services for the dead buried in Saxton. Therefore, we must assume that Richard's chapel was not an insignificant building, that it was a large free-standing edifice (unlike the first which pre-dated the battle of Towton) and that it had new foundations, was sumptuously built of local stone and was sited in a prominent position relatively close to the London road. This summarises Leland's description, and given that he noted the chapel in his work, along with many other historical buildings he passed during his visitation, it is clear that any further archaeological work needs to concentrate on a structure much larger than previously thought. The fine examples of local medieval chapels at Lotherton Hall and Lead may be considered probable architectural styles, but not necessarily facsimiles of the much greater half-built chapel at Towton.

As explained earlier, surviving evidence reveals that the original chapel of St Mary had a cemetery, and that Richard III ordered the reburial of bones from the battlefield here and in the cemetery at Saxton. If these were purposely exhumed from the shallow battlefield graves in about 1483 (twenty-two years after the battle) and re-interred in or around the chapel by the Hungates, then these were *not* the bones found by workmen and archaeologists in 1996. Confirmation of this fact is that complete cadavers, in situ, were excavated from beside Towton Hall and not a mass of random bones, which might be expected after exhumation and reburial. However, as noted by Leland, it was the local Hungate family who were ultimately responsible for the clearance of the battlefield plateau and

Archbishop Thomas Rotherham 1423–1500. *(Author)*

that the original mass graves, which were certainly there in abundance at one time, are a mystery no longer. In short, the graves that Richard III mentioned in his decree above are no longer there.

After its foundation, it is believed that work on the Towton Chapel flourished for a while, and by February 1484, a new chaplain had been decided upon. John Bateman was to receive seven marks a year from the wardens of Saxton parish church, although it is doubtful that he ever took up the position.[12] The chapel was not yet finished, and civil unrest was once again brewing in the kingdom. The building work was not progressing, and in 1486, after the battle of Bosworth and the death of Richard III, Archbishop Rotherham was offering indulgences to anyone who would give alms to finish off the construction. He reported that:

a certain chapel has been expensively and imposingly erected
from new foundations in the hamlet of Towton, upon the battlefield where the bodies of the first and greatest of the land as
well as great multitudes of other men were first slain and then
buried and interred in the fields around. Which chapel in so
far as the roofing, the glazing of windows, and other necessary
furnishings is concerned has not yet been fully completed, nor
is it likely that the building will be finished without the alms
and help of charitable Christians in the diocese.[13]

In July of the same year, the Langton family sued in the local
court for the theft of 460 tiles from their premises and that
these might have been intended for the Towton Chapel roof.
However, by 22 December 1502, Thomas Savage, Archbishop
of York, was still desperately trying to drum up support to
complete the chapel:

> Whereas the Chapel of Towton in the parish of Saxton in which
> chapel and ground about it very many bodies of men slain in
> time of war lie buried. Now forasmuch as the said chapel is not
> sufficiently endowed with possessions and rents as to sustain it
> and have divine service celebrated therein, without the chari-
> table alms of Christian people elsewhere. Whereupon William
> Archbishop of York hereby granted his license and authority to
> Dom. Robert Burdet, chaplain, to celebrate divine service in
> the said chapel, and to the inhabitants of the town of Towton to
> found a guild or fraternity in the same chapel to the honour of
> St Mary the Virgin, St. Anne and St Thomas the Martyr.[14]

In 1546 further grants were offered to those who would assist
with donations to the fabric and endowment of the chapel.
Indulgences 'of 40 days for the Chapel of Towton to be newly
built' give the impression that patronage was still desperately
needed. Earlier offers of indulgences (time off from purgatory)
had been largely unsuccessful. But among the grants made

The indulgence of Thomas Savage, Archbishop of York, intended to raise funds for the refurbishment of the 'Toughton Capella'. *(Borthwick Institute)*

in September 1511 was one to Henry Lofte (hermit) of the order of St Paul who purchased several indulgences from 'the Chapel of St James of Tolton [Towton's original name] in the Parish of Saxton, County of York, to the intent that he shall leave the said pardon and pray for the king and queen consort and the souls of the late king and queen'.[15]

With a new king on the throne and Richard III branded a villain by this time, it was probably thought that the building could be put to better use as a chapel of ease. However, even lucrative promises of indulgences did nothing to induce further investment or interest in the building work. Evidently, the fact that the Tudors were in power dissuaded many wealthy people from contributing, and despite several attempts at regeneration, the chapel soon became a political embarrassment. The founder, after all, was a 'child killer and tyrant' in Tudor eyes, and even though many Lancastrians may have had deep feelings for those soldiers who perished at Towton, the overriding factor appears to have been against any form of further battlefield commemoration.

John Leland's final glimpse of the ruin in the 1540s shows that the chapel was a resilient creation despite its traumatic history. However, we may safely assume that after this date the battlefield chapel became ruinous, and materials from it were used to extend Towton Hall centuries later.

A sketch of Towton Hall made by the antiquary John Warburton in 1718. *(Author)*

Admiral Edward Hawke of Towton was responsible for some of the re-building work in about 1776. Various features, including the Chapel Room, substantiate the claim that this part of his house was renovated with reclaimed medieval stonework. With a chimney of brick as evidence of a later construction, we may conclude that this extension is not part of the imposing free-standing chapel that Leland saw in the 1540s and therefore not the edifice commissioned by Richard III as some might believe. Further evidence can be brought to bear if we consider that the trench graves discovered in 1996 were found partly under this room, continuing past the hall's north wall into the void and under the chimney. The so-called 'wall of dead' found abutting the cellars in 1797 also confirms the limits of the original fortified manor house that once stood there, and along with complete cadavers found in 2006, this suggests that graves were dug initially beside the hall and chapel in 1461 and not in it.[16]

The final word on this investigation has clearly not been heard. The crest of Chapel Hill shows no sign of building work or stone foundations. Some archaeological work has been done in and around the hall by the Towton Archeological Project, and more graves in the area will undoubtedly be found, but the chapel may continue to remain an enigma mainly due to Tudor neglect and the need for local building materials.

However, if the search for the chapel is to continue, any further archaeology must concentrate on the elusive Chapel Garth 'to the north of the [original] village'[17] as mentioned in *Drake's Eboracum*, although where precisely this enclosure is today remains a mystery worthy of further illumination.

The Tomb of Lord Dacre

After the battle of Towton, many mass graves were dug in the immediate vicinity to bury the dead. But one grave, in particular, stands out from the rest as unique to the medieval period because of its location and of a legend that has baffled historians for at least two centuries.

The rectangular stone tomb of Ranulf, Lord Dacre of Gilsland, lies to the north side of Saxton Church, the focal point of many unmarked burials there in 1461. Most of these burials, as explained, were probably Yorkist soldiers. However, after the battle, because the area was predominantly Lancastrian territory, it is thought that some of the royal army, including Lord Dacre (and allegedly Lord Clifford), were also buried at Saxton instead of transporting their bodies home.

Lord Dacre (*c.* 1412–61) was a Cumberland landowner, a peer of the realm, and he and his younger brother Humphrey fought for the Lancastrians at Towton. Like all prominent families in the Wars of the Roses, the Dacres had to choose sides in the conflict. Some were killed or attained by the Yorkist regime due to their staunch loyalties to King Henry VI, and Ranulf, or more commonly *Ralph* Lord Dacre, was no exception. He was almost fifty years old when he died at Towton, and more erroneously, it is thought he was killed in North Acres to the left of the Lancastrian battle line. Local legend has it that an arrow struck him as he removed his helmet to drink a cup of wine. Also, a rhyming couplet that 'The Lord of Dacres was slain in North Acres' by a *lad in a bur tree* is prominent among Towton oral tradition along with the myth that he was buried in Saxton churchyard with his horse. But are all these stories true, or are we dealing with unsupported facts?

Dacre died, and that is a fact. But in my opinion, a fifty-year-old man drawn into the carnage of hand-to-hand combat is a man vulnerable to more than just a stray arrow. Unfortunately, there are many examples of men dying from a heart attack, stroke and exhaustion in battle even though their retainers and household men probably did most of the actual fighting – and dying. They were sworn to protect their master; therefore, given that arrows were available in their thousands on the day of battle, especially after the initial archery duel, and that Dacre was, like many others, exhausted in the confines of his armour, then the cause and effect of his last moments in North Acres rings true.

Humphrey Dacre may have seen his brother die. However, he was a younger and luckier man. He managed to escape the battle despite being later attained for treason. His punishment by Edward IV was assured after such a decisive defeat, but aside from this, who took care of Ralph's burial and commemoration immediately after the battle was over if Humphrey was on the run? Edward IV had issued orders of no quarter before the

battle, and the rout of the Lancastrians was followed up mercilessly to the gates of York. Therefore, it's highly doubtful that
any of the defeated army were present on the field when the
battle ended unless they were dead or dying. After the event,
Lancastrian executions were in progress, and we know certain
prominent nobles were beheaded by Edward IV in York the
following day. So, was it the impartial heralds who arranged
Lord Dacre's burial at Saxton? Obviously, the tomb itself must
have been constructed much later when Edward IV pardoned
Humphrey Dacre for his crimes, but who did this, and why
was Ralph Dacre singled out from the many who died on
Palmsunday Field to be commemorated?

Closer scrutiny of the tomb reveals that Humphrey's son,
Thomas Dacre, later married into the Greystoke family and
became known as Baron Greystoke in 1488. Therefore, given
this change of title, the tomb could have been erected as much
as twenty-five years after the battle of Towton if the original
translations of the inscription and the Dacre heraldic arms can
be believed.[18]

However, let us suppose that Lord Dacre's body was identified on the battlefield sometime on the 29th (or early the
following day) and noted by the heralds. Dacre's prominence
as a noble would have assured his place in consecrated ground,
and it is clear from chronicled evidence that Edward distributed rewards 'among such as brought the bodies of the slain
and gave them burial' therefore was the new king responsible for Dacre's interment even though he was his enemy? It
appears he was far from heartless when it came to the slain
and proper burial rites. However, the heralds as official 'battlefield referees' would have organised the detail of the burial,
although this feeling of purpose would not have extended to a
fashionable tomb. Therefore, can we be sure Dacre's grave was
marked permanently in 1461? The heralds and clergy were the
obvious choices to arrange mass burials, as they were known
for their impartiality and proper observation of all things

chivalrous. Still, they must have been shocked by the carnage at Towton, not to mention how monumental their task would be to count and bury all the dead. Indeed, was this task ever possible given the spread of bodies alluded to previously?

Evidently bodies had to be buried in mass graves, and Lord Dacre's tomb is situated in Saxton churchyard. But legend has it that Dacre is not alone in his grave, his mode of burial is far from normal, and more to the point, what is a random horse doing in his grave, as some sources and letters have revealed?

The simple truth is that we cannot be sure if a horse is buried in Dacre's grave or not. Or that he was buried (as some say) in a standing position or mounted on the animal. Surely the sheer amount of battlefield dead was enough for gravediggers to contend with without burying someone with a horse? In short, it is a logistical nightmare to do this and would make no sense, unless there was a precedent. But rather than accept this as apocryphal, can we hazard an educated guess as to why the story has persisted based on archaeological evidence: for instance, the existence of Anglo-Saxon sixth- and ninth-century human–horse burials which *can* be verified and are not clouded by legend?

According to recent archaeological fact, the Anglo-Saxons buried their warrior class with their horses in abundance. One of the many burials at Sutton Hoo is illustrative of this. Another is one at Lakenheath. There are others in Britain, and Pamela Cross of Bradford University has done some interesting work on this subject proving the pagan significance of such human–horse burials. Here is an extract from her article in the magazine *Saxon*:

The behaviour behind these types of burials is complex and much of it appears to have ritual significance. Part of it probably represents feasting residue, part of it sacrificial rites probably associated with fertility and good luck. The human–horse burials certainly seem to have an aspect of status and prestige but may also have other meanings. Within the Celtic-Northern traditions there are indications that Odin and Frey/Freya, Epona and Rhiannon may figure in horse ritual practices. And more generally, the horse is often symbolically linked both with the sun and with boats. Some feel that the horse represents a means of journeying into the next world, some that it is simply a valuable possession. The actual meanings are probably as multi-layered and diverse as the people involved in these practices.[19]

In these cases of ritualistic burial, the horse is a symbol of prestige in warfare. Therefore, it is natural to suppose that horses profoundly affected the development of warrior funerary culture later. We know this tradition is Anglo-Saxon and had Germanic origins, but did it survive into the late medieval period? After all, the horse was still central to status, knightly prowess, chivalry and featured in many funeral rites in the Middle Ages?

Given there was little difference between this *Anglo-Saxon* way of thinking and chivalric horse veneration in the medieval period, are we any closer to the truth given that Dacre and his kind generally thought the same way about their horses? Another explanation could be that, like at some other sites where *single* horse burials have been discovered, historians could have mistaken the story about Lord Dacre and his horse in Saxton churchyard for centuries.

To explain this further, Saxton Church dates from the eleventh century, but the village itself pre-dates this, appearing in the Domesday Book of 1086. Saxton was formally known as *Seaxtun*, meaning 'town or settlement of the Saxons'. Therefore, could there have been a bizarre coincidence in 1461 where Lord Dacre's burial and a *single* ritual Anglo-Saxon horse burial shared the same space? There is certainly no late medieval precedent for such a burial rite, and we may conclude that Dacre was not a pagan. Therefore, what is really buried in his tomb, and what is the written evidence allegedly proving that this is a fifteenth century human–horse burial with Lord Dacre sitting, or standing, in his grave?

Lord Dacre's strange upright burial was first reported in 1749 when his tomb had metal clamps securing it. This grave was later broken into to bury a *Mr Gascoigne* who may have been related to the local gentry at Parlington, Lotherton and Craignish in Scotland. While digging this Gascoigne grave – called an abomination by Richard Brooke, who visited the site in 1848 – the skeleton found was allegedly unearthed in a standing position. And later, when another grave was dug beside the Dacre tomb, a horse's head was found with its vertebrae extending into the grave.[20] A letter sent from Saxton vicarage dated 23 January 1882 confirms these two burials, although most of the excavations in Saxton churchyard were local, amateurish, and not recorded by competent archaeologists. The letter is, however, an eyewitness report, albeit second hand, and it reads:

My Dear Sir,

When I was at Craignish we had some conversation about the battle of Towton, which was fought in this parish on Palm Sunday (March 29th old style) 1461. I then said that I would try to get hold of a pamphlet which I had seen on this subject and let you have it to read. I have not forgotten my promise but regret that I do not recall where to lay my hand upon this source of information. I have lately had some conversation with the son of the old sexton who dug the grave close to Lord Dacre's tomb, and who himself was assisting. He tells me that when they had got down about 6 feet, they came upon the skull of a horse, and from the position of it, and the vertebrae of the neck, it was made plain that the body of the horse extended actually into Lord Dacre's grave. This discovery is a wonderful verification of the tradition in the village that Lord Dacre's horse was actually buried with him in the churchyard. I have in my possession a portion of this skull which I hope someday to have the pleasure of showing to you. The body of the horse undoubtedly yet lies in Lord Dacre's tomb, as I understand the sexton did not make any excavations further than were necessary in digging the grave he had in hand.[21]

The above horse's skull is now reputedly in the British Museum, and ironically the above letter from George M. Webb, the Vicar of Saxton, was addressed to another of the Gascoigne family, in this case, Colonel Richard Gascoigne, who was related to the one so mysteriously buried in, or adjacent to, the Dacre grave.

According to the same tradition Lord Dacre is supposed to be buried in an upright position. However, there is no mention of this in the letter as Dacre's grave was not disturbed further. Therefore, the legend is difficult to justify unless we can prove it by finding other examples of this kind of burial in Britain during the medieval period.

Sadly, I have found no evidence of this to date. However, at the east end of the north aisle of Bolton Priory Church, North Yorkshire, there is a chantry belonging to Beamsley Hall, and in the vault, according to tradition, the Mauleverer and Clapham family tombs were found exactly in this orientation. The reason for this strange burial custom was said to originate from the Mauleverer family, *who refused to bow down to any man even in death*. However, this type of burial was disproved in 1812, to a certain extent, when T.D. Whitaker visited the site and wrote:

> I have looked into it [the vault] through an aperture in the pavement, but could discover no remains of coffins, except one of the Morley family. Perhaps this unnatural position of the bodies had caused them to collapse, in consequence of which they may have been removed.[22]

It seems the latter may have been the case. William Wordsworth, the famous poet, later wrote about Thomas Clapham's son, John Clapham, a participant in the Wars of the Roses, and his poem rings true with the Dacre mode of burial at least in a romantic sense:

> Pass, pass who will yon chantry door,
> And, through the chink in the fractured floor,
> Look down and see a grisly sight,
> A vault where the bodies are buried upright!
> There, face by face, and hand by hand,
> The Claphams and Mauleverers stand,
> And, in his place, among son and sire,
> Is John de Clapham, that fierce esquire,
> A valiant man, and a name of dread,
> In the ruthless wars of the White and Red,
> Who dragged Earl Pembroke from Banbury Church,
> And smote off his head on the stones of the porch.[23]

This same John Clapham was a supporter of the Earl of Warwick, and he took part in the Battle of Edgecote (Danes Moor), fought on 24 July 1469. He was personally responsible for the beheadings of the Earl of Pembroke and his brother near the south porch of Banbury Church. A small, plain rusty sword survives in a branch of the Clapham family today, which may have belonged to John, although this cannot be confirmed as the murder weapon.

However, some of the legends surrounding Lord Dacre's tomb seem to ring true, in part, and have definite links with the northern gentry that existed in 1461. In the fifteenth century, prominent local families such as the Gascoignes, Scargills, Multons, Sallays and Hungates (some of whom were the lords of Saxton and Lead) would have been at least partly interested in Lord Dacre's burial – along with the Dacre family when it was safe for them to do so. They may have even fashioned the Dacre tomb themselves to commemorate not only Ralph's death at Towton but also the great outpouring of grief for all those Lancastrians lost in the battle. Even in 1468, when their attainders were reversed, the feeling was strong enough to warrant a lasting memorial to one knight who held such staunch Lancastrian sympathies.

Today, we can see these local feelings in the patriotic tone of the contemporary Lancastrian inscription on Lord Dacre's tombstone. It shouts to us across the ages and tells of a long-forgotten warrior class that had been soundly beaten on their home ground in more ways than one. The Dacre inscription has, over the years, been translated in several ways, but this is my translation which follows *Eboracum* (the earliest) closely:

Here lies Ranulf, Lord of Dacre and Gilsland, a true knight, valiant in battle in the service of King Henry VI, who died on Palm Sunday, 29 March 1461, on whose soul may God have mercy, Amen.[24]

The blackened tomb, about 2½ft high, displaying Lord Dacre's heraldic achievements on all four sides, is today in a bad state of repair. Wrenched open, defaced and broken in two pieces by the curious and the disrespectful, it is now only 'protected' by iron rails and an enduring legend. Whether Dacre was buried with his horse, on his horse, or in a standing position are questions that may never fully be answered. However, in the parish records of Sherburn-in-Elmet, there is an interesting note in the burial register of 1754–78 that includes a memorandum. Among the lists of vicars, a note about the new church clock, a new bridge at Milford Beck and the repair of Church Fenton vicarage, there is a note about Lord Dacre. In 1787, an entry reads 'the vicar dug up the *skull of Lord Dacre* in Saxton Field', which further complicates an already complicated story and calls into question the veracity of such claims and local traditions.[25]

However, legends and traditions aside, the Dacre tomb is still a remarkable survival of the fifteenth century, and as such, it deserves better conservation. Proof of whatever is in the grave (or extending into it), may put the legend to rest once and for all. But the fragile tomb must not be disturbed again, in my opinion. If it ever is, it will be a sad tribute to a man who saw the terrible battle of Towton first-hand and was buried on the battlefield where he lost his life fighting for a cause he believed in.

The Longest, Biggest and Bloodiest

Due to the comprehensive work carried out on the bow and arrow in recent years, some battles of the Wars of the Roses need revision. This need is addressed here regarding the length of the Towton campaign and, in turn, the casualties inflicted, particularly on the 'Battle Cross Ridge' where the Lancastrians fell foul of the Yorkist arrow storm. Also presented below is a possible explanation of why contemporaries confused dates and timings during the campaign, leading to the common misunderstanding that the battle lasted ten hours, was fought at night, or alternatively, took one and a half days to decide the outcome.

Casting our mind back to the battle, Lord Fauconberg's 'vaward' comprised wholly of archers was the first to engage the Lancastrians at Towton. The ruse Fauconberg used, if we can believe Edward Hall, is clearly explained. But the devastation caused by the bow is more difficult to visualise and come to terms with without understanding the weapon's mechanics. In my view, the casualties incurred by Yorkist arrows were well above the average expected in medieval battles due to the size of the contingents of archers employed, the effect of the weather conditions and the Lancastrian inability to counterattack. The Yorkist arrow storm proved catastrophic for Lord Fauconberg's counterpart Thomas Hammes 'captain of all the footmen'[26] whose own archers suffered from a commander's worst nightmare – the unforeseen elements of battlefield conditions. The situation led to profound Lancastrian casualties and ultimately an uncoordinated advance led by unwieldy bodies of men suffering from shock and fractured morale.

It was estimated some years ago by Simon Stanley and Robert Hardy, by practical means and historical comparison with Mary Rose replica bows, that the medieval archer was equipped with a 120-pound (draw weight) bow and war arrows (Type 16) that weighed approximately three to four ounces. MRA (Mary Rose Approximation) bows have been shot rapidly by Stanley, a world record–holding archer, at a rate of about ten arrows per minute at a range of 240yd without arrows losing a critical amount of their initial velocity. Test shots across North Acres in 1996 measured over 270yd without a following wind, therefore the medieval archer's paradox is no longer a theory, and no doubt should prove that medieval soldiers could handle such a formidable weapon with ease. The physical and tactical aspects of the bow and arrow are a prominent feature of the historical work done by Strickland and Hardy in *The Great Warbow*. However, what is more remarkable is the lethal striking power of the arrow even at optimum range. The mathematics can be read in detail in the above work (now standard philosophy),[27] but the reality of ten thousand arrows falling en masse at Towton must have been appalling.

The penetrative force and range of the warbow have been compared to a musket ball of the eighteenth century. At a range of 240yd and falling at a rate of up to 146 joules from a bow with a draw weight of 120lb, a 75g war arrow would have penetrated armour of wrought iron.[28] Against lesser armoured men, such arrows would have killed outright. At best, a shaft would have maimed an individual probably for life. A ricocheting arrow bouncing off fluted plate armour would also have incapacitated or caused various types of shock to occur, even if it was headless. Thousands of arrows falling at once would have caused massive disorder and confusion in the ranks. The science of terminal ballistics shows that the penetrative force of an arrow had no equal other than the crossbow, which was extremely slow to operate. A comment by Gerald of Wales in the twelfth century substantiates the power of the bow when he saw a man at arms shot 'through his thigh, high up, where it was protected inside and outside by iron cuirasses ... then [the arrow went] through the skirt of his leather tunic and penetrated part of his saddle. Finally, it lodged in his horse, driving so deep that it killed the animal'.[29]

A great many wounds from arrows were deemed lethal due to infected material entering the bloodstream. As stated earlier, some wounds never healed. Therefore, survival depended on not being hit or wearing enough protection to withstand the arrow storm. However, most men in the army could not afford armour plate, and despite the serviceable English jack and sallet helmet, it is certain that arrows negated such defensive equipment even at long range. Literally, tons of arrows were unleashed during one volley at Towton, but supplies were limited, hence the arrow strike had to be effective and of short duration. Soldiers stood and faced the inevitable. Swathes of casualties and disorder would have caused multiple collapses in the ranks as arrows fell, and in only a few minutes, the mounds of dead and dying would have considerably affected morale and movement. Anyone who questions the high casualty rate at Towton must therefore take this phase of the battle into account and acknowledge that the actual cost in life among the Lancastrian host was unusually high. Caught in the most dreadful 'shower' ever unleashed on Englishmen, there is no comparison in history. I am inclined to believe that even after a few volleys of arrows, at least 5,000 men were killed during this phase of the battle. The mathematics of men to arrows delivered is self-evident, even allowing for arrows falling harmlessly, and if we calculate that each archer had a minimum of twenty-four arrows at his disposal, the above figure is still strikingly low in comparison to what it could be.

The archer Simon Stanley drawing a replica Mary Rose bow. *(Robert Hardy)*

Apart from the archery duel at Towton, which lasted (in my opinion) only a few minutes, it is certain that the ten hours of hand-to-hand fighting mentioned by the chroniclers needs some revision. *Hearne's Fragment* even says that the battle lasted a day and a half and was fought at night, which is, of course, a physical impossibility on such a scale. Evidently, there needs to be some synthesis, and a chronology must be established to determine logically the times associated with certain events in the Towton campaign. My original timings stand, but a breakdown of a possible reason why the chroniclers got some aspects of the campaign wrong due to interpretation, an unfamiliarity with the topography and garbled news from the field is given below.

It is clear from analysing the contemporary evidence that most chroniclers were confused and thought that there was one continuous fight beginning with the battle of Ferrybridge on 28 March (Palm Sunday eve), which developed into 'a great conflict' that ended with a rout the next day. Given that the battle of Ferrybridge began at about midday on 28 March and the battle of Towton (including the rout) lasted for most of the following day, the mistaken calculations in *Hearne's Fragment* can be partly reconciled. George Neville's Palm Sunday battle, lasting ten hours, also fits the general chronology mentioned by Hearne, given that Neville received news second hand and that the dead were spread over 6 miles of countryside from the initial battle of Ferrybridge.[30] However, in all examples, it is quite clear to me that the fighting was not continuous due to the physical, mental and, more importantly, the logistical factors involved in moving pre-mechanised armies loaded with food supplies, camping equipment, and, critically, barrels of arrows, onward without a rest.

As stated previously, the chroniclers of Towton (of which there are few) were far removed from the event. Even the battle location was misinterpreted chiefly because contemporary writers were ignorant of local topography, distances and names. The first to receive word of Edward's victory from a reliable source, George Neville, neither mentions Towton or Saxton in his letter to Coppini. In fact, the only prominent places revealed by him are 'Pomfret' (Pontefract) and 'Feurbirga' (Ferrybridge), the latter being the location where, in his opinion, the Lancastrians were routed.[31] The *Croyland Chronicle* says that the Yorkists 'made immense havoc among them [the Lancastrians] for a distance of 10 miles, as far as the city of York'.[32] The villages of Towton and Saxton are not mentioned here either, and from this we might construe that the fight at Ferrybridge was the only battle of the campaign. Neville's dubious claims could easily be discarded out of hand as a summary of what he heard. However, his unique information regarding the fight at Ferrybridge is confirmed by the Croyland continuator, who describes that the battle was fought on 'a level spot of ground, situated near the castle of Pomfret and the bridge at Ferrybridge, and washed by a stream of considerable size'.[33] Add to this the fact that Neville says that a bridge was broken behind enemy lines and that men drowned as a result, and the case against a larger battle the next day at Towton becomes even more damning.

Similarly, some chroniclers thought the battle was fought at 'Shurborne' (Sherburn), while others considered that York was the only place worth noting (presumably because it had a substantial castle and Edward arrived there after the battle). The truth is that official records, namely Edward's attainder document, local tradition, and archaeology concur that the accepted site of the battle of Towton is correct. The fact that bridges were broken, men drowned in rivers, and a running battle ending in 'a great conflict' is proof of what likely occurred over one and a half days. Other contemporary chronicles and letters provide more details, but it is certain that messengers from the north, and even those involved in the conflict, were unsure of events at first. However, we may construct a possible scenario from the available evidence and conclude that due to Lord Clifford's harassing tactics at Ferrybridge and the subsequent skirmish at Dintingdale[34], the chronology was extended by writers. Indeed, as George Neville suggests, Lord Clifford's withdrawal from Ferrybridge may have been a bloody rout rather than an orderly retreat. Indeed, the skirmish at Dintingdale resulting from this mopping up operation by Fauconberg is partly confirmed by him, although not by name, as the place where 6 miles of dead bodies extended from before the battle of Towton.

As a result of the division in the Yorkist army, the vaward would have had no option but to advance against the Lancastrians the next day. While their main body under Edward was still arriving and positioning itself on the battlefield, Fauconberg's archers may even have engaged the enemy alone.[35] In Waurin's account, Edward, some 4 miles distant from the battlefield, received intelligence at first light that the Lancastrian army was advancing and 'in the field'. Knowing this, he immediately marched against them. Sent via Castleford to envelop Clifford's flank, the chances are that Fauconberg's vaward, like most medieval armies, was much enlarged and that it partly covered Edward's advance to Saxton. However, regarding the Duke of Norfolk, who commanded the rearward, this division was always separated from the main body. Therefore, it was pure luck that the dangerous partition in the Yorkist army was not exploited to the full by the Lancastrian high command, or Edward's army might have been destroyed when it was most vulnerable to attack.

A glance at the chronology shows the possible duration of each of these events, which supports the ten hours of fighting recorded by George Neville and the one and a half days' battle described by *Hearne's Fragment*. After the initial dawn attack, the battle of Ferrybridge probably lasted no more than a few hours, but the subsequent rout from the River Aire was pursued to Dintingdale, therefore militarily speaking Ferrybridge lasted most of the afternoon. The next day the battle of Towton was fought essentially in the afternoon (three or four hours at the most), with the rout being followed up into the evening. As can be seen, it was not the actual fighting that lasted ten hours; instead, it was the military manoeuvres and the protracted routs and pursuits that caused writers to mistake two battles for one.

As for how big the armies were at Towton, it may seem logical to calculate how many men fought as a multiple of how many were killed. However, as previously mentioned, this theory is hampered by the unique aspects of the routs from Ferrybridge and Towton. Similarly, it is a fruitless enterprise to try to calculate the death toll from the 'apparent' absence of graves or from the musings of monkish chroniclers who threw their hands up in abhorrence to the bloodletting. From the documented evidence detailing how many men the City of York mustered to fight at Towton (roughly ten per cent of the population according to the York Civic Records) we may judge that the Lancastrian army was deficient of volunteers.[36] But again, we would be wrong in assuming that their army, when fully mustered, was any smaller than the force which fought at the second battle of St Albans a month earlier, where some 3,000 men perished. Clearly, some Scottish contingents would have gone home after pillaging the English countryside. Still, most northern lords would have re-commissioned their tenants into Lancastrian ranks, and others were retained for life by their lords and called upon to fight for Henry VI or forfeit their lives. As explained earlier, some chroniclers recorded great multitudes of men in both armies. Therefore, it is apparent that we need to look elsewhere for a guide to how large the armies were at Towton.

In Chapter Six, I compared known unbiased musters and recruitment methods with the average number of men employed in noble retinues and militias. From this, I approximated armies in the region of 20 to 25,000, and I stand by these figures for several reasons. To establish the mathematics further, William Worcester, gentleman bureaucrat and antiquary, was in London when Edward of March entered the city after the battle of Mortimers Cross. He calculated that there were 8,000 men in Edward's army, and later at Clerkenwell, he estimated that this figure had been reduced by half. It is unreasonable to suggest that less than 8,000 men marched from London to fight the Lancastrians at Towton. Indeed, we would expect that Edward's original army of the Marches was augmented, essentially by additional troops from London and the southern shires, namely Kent, who it is said flocked to him in 'countless multitudes'.[37] If we add to this the combined strength of the Earl of Warwick and the Duke of Norfolk, who were both well connected and carried the king's commission to recruit every man between the ages of sixteen and sixty, then

		LANCASTRIANS	YORKISTS
	Date/Time	Event	Event
	27 March	Somerset's army concentrates in the vicinity of Tadcaster/Towton	Edward's army arrives at Pontefract Castle (without Duke of Norfolk's men)
			Edward sends Lord Fitzwalter to repair bridge at Ferrybridge (broken by Lancastrians)
	28 March DAWN	Lord Clifford with 'Flower of Craven' sent to Ferrybridge to harass Yorkist advance	Lord Fitzwalter attacked by Lord Clifford at Ferrybridge
	28 March AM		Edward's army moves to Ferrybridge.
	PM		The battle of Ferrybridge is fought Edward sends Fauconberg with the vaward to attack Clifford's flank via Castleford
	28 March PM/EVE	Clifford retreats to Towton, but is attacked by Fauconberg at Dintingdale/Barkston Ash	Edward's army crosses Ferrybridge and marches to Sherburn where he camps (now without Fauconberg and Norfolk)
	28 March NIGHT		Fauconberg camps at Saxton/Lead
	29 March DAWN	Somerset moves onto the plateau and takes up position on the 'Battle Cross Ridge'	Fauconberg's vaward moves onto the plateau and Edward strikes camp at Sherburn
	29 March 9.00 AM		Fauconberg's vaward engages the enemy while Edward moves onto the plateau (Norfolk is still on the road)
	29 March AM	Somerset advances. Northumberland is slow to engage the enemy	The battle of Towton is fought on the southern ridge. Edward's army is pushed back towards Saxton
	29 March MIDDAY		Norfolk arrives and attacks the Lancastrian left is pushed back
	29 March PM	Somerset's line breaks at midday and his army routs towards Towton and the rivers Cock and Wharfe	Orders of 'no quarter' cause a spate of indiscriminate killing (including prisoners)
	29 March PM/EVE		Edward remains on the field with the majority of his army who are not pursuing the enemy (heralds count the dead and graves are dug)
	30 March		Edward enters York with the army (clearing the battlefield continues)

Chronology of the Towton campaign. *(Author)*

an army of 20,000 men is not an impossibility. The strength of the Yorkist force gains further credibility if we consider that 20,000 Yorkists (the whole of Edward's army minus its casualties) were sent out from the City of York after the battle of Towton to pursue the Lancastrian refugees into the north.[38]

The strength of the Lancastrian army presents more significant problems due to lack of evidence, and regarding casualties, there is a tendency to inflate figures out of all proportion. However, stress must be placed on the fact that Towton was a notably bloody battle and that a good percentage of the men who fought there were killed in the rout, executed or drowned in rivers that hampered their escape. There was no place to run for those caught up in the aftermath of the battle, and the rivers that the Lancastrians crossed, without a thought to their later significance, play a big part in understanding the Towton death toll. Like the heralds, we have no way of knowing the final figure of those who drowned, and the option to subtract the bloodiest from the biggest anachronisms is our only way forward. Clearly, the 28,000 dead is the place to start, and this is a staggering figure for us to comprehend today. For those who compared the casualties at Towton to those of the Somme, where 60,000 men lost their lives, of which 21,000 were killed in the first hour of attack (perhaps in the first few minutes), this is another great enigma. Another factor to bear in mind at Towton is the one-sided archery duel and the effects of the medieval equivalent of the machine gun on closely compacted troop formations that had no cover or means of responding to the Yorkist barrage. The work done by Strickland, Hardy and Stanley proves that the bow and arrow were specifically built to maim and deal out death on a massive scale, the practical verification and proof of this, expounded by Simon Stanley in trials, being that no one was safe from such a large concentration of archers. But how many were killed in this phase of the battle?

Given that half the Yorkist army comprised archers (10,000) and each man had a full complement of arrows in his bag (24), we can calculate that even if half of the arrows shot missed flesh and blood, then 120,000 did not. The death rate was, therefore, a question of surviving such wounds in an environment where personal safety and battlefield surgery was limited. It is no wonder the situation instigated an immediate advance by the Lancastrians on their enemies. Like their ascendants at the battle of the Somme, the Lancastrians had probably lost a quarter of their strength in only a few minutes. If 5,000 men were killed (and this is a conservative estimate even if we suggest that smaller armies took the field at Towton), then many more died and were maimed in the brutal hand-to-hand combat that followed.

Although we may be sure that the damage done on both sides was severe, it presented an even greater problem to those whose job was to record it in official documents (for example, the heralds). Their overall casualty figure must remain suspect. However, the total given by the heralds is still an impeccable source of truth. Moreover, it is a unique survival of the Wars of the Roses by a group of men who saw the battle unfold into widespread carnage. Therefore, how did the heralds calculate their final figure over such a massive area? Did both sides settle on an approximation of the casualties? What did the heralds base their calculations on, and why did they come up with a figure of 28,000 and not inflate or round it off as partisan chroniclers tended to do after the event? Alternatively, did the heralds exaggerate and lie at the behest of Edward IV and the Yorkist propaganda machine? Perhaps we should simply say that Towton was the bloodiest medieval battle and suggest that others such as Boudica's Revolt in AD 60/61 and Marston Moor in 1644 are comparable in their eras. As a matter of interest, the more level-headed contemporary chroniclers computed that 10,000 to 20,000 were slain at Towton – a massive fellowship of death by any standards of warfare. Polydore Vergil, who had no real cause to be partisan, recorded that 'there was wanting of both parties about twenty thousand men [of which] the number of prisoners and wounded persons, whereof some were cured, and some died, were fully ten thousand'.[39]

Does Vergil's comment approach the truth and confirm that the Lancastrians lost over fifty per cent casualties at Towton, or does the herald's death toll mask something far more sinister and disturbing that occurred after the battle was over? Commemoration betrays genuine feelings of loss, releases guilt and opens political opportunities after the event. With a change of administration, pressures ease in any era, and the resulting outpouring of energy becomes manifest in memorials to those that made the ultimate sacrifice. This emotive action is apparent after all conflicts and was evident at Towton in the reign of Richard III, but in the Tudor period, Lancastrian grief was left wanting.

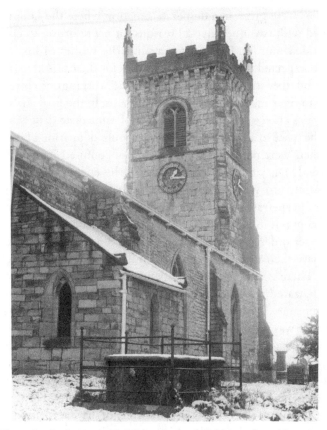

Where the dead were buried. After the battlefield was cleared bones were newly interred on the north side of Saxton Church and also near the original Towton Chapel. Lord Dacre's tomb is in the foreground. *(Author)*

Indiscriminate Slaughter or Selective Killing

At the battle of Agincourt in 1415, Henry V issued orders that all his French prisoners were to be immediately put to death, and as a result, there was a massacre of unarmed knights and men at arms who might otherwise have been ransomed. However, these executions were not carried out to the full, and Henry's orders were given in a desperate situation where the king was faced with two unequivocal reasons for *not* resorting to cold-blooded murder. First, it was against the wishes of his men who expected to be paid great ransoms for their prisoners, and second, that it was expressly against the workings of chivalry not to offer mercy to those of equal status. In the final analysis, Henry's choice was restricted to one of immediate danger, and in the space of a few minutes, several groups of unarmed French soldiers were put to death in a frenzy of confused activity that earned Henry the title of 'cut-throat' by his enemies.

Agincourt was not the first or the last time such massacres were perpetrated on the medieval battlefield. In fact, twenty years previously, at the battle of Nicopolis, the French commander ordered the deaths of a thousand prisoners who were to have their throats slit rather than burden his army the next day. There is also plenty of evidence that similar killings were perpetrated under explicit orders of no quarter or because of reprisals. Under normal battlefield conditions, a captured knight was ransomed, which in some instances might mean that he was set free on the promise that payment for his life would be forthcoming. His captor might even treat him to a banquet at his own expense or imprison his hostage in lavish apartments in one of his castles as befitting his status. However, by the Wars of the Roses, the ransoming of prisoners after battles was replaced by the headman's axe and soldiers were more concerned with looting the battlefield and their victims rather than restraining captives.

This same treatment of the vanquished was a dominant feature after the battle of Towton. However, before the excavation of the grave in 1996, we might be forgiven for thinking that there was wholesale slaughter in the rout from the battlefield. Indeed, every chronicler without exception emphasises an unusually high casualty rate among the gentry and the common soldiery in this phase of the battle. The opinionated Croyland continuator related that 'the king's army eagerly pursued them [the Lancastrians], cutting down the fugitives with their swords [and] just like so many sheep for the slaughter made immense havoc among them',[40] the impression being that the rout was more like a pogrom rather than a clearing-up operation. It is also said that orders of no quarter were a feature of both sides' psychology before the battle commenced, that noted lords were to be hunted down and that it was forbidden to show mercy to anyone upon pain of death. But can this killing frenzy be substantiated in any way? Were there massacres at Towton, and if so, how can we be sure that this was a selective operation?

Edward Hall is our only source for the 'no quarter' order that was a precursor to the battle. Writing in 1542, he knew men whose grandfathers had fought in the Wars of the Roses. His own grandfather Sir David Hall had been slain along with the Duke of York at the battle of Wakefield in 1460, and he likely knew what occurred when battles turned into routs. A good portion of this knowledge found its way into his history, and on balance, there is reason to accept that some of his work detailing the Towton campaign can be confirmed by other sources. Hall also probably visited the battlefield in the Tudor era. He knew of local traditions associated with the River Cock and areas of the battlefield, such as Dintingdale, where Lord Clifford was killed. However, two separate passages in his work relate that before the battle Edward IV 'made a proclamation, that no prisoner should be taken, nor one enemy saved', while a few lines later he reiterates that the 'taking of prisoners was proclaimed a great offence'.[41] Men were even warned that they would be killed if they showed mercy to captives. Therefore, even if we take away the notion that there was an unusually high incidence of blood-feuding in the armies by 1461, the official Yorkist line was clear and that Edward's custom of saving the commons but killing the lords (as related by Commynes in his work) was not observed at Towton. Indeed, it is almost certain that Edward did not even coin this mandate to limit collateral damage among the common soldiery at this early date.

What else can we judge relevant from contemporaries that might point towards a purposeful elimination of hated Lancastrians? Indeed, there were men, other than those who were being pursued by blood feuding relatives, who had a price on their head and presented a continuing threat to the Yorkist regime and their future success on the battle-field. Chroniclers tell us that the Yorkists singled out Andrew Trollope and several other named men for extinction before the battle commenced. On 6 March 1461, a price of £100 was placed on the head of Thomas Tresham, Thomas Fitzharry, William Grimsby and the two 'bastards of Exeter' who the Earl of Warwick had every reason to view with hate for executing his father at Wakefield.[42] The esquire and turncoat named Lovelace had the reputation of being the most expert in warfare in the whole of England, and Warwick had made him captain of Kent in 1461 with disastrous consequences. It is a well-known fact that there were verbal orders to kill such men in battle, and feuding enemies formed up opposite each other to settle old scores. The political circumstances of the Wars of the Roses dictated that it was essentially the nobles and gentlefolk who took command of these belligerent divisions. Still, there were exceptions and most soldiers who had proved their worth in the Hundred Years War rose through the ranks and retained high profile positions in English armies of the period. Some of these 'experts' were knighted on the battlefield for their services to the crown and soon commanded contingents and even whole divisions in the wars. These 'chief captains' were retained for their cunning in war and were also sought out and put to death if they were found on the losing side. Warlike leaders like the London mercer John Harrow and Captain Hanson of Hull were also executed with the Earl of Salisbury after the battle of Wakefield in 1460 in reprisals that were made to look like accidents.

The heavy casualties suffered in noble families at Towton were bitterly remembered in Yorkshire long after the battle, and this is reflected when the Percy family would not stir themselves to help Edward IV win back the throne in 1471. The biased Yorkist chronicler of the *Arrivall*, Edward's official record of the campaign, shows that when he landed in Yorkshire and rode to York in 1471, the king was openly resisted by some nobles who had vivid memories of Towton. However, the Earl of Northumberland chose a different tactic and 'sat still' while others:

> would not so fully and have determined themselves in the king's right and quarrel as the earl would have done himself, having in their remembrance, how the king [Edward], at his first entry and winning of his right to the Realm and Crown of England, had won a great battle in those same parts [Towton] where their sons, their brethren, and kinsmen, and many other of their neighbours were killed. Wherefore, and not without cause, it was thought that they could not have borne him very good will and done their best service to the king at this time and his quarrel. And so, it may be reasonably judged that this was a notable good service, and politically done by the earl. For his sitting still caused the City of York to do as they did, and no worse, and every man in all those parts to sit still also, and suffer the king to pass as he did, notwithstanding many were right evilly disposed of themselves against the king, and especially his quarrel.[43]

So, ten years after Towton, the scars had not healed, and those families who had suffered indirectly from the 'great battle of Towton' still held a grudge. Evidence suggests there was a muted reluctance to take up arms even if it meant incurring the king's wrath if he was restored. Most chroniclers saw the Earl of Northumberland's decision as pivotal to Edward's success in 1471. Still, the hope, especially regarding those that had suffered a death in the family at Towton, must have been that Edward would fail miserably in his enterprise to retake the throne.

As indicated, commemoration was an important pastime for both sides many years after the battle of Towton, and this observance continued well into the Tudor period, the preoccupation being chiefly with Lancastrian losses and a gruesome landscape of thousands of bones surfacing on the battlefield. This visual remembrance culminated in the building of the Towton Chapel, furnishing Lord Dacre's tomb, and, more recently, renovating the wayside cross to mark the site in 1929. Even more recently, a stone in Saxton churchyard dedicated to the men who died in battle has also been erected by the Towton Battlefield Society, but who do we commemorate so generously with our stones and sentiment? Who are the dead in the graves discovered in Towton? What kind of men fought in the battle? And is it in any way relevant today?

Some aspects of history are increasingly hard to visualise without the writer resorting to a novel description of what occurred there. And I have been accused by some of this with Towton. Rather than sticking to the facts, the writer tends to colour events, and a bloody battle such as Towton is even more alluring. The unique final stages of the carnage defy rational explanation or chronicled description. The rout unquestionably contained incalculable tragedies and countless lurid scenes of violence that beggar description. However, I make no apologies for my passion. It is based on firm factual evidence, and chief among these 'fictions' about Palmsunday Field is undoubtedly what befell a certain group of Lancastrian soldiers in the rout from the battlefield. This act of violence warrants some explanation. Therefore, I will try to follow the facts when describing their fate and leave imagination to the reader.

Although we cannot possibly relate the whole story of the men who were randomly thrown into the grave pits near Towton Hall, the marks imprinted on their bones are proof enough that they all died sickeningly and brutally. We may be shocked by their injuries and blame the violent times in which they lived. Conditioned as we are to both real and pretended violence, the mental block that readily accepts such acts of cruelty numbs the senses. This is especially true if such acts are part of warfare in another age. For want of a better word, this 'numbness' cushions us in our everyday lives to go about our business free from anxiety. Admittedly when violent action occurs closer to home, we are appalled and shocked by it. Faced with the rawness of such behaviour, we would do almost anything to survive death. That said, military history sadly produces the most numbing human responses of all in those that view battles from afar. Even in conflicts today, we have no accurate perception of what is going on, and this is undoubtedly why war is so readily pursued in the world by those not embroiled in it directly.

For all the above reasons, the battle of Towton becomes a quaint tapestry of far-off things that have no significance today. However, what can we glean from the 1996 grave – our only human connection with the effects of medieval warfare?

The man known as Towton 16 is probably the best experience to try to identify with, although other individuals died with him who suffered greater injuries, including various acts of mutilation and overkill. Shortly after examination, experts reconstructed Towton 16's face for the programme *Blood Red Roses*, and he immediately became a character who had a story to tell. He was in his late forties and had probably fought in previous battles or the Hundred Years War. Alternatively, he may have been a thug who had received his distinctive healed blade wound to the jaw because of a local brawl in a tavern. Towton 16 may also have been an archer considering his size, proportions and the transformations apparent in his elbow. Alternatively, he also could have been a yeoman or gentleman of some distinction, in other words, a leader of men. Most Englishmen had at some time in their life been 'brought up to the bow', and like his partners in death, Towton 16 was probably used to handling various weapons – one of the many reasons why his lord recruited him.

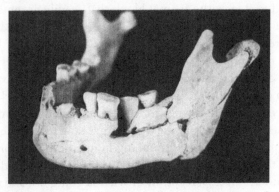

The well-healed jawbone of Towton 16. Previous experience of violence prior to Towton did not affect the willingness of soldiers to fight again. *(Bradford University)*

In the latter stages of the rout at Towton, we have seen that many of the Lancastrians fled to the rear, to their campsite and ultimately to the river crossings that led to York and freedom. As previously detailed, contemporary accounts indicate that some of these men had been captured and made prisoners by the Yorkists. It is doubtful that the Towton grave contained actual battlefield dead (transported there to be buried) or that these were bones reburied by the Hungates in the Tudor period. Therefore, we must assume that the grave was dug in the village to bury those men killed in the village, not in the rout. I believe that Towton 16 was one of these men. I also suggest that he was not an ordinary soldier at all and that he was killed, along with others of equal status, because of who he was and the threat he posed to the Yorkist regime. This scenario is made even more plausible if we consider how and where Towton 16 died. A total of eight blade, blunt and puncture wounds were found in his skull, and these are consistent with those inflicted on others in the grave who were clearly not wearing their helmets when they were killed. Injuries were delivered from both the front and back, all were to the skull, and several different weapon types were used. The killing took time to complete – time that would not have been available under normal battlefield conditions. Admittedly the battlefield was a frenzy of confused activity, and that several attackers could strike at an individual at once in combat. However, there is evidence to believe that the men in the grave were killed by repeated blows close to Towton village and that defence wounds to the forearms and hands were present, denoting that they were not bound. Indeed, many of these men may have been expecting to be freed. It is interesting to note that there was not a single wound in the chest/ribcage or back, although there are cuts to the neck area amounting to approximately fifteen per cent of the overall postcranial perimortem trauma.

What are we to make of these forensic facts? Why did all the men in the grave die from repeated blows to the head? Why were there no helmets in place when they were attacked? Were some of the soldiers mutilated after death, as the forensics suggest? Who were they to deserve such treatment and overkill? The author of *Gregory's Chronicle* may have revealed the answer when trying to account for the terrible price paid by some of the Towton soldiers. He begins by relating the dreadful casualty list and continues by counting 'many more [men] I can rehearse; but with these and others that were slain in the field is a great number, besides forty-two knights that were slain thereafter'.[44] Could these forty-two knights, and those 'that were slain thereafter', have been those who were captured, made prisoner and executed near Towton Hall? Were they executed in some sort of enclosure that existed around the original chapel in 1461? Even more critically, are we seeing the extermination of a warrior class of captains that posed a threat to the Yorkist military machine? In short, did Edward IV condone a massacre of unarmed gentry just because they were Lancastrian?

We are told that few Lancastrians of note escaped from Palmsunday Field, although a proportion of the peerage did flee and lived to fight another day. Like Henry V, Edward IV was probably in no mood for merciful acts or appeals for ransom after such a brutal battle. Indeed, he was in a similar situation to his ancestor at Agincourt, but on a much wider scale against multiple enemies who had deeply rooted feelings against his family and his usurpation. Edward had to establish himself as a strong monarch, and in English shires, where unrest, infighting and rebellion were endemic, there had to be a final solution. The political answer to this transferred to the battlefield was to annihilate his enemies' will to combat, remove their leaders and teach his subjects a lesson they would not forget. Towton 16 was a man typical of his breed, and many like him were useful in war and hunted in defeat. The humbler soldier was remarkable in being prone to acts of violence in everyday life. In the peak of fitness and ready to kill to claim wages and booty, these were the cannon fodder of the Wars of the Roses; and many thousands certainly paid for their master's ambition in blood at Towton. However, the evidence proves that it was their masters who suffered summary execution after battles had ended. Was it the memory of these men that urged Richard III to build a grander Towton Chapel on existing foundations and re-inter the unnamed dead in hallowed ground? What prevented his brother Edward from recognising the existing chapel of St Mary as a place of commemoration? Did Richard know of the executions carried out there by his brother, and did he seek reconciliation from the northern nobility in the hope of appeasing those who still held bitter memories of Towton? Perhaps we shall never know.

Towton 16 may have been just another unlucky soldier, or he may have been a landowner of some means, but as explained, many men were hunted down in the protracted rout long after the battle of Towton. However, Edward's revenge eased after many families sought to bury their dead and reverse their attainders. Indeed, it was more probable that the king later pardoned those who had fought against him rather than erase their good names and alienate their offspring. The fine tombs of Dacre, and particularly Lord Welles' alabaster effigy at Methley, are proof that Edward allowed his 'enemies' to be commemorated in return for their family's allegiance, particularly in the north of England. Not being lenient would have aggravated the tension felt in pro-Lancastrian territories that could and later did oppose the king's rule through localised rebellion.

Lionel, Lord Welles, the sixth baron of that name, was born in 1406 and was a predominately Lincolnshire landowner. He served as Lord Lieutenant of Ireland early in his career and became a joint deputy of Calais. In the Wars of the Roses, Welles fought at the battles of Blore Heath, where he was captured, and at the second battle of St Albans. He was a staunch Lancastrian supporter of Henry VI, but his luck ran out when at the age of fifty-five he was slain at Towton. Recognised among the heaps of dead and conveyed to Methley, one of his manors in Yorkshire, he was buried alongside his first wife, Joan Waterton, in a tomb eventually installed in the Waterton Chapel at St Oswald's Church. But it was not without some petitioning that his offspring could recover from the stigma of the great battle and its bloody aftermath. Richard Welles, Lionel's son, fought alongside his father at Towton and survived, but when King Edward attainted his father in 1461, Richard did not immediately succeed to the barony, and it was only in the following year that he was able to obtain a pardon and properly commemorate his father's memory. Richard managed to make his peace with the Yorkists thereafter. However, his eldest son, Sir Robert, was determined to carry on the fight and openly declared for Warwick and the Duke of Clarence in the Lincolnshire Rebellion of 1470, after which his father, Richard (Lionel's son), was promptly executed. Sir Robert fought at the battle of Empingham (commonly called Losecoat Field) in 1470 but was defeated and executed at Doncaster, dying without issue. Even ten years after Towton, the memory of the battle and the burning fires of Lancastrian revenge had not been extinguished. Eventually, the barony of Welles passed to others who were more supportive of Edward IV and the Yorkist regime.

Another participant and subsequent financial casualty of the battle was Sir Robert Bolling of Bradford, who fought in Lord Clifford's retinue 'The Flower of Craven'. According to the evidence below, Bolling was at the second battle of St Albans, Ferrybridge and Towton. It is likely that he was also involved in the skirmish at Dintingdale where Clifford lost his life. J. James, in his *History of Bradford*, quotes the following extract from Bolling's petition to Edward IV in 1475, where he pleads for the king to reverse his attainder due to the poverty and continuing misery of his family:

> I humbly beseech your Highness, your true liegeman, Robert Bolling, in the Shire of York, gentleman, that in the parliament held at Westminster, on the 4 November, in the first year of your noble reign, I was convicted and attainted of high treason, whereby it was ordained that I should forfeit all manors and lands etcetera that I held the 4 March last past. Let your Highness be credibly informed that your suppliant was never against your Highness in any field or journey, except on that dread Palm Sunday, in the first year of your most noble reign, whereto I was driven, not of mine own proper will, nor of malice towards your good Grace, but only by compulsion, and by the most dread proclamation of John, then Lord Clifford, under whose danger and distress the livelihood of your suppliant lay.[45]

Both Bolling and his son Tristram may have fought for what they believed in at Towton, but they also may have been pressured into following Lord Clifford 'on pain of death'. An existing summons from Clifford before the second battle of St Albans orders 'Robert Bolling and his son Tristram Bolling, to repair forthwith and not to fail me, at their peril, to join His Majesty at Doncaster',[46] so this latter cause for concern may have been Bolling's evidence that he was coerced into fighting. Many orders like this survive from the Wars of the Roses and they are similarly harsh in tone. However, both Bollings managed to survive the Towton campaign despite being convicted of high treason and having their lands forfeit to the crown. Edward listened to Bolling's plea for mercy, but it seems he was hardly forgiving. He only returned the Bolling family lands years afterwards. Fourteen years to be exact, while the family experienced near poverty in the meantime.

Despite this, Robert Bolling lived into old age and was buried in Bradford Cathedral while his son Tristram died in 1502 and was buried in the same church bequeathing 'in honour of my mortuary my best horse with saddle and bridle, jack, salet, bow, harness, sword and bucklers, that I used in the war'.[47] Clearly, the Bollings were typical victims of the strict feudal laws that bound man to master – in this instance, Lord Clifford. But as Lancastrian partisans, they were also guaranteed to become marked men purely because of where they lived and who they served. Most of the soldiers who fought against Edward at Towton and were attainted were punished in one way or another, placing great stress on their finances and families. Ill feeling towards the king was inevitable after this. Thus, the civil wars continued in the hearts and minds of those who suffered the backlash of 1461. The graves on Towton field may have been a living testament to Edward's decisive victory, but the wars went on despite the great slaughter that scarred the families of England.

Daniel Defoe, the famous author, wrote his *Tour Through the Whole Island of Great Britain* in 1724–27 and, in letter nine of his travels, he recalls his visit to Towton battlefield with abject sadness. His sorrows and frustrations resound loud and clear even today in the minds of those who visit the site and wonder at the thousands that died there in such a tragic and brutal way:

> On this road we passed over Towton, that famous field where the most cruel and bloody battle was fought between the two houses of Lancaster and York in the reign of Edward IV ... Tradition guided the country people, and they us, to the very spot. But we had only the story in speculation, for there remains no marks, no monument, no remembrance of the action, only that the ploughmen say that sometimes they plough up arrow-heads and spearheads, broken javelins, helmets, and the like; and we could only give a short sigh to the memory of the dead and move forward.[48]

Defoe mournfully agrees with the same feelings of loss and indescribable fascination that some people with imagination feel about Towton today. The disbelief that an event of such horrific proportions could have occurred in such a pleasant place is a re-occurring question that visitors often ask me when confronted by the evidence.

The enigma of battlefields as a place of historical contemplation and spiritual veneration is an equally difficult question to answer. Conflict archaeology and world history prove the point that Towton is not alone in this 'other worldly' fascination with the past, even to the extent that some battlefields and historical sites may have a particular 'aura' pervading them. Who can account for the stillness and fascination that many feel when encountering places in Europe where thousands died in two world wars? And for many, Towton battlefield is one of these sites. I too have felt the 'presence' of its history on more than one occasion trudging across North Acres in the snow or gazing at compacted bodies in a mass grave, although many people have witnessed and felt far stranger things that have no scientific or reasonable answer.

Many years ago, I was told that a reputable medium visited the battlefield and was bruised on the shin by some ethereal force that 'kicked her'. She said that the Towton dead 'wish to leave' the battlefield, and although I don't hold with spiritual assumptions generally, this kind of story proves that there is more to the battlefield than meets the eye. People are affected by the site psychologically, and some of those who live and breathe Towton are willing to camp there in all weathers, commemorate the battle with red and white roses, hunt for ghosts, and generally recreate the event in any way they can. Yet others I know with tough constitutions have felt physically sick on the battlefield plateau, and once in the nineteenth century, it is said, a local farmer arrived at a local pub with snow heaped on his shoulders in the middle of summer to confound the clientele.

For me, the battle of Towton reminds us that military history repeats itself. After major conflicts politicians and analysts remind us that we should act quicker to contain a crisis. But it seems that every time war rears its ugly head, this chance is either missed, or a pre-emptive strike aggravates the situation. History matters in any age, and most of it is written by the winners. The Tudors, for instance, covered their tracks well in the late fifteenth century and used the Wars of the Roses as an example of a terrible and best-forgotten past. No lessons were learned, rebellion and civil war happened again in Britain, and the real meaning of internecine strife, like that displayed at Towton, was overlooked. After all, the Tudors were the morally superior winners of the wars, and after Bosworth, they took the high ground in more ways than one. By usurping the throne and uniting the Houses of York and Lancaster, they claimed to have pitched right against wrong. But there is never right or wrong in warfare. Both sides lose, and history shows us this even today when there is a tendency for countries to rush off to war time and time again, no matter what their reason or ideology.

Like Daniel Defoe, once you know the traumatic side of a battle, the only way is forward to educate and hopefully learn from the past. And the history of Towton battlefield pulls you towards the past like a magnet. As battles go, the medieval era saw none like it. As explained, contemporaries found the death toll shocking. But did those in power learn from it – far from it? Commemoration is one way to remember a conflict. Another is to educate, and it is this act of education, more than religious, political or spiritual observance, that adds flesh to the bones once buried in Towton and Saxton fields. Even today, the site is publicised through oral tradition with its many tours and visitors – and long may it continue. For me, Towton is a lifetime interest, and thankfully 'Palmsunday Field' is not the forgotten battle it once was.

Appendices

1 King Edward IV's Act of Attainder

The following is an extract from King Edward IV's Act of Attainder, passed against the Lancastrians after the battle of Towton. It is useful in so much as it contains some of the names of those who fought for King Henry VI on Palm Sunday, 29 March 1461.

And where also Henry Duke of Exeter, Henry Duke of Somerset, Thomas Courtenay, late Earl of Devonshire, Henry, late Earl of Northumberland, William Viscount Beaumont, Thomas Lord Roos, John, late Lord Clifford, Leo, late Lord Welles, John, late Lord Neville, Thomas Grey Knight, Lord Rugemond-Grey, Randolf, late Lord Dacre, Humphrey Dacre Knight, John Morton, late Person of Blokesworth in the shire of Dorset Clerk, Rauf Makerell, late Person of Ryseby, in the shire of Suffolk Clerk, Thomas Manning, late of New Windsor in Berkshire Clerk, John Whelpdale, late of Lichfield in the county of Stafford Clerk, John Nayler, late of London Squire,

John Preston, late of Wakefield in the shire of York Priest, Philip Wentworth Knight, John Fortescue Knight, William Tailboys Knight, Edmund Moundford Knight, Thomas Tresham Knight, William Vaux Knight, Edmund Hampden Knight, Thomas Findern Knight, John Courtenay Knight, Henry Lewes Knight, Nicholas Latimer Knight, Walter Nuthill, late of Ryston in Holderness in the shire of York Squire, John Heron of the Forde Knight, Richard Tunstall Knight, Henry Bellingham Knight, Robert Whitingham Knight, John Ormond otherwise called John Butler Knight, William Mille Knight, Simon Hammes Knight, William Holland Knight called the Bastard of Exeter, William Joseph, late of London Squire, Everard Digby, late of Stokedry in the shire of Rutland Squire, John Mirfin of Southwalk in the shire of Surrey Squire, Thomas Philip, late of Dertington in Devonshire Squire, Thomas Brampton, late of Guines Squire, Giles Saintlowe, late of London Squire, Thomas Claymond, the said Thomas Tunstall Squire, Thomas Crawford, late of Calais Squire, John Audley, late of Guines Squire, John Lenche of Wich in the shire of Worcester Squire, Thomas Ormond otherwise called Thomas Butler Knight, Robert Bellingham, late of Burnalshede in the shire of Westmorland Squire, Thomas Everingham, late of Newhall in the shire of Leicester Knight, John Penycock, late of Waybridge in the county of Surrey Squire, William Grimsby, late of Grimsby in the shire of Lincoln Squire, Henry Ross, late of Rockingham in the shire of Northampton Knight, Thomas Daniel, late of Rising in the shire of Norfolk Squire, John Doubigging, late of the same Gentleman, Richard Kirkby, late of Kirkby Ireleth in the shire of Lancaster Gentleman, William Ackworth, late of Luton in the shire of Bedford Squire, William Weynsford, late of London Squire, Richard Stuckley, late of Lambeth in the county of Surrey Squire, Thomas Stanley, late of Carlisle Gentleman, Thomas Litley, late of London Grocer, John Maidenwell, late of Kirton in Lindsey in the county of Lincoln Gentleman, Edward Ellesmere, late of London Squire, John

Dawson, late of Westminster in the shire of Middlesex Yeoman, Henry Spencer, late of the same Yeoman, John Smothing, late of York Yeoman, John Beaumont, late of Goodby in the shire of Leicester Gentleman, Henry Beaumont, late of the same Gentleman, Roger Wharton otherwise called Roger of the Halle, late of Burgh in the shire of Westmorland Groom, John Joskin, late of Branghing in the shire of Hertford Squire, Richard Lister the younger of Wakefield Yeoman, Thomas Carr, late of Westminster Yeoman, Robert Bolling, late of Bolling in the shire of York Gentleman, Robert Hatecale, late of Barleburgh in the same shire Yeoman, Richard Everingham, late of Pontefract in the same shire Squire, Richard Fulnaby of Fulnaby in the shire of Lincoln Gentleman, Laurence Hill, late of Much Wycombe in the county of Buckingham Yeoman, Rauff Chernok, late of Thorley in the county of Lancaster Gentleman, Richard Gaitford of Estretford in Cley in the shire of Nottingham Gentleman, John Chapman, late of Wimborne Minster in Dorset shire Yeoman, and Richard Cokerell, late of York Merchant; on Sunday called commonly Palm Sunday the 29th day of March the first year of his reign, in a field between the towns of Sherburn-in-Elmet and Tadcaster, in the said shire of York, called Saxtonfield and Towtonfield, in the shire of York, accompanied with Frenchmen and Scots, the Kings enemies, falsely and traitorously against their faith and liegeance, there reared war against the same King Edward, their rightwise, true, and natural liege lord, purposing there and then to have destroyed him, and deposed him of his royal estate, crown, and dignity, and then and there to that intent, falsely and traitorously moved battle against his said estate, shedding therein the blood of a great number of his subjects. In the which battle it pleased almighty God to give unto him, of the mystery of his might and grace, the victory of his enemies and rebels, and to subdue and avoid the effect of their false and traitorous purpose.

Rot. Parl. 1st Edward IV. 1461, Vol. V fo. 477–8.

2 Sir William Plumpton's Contingent

On 13 March 1461 Sir William Plumpton was summoned by King Henry VI to attend him in York with as many men as possible. The resulting contingent raised by Sir William went into action at Towton, sixteen days later, where Plumpton's eldest son was killed in battle:

> To our trusty and well-beloved knight, Sir William Plumpton. By the King R.H.[1] Trusty and well-beloved, we greet you well, and for as much as we have very knowledge that our great traitor, the late Earl of March,[2] hath made great assemblies of riotous and mischievously disposed people, and to stir and provoke them to draw unto him, he hath cried in his proclamations havoc upon all our true liege people and subjects, their wives, children, and goods, and is now coming towards us, we therefore pray you and also straitly charge you that anon upon the sight hereof, ye, with all such people as ye may make defensible arrayed, come unto us in all haste possible, where so ever we shall be within this our Realm, for to resist the malicious intent and purpose of our said traitor, and fail not hereof as ye love the security of our person, the weal of yourself, and of all our true and faithful subjects. Given under our signet at our City of York, the thirteenth day of March. (1460–61).

> *Plumpton Letters* (ed.) Thomas Stapleton,
> Camden Society 1839, letter 1.

3 'The Towton Dog Collar'

The following story appeared in the *Yorkshire Evening Post* on 20 April 1926:

£1,500 COLLAR FOUND AT TOWTON BATTLE RELIC; WOMAN RECALLS PLOUGHMAN'S TREASURE

Mrs. Davis, a widow, now living in Hunslet (Leeds), took an especial interest in the story of the battle of Towton because of her birth in Saxton village where her father, Mr. Edward Warrington, was the village shoemaker and the clerk and sexton of Saxton Parish Church. He had much to do with the restoration and proper preservation of Lord Dacre's tomb in the churchyard. Mrs. Davis is now 69, and we give the story as she tells it.

'I wrote to you about a supposed-to-be brass ring', she said, 'which was turned up by the plough in one of the fields on Saxton Grange Farm about 55 years ago. I could go very nearly blind-folded to the spot now. Mr. Henry Smart had the farm then, and I was a girl of about 14 working there. Tom Ambler, who came from Church Fenton, was there as second wagoner. He ploughed this ring up in the field and said it would make a nice collar for the dog, a black retriever we had on the farm. I have put the collar on and off many a time. I called it a ring, but it was quite a big collar. It was all caked up and clogged, but as we brushed the dirt off it, we found that it was made of moveable parts in such a way that when it was small – closed up like – it was broad, and as it stretched out it went narrower. It was fastened with a sort of clasp.

'It was a battle relic right enough. We thought it was just a brass collar at first and then one day Mr. Benjamin Hey of Sherburn came shooting with Mr. Smart. They took the retriever with them and looking at the collar Mr. Hey asked where it came from and then said, "I'll give you £5 for t'collar Harry."

'Mr. Smart said, "Nay, if it's worth £5 to you it's worth £5 to me," and they began to examine it. The dog had been wearing it about eight months and it had begun to shine and some things on it that we took for studs had begun to glitter. They turned out to be gems and rubies, and what we thought was brass was gold.

"I'd have it valued Harry," said Mr. Hey, and they took it to York and the man they took it to offered them £600 for it straight away. They sold it and the last we heard of that collar was that it had been sold at one of the sale rooms in London for £1,500. I think it was at that place – you know Christies. And all that Tom Ambler, who ploughed it up, got was two pints of beer. I served him with it out of the barrel in the kitchen.'

Could this collar have been a chain of office, a livery collar worn by a noble at the battle of Towton, or something more ancient perhaps? What makes the story more interesting, and personally ironic, is the fact that I may be related through my paternal grandmother to the Tom Ambler of Church Fenton who unearthed it.

4 Sir William Gascoigne IV

The Gascoigne family of Gawthorpe Hall, Yorkshire, are firmly connected with the battle of Towton in that one of their number was more than likely slain (or severely wounded) there in the service of the Earl of Northumberland in 1461. Sir William Gascoigne's premature death illustrates how vulnerable some individuals were at the height of the Wars of the Roses and how the English gentry failed to avoid involvement at Towton when most northern knights were tied into various indentures and other forms of local recruitment.

Edward IV's Act of Attainder lists some of these men in detail, and as official documents go, if your name was included in it, you were a marked man. Like similar attainders in the Wars of the Roses, the document records those charged with high treason, and after Edward's victory in the Towton campaign, the list, as can be seen, was a particularly long one. It plucked out individuals to forfeit their land, property, titles, and (if caught) their heads. However, in Sir William Gascoigne's case, his name is missing from the document despite his renown as a Lancastrian soldier. He had fought with his master, the Earl of Northumberland, at least twice. He was even knighted on the battlefield, but unlike his master, he and his family managed to avoid forfeiture.

William's last resting place has been debated for some years. His tomb was thought lost to history, but a probable location of his effigy can be re-established if we consider Gascoigne's many family connections, heraldic protocol, the nuances of late medieval burial rites, and that a deceased's wife, despite remarrying, was sometimes buried with her first husband.

Although the date of William's death can only be narrowed down to a few years (1461–63), we know that his father (another William) outlived him. The younger Gascoigne's birth is also uncertain (probably 1426), but there is no doubt he was born into an already prominent Lancastrian family who were significant landowners in Yorkshire during the fifteenth century. It is alleged that William married twice, although recorded history is more certain about his second wife, Joan, than his first. Joan was the daughter of John Neville of Oversley in Warwickshire (a Lancastrian branch of the Neville family), and after his death, the Gascoignes inherited property and manors that increased their notoriety.

William and Joan had five children together, and as mentioned above, William was technically the fourth recorded Gascoigne of Gawthorpe Hall, although he was never head of his family due to his father's death in 1465. This senior William, the third recorded Gascoigne of the medieval era, was a prominent local knight in the early Wars of the Roses but was not militarily involved in the conflict. However, he was a commissioner tasked with recruiting troops to fight in the wars, and his son (who married Joan Neville) did not avoid warfare. It seems this Gascoigne was always the more likely one to put his trust in the sword rather than the law or the church despite serving in the Lancastrian royal household and being appointed coroner in the West Riding between 1454 and 1457. Later, William was also assigned to the King's Bench like some of his ancestors, but it is recorded that he served his northern master, Henry Percy, Earl of Northumberland, in a purely military capacity when the dynastic wars for the throne erupted in England during 1460–61.

Gascoigne's Lancastrian sympathies and family ties to other Yorkshire lords marked him out as a likely candidate for knighthood, and after he took the royal oath at Coventry, he fought at the battle of Wakefield in December 1460. It is said he was knighted on the field by the Earl of Northumberland in person, and along with three other worthies who also received the accolade, he continued to support Margaret of Anjou in her ambitious plan to recapture Henry VI once the Duke of York's head was firmly fixed to Micklegate bar.

The Lancastrian sweep south to London provided the next opportunity for Gascoigne to prove himself as a staunch royalist supporter. William fought at the second battle of St Albans in February 1461, freeing Henry VI from Yorkist control before having to retreat north with the royal army to await the Yorkist response under Edward IV, whose notoriety saved London from widespread pillaging.

Towton, however, was William's last throw of the dice for Lancaster, it seems. He more than likely fought and died there for the royalist cause, and unless he died of his wounds (or for other reasons) after the battle, William was certainly dead and buried by the end of 1463 as in January 1464 (modern dating) his wife Joan obtained a licence to marry Sir James Harrington, a Yorkist knight whose father and brother had died fighting for the Duke of York at the battle of Wakefield.[1]

Joan's marriage was an understandable necessity, given the upheavals of 1461. However, it is unknown where either Joan or William, her first husband, were buried as their

memorials are missing from the Gascoigne family mauso-
leum at Harewood's church close to where Gawthorpe Hall
once stood. William's father, who died in 1465, is interred
here with his wife Margaret Clarell beneath an impressive
monument, but William IV and his wife Joan may not have
been buried in the church, making two other Gascoigne
effigies in the old church at Wentworth possible contenders
for, at least, their effigies. Early photographs of this tomb
before restoration depict Joan at her husband's side, and the
monument has all the hallmarks of a mid-fifteenth century
alabaster, including the appropriate heraldry of William
Gascoigne's family lineage.

In their book *The Medieval Monuments of Harewood*, P. Routh
and R. Knowles discuss the possibility that Sir William
Gascoigne and his lady are commemorated here in a tomb that
may previously have been situated at Monk Bretton church:

> Here [At Wentworth] we have remaining two canopied tomb-
> chest panels with knight weepers and shields, a lady's head
> showing flowing hair bound with a decorative orle, and the full
> figure of a knight, his short-haired head resting on a now crest-
> less helm, an SS collar round his neck. The plate body armour
> is covered by a sleeveless surcoat or tabard, carved unmistak-
> ably with the quartered arms of 1&4 Gascoigne, 2 Mowbray,
> 3 Wyman ... and as the effigies appear to date to the mid-
> fifteenth century, research reveals no alternative candidates
> for their ascription, and it seems likely that they represent
> Sir William Gascoigne and Joan Neville.[2]

Removal of the two monuments to Wentworth may date from
the Dissolution, and Routh and Knowles state that the effi-
gies may have once been 'rescued' from the church at Monk
Bretton (a former holding of the Harringtons) by Margaret
Gascoigne when she married Thomas Wentworth in the
Tudor period.

It is difficult to judge who the missing Gascoigne might be other than William IV, who fought at Towton. However, the reader must speculate where William's *actual* remains lie buried. For example, William may have been thrown into a mass grave at Towton, interred at Harewood (with his family) or buried at Monk Bretton church. The interesting twist in the tale is that Gascoigne was never attainted for his actions at Towton and because his name is absent from Edward IV's list of 'traitors', we may wonder how the family survived the king's wrath and the propensity for other Yorkist lords to land-grab his estates.

The fact that William's father was still alive (and still heavily partisan) before his son's death is likely key to this failing. Even though his own tomb was prepared and waiting, complete with a Lancastrian livery collar, it seems William's father swallowed his pride and grief by pleading with the king to pardon his son. And this can be proved by the existence of a 'general pardon for William Gascoigne the elder, knight', dated 15 July 1461, which saved the family name.[3]

After the battle of Towton and the demise of that generation of Gascoignes, William and Joan's son succeeded to the title as the fifth Gascoigne of Gawthorpe Hall. This William married Margaret Percy, and their splendid fifteenth-century tomb can also be seen at Harewood. After the Earl of Northumberland died at Towton and his title was forfeit, the earldom passed to John Neville, Lord Montague, brother to the Earl of Warwick. However, when Montague and Warwick rebelled and were killed at Barnet in 1471, the Northumberland earldom became vacant. And following the release of Margaret's brother, Henry Percy, from prison, a strong association was forged between William Gascoigne V and the Percys once more, enabling a resurgence of the family in Yorkshire when Henry Percy recovered his dead father's title in 1473.

William frequently served on West Riding peace commissions and musters throughout the Wars of the Roses, and he was made a Knight of the Bath in 1478 and a Knight of the Body of Richard III in 1483. He gained permission to rebuild Gawthorpe Hall and crenellated the building before Richard died at Bosworth in 1485. However, it still seemed Gascoigne held secret Lancastrian sympathies despite his allegiance to Edward IV and Richard III, probably due to his father's death at Towton. For instance, no evidence survives that William V ever fought in any battles of the wars, either for York or Lancaster, and we may speculate about his feelings when pressurised to muster his northern retainers before Bosworth at Richard's command. It was probably no accident that he too 'stood still' alongside his brother-in-law Percy, Earl of Northumberland, when both could have helped their Yorkist sovereign, Richard III, retain his crown.

William died in 1488, and it is not difficult to imagine that this Gascoigne of Gawthorpe was a very prudent man. He probably never forgot the Yorkists killed his father, and as such, made it his business to stay clear of party politics throughout his life, especially if it involved buckling on his sword and marching off to war.

Notes

Chapter One
1. A.B. Hinds, ed., *Calendar of State Papers and Manuscripts in the Archives and Collections of Milan*, vol. 1, 1912, pp. 61–2.
2. *Ibid.*, p. 62.
3. *Ibid.*, p. 60.
4. *Ibid.*, pp. 64–5. Enclosed in the dispatch is a list of the lords who were slain, Lord Fitzwalter being the only notable Yorkist casualty.
5. *Ibid.*, p. 66. A similar list of the dead to note 4 is also supplied with this letter.
6. *Ibid.*, p. 68.
7. *Ibid.*, p. 73.
8. *Ibid.*, p. 69. He also mentions that the battle lasted 'a whole day and a half'.
9. J. Gairdner, ed., *The Paston Letters*, vol. 3, 1904, pp. 267–8. Note that the list of named Yorkist casualties has increased.
10. J. Keegan, *The Face of Battle*, 1976, pp. 87–8.
11. Shakespeare, *Henry V*, Prologue.
12. J. Gairdner, ed., *Three Fifteenth-Century Chronicles*, Camden Society, 1880, p. 94.
13. H.T. Riley, ed., *Registrum Abbatis Johannis Whethamstede*, 1, 1872, p. 247.

14. G.L. Harriss and M.A. Harriss, ed., *John Benet's Chronicle for the years 1400–1462*, Camden Miscellany, 24, 1972, pp. 206–7.

15. 'London Chronicle for 1446–1452' in C.L. Kingsford, *English Historical Literature in the Fifteenth Century*, 1913, pp. 297–8.

16. J. Gairdner, ed., *The Paston Letters*, vol. 3, 1904, p. 13.
    Henry's mental condition has been likened to catatonic schizo-phrenia, but see M.E. Smith, 'Henry VI's Medical Record: A Preliminary Survey', *The Ricardian*, no. 43, December 1973, for a link to porphyria.

17. See C. Oman, *The Political History of England 1377–1485*, 1920, p. 367.

18. J. Gairdner, ed., *The Paston Letters*, vol. 3, 1904, p. 28.

19. For a full account of the battle see C.A.J. Armstrong, 'Politics and the Battle of St Albans, 1455', *Bulletin of the Institute of Historical Research*, vol. 33, no. 87, 1960. See also A.W. Boardman, *The First Battle of St Albans 1455*, 2006.

20. J. Gairdner, ed., 'Gregory's Chronicle' in *The Historical Collections of a Citizen of London*, 1876, p. 204.

21. H.T. Riley, ed., *Registrum Abbatis Johannis Whethamstede*, 1872, pp. 376–8.

22. See R.I. Jack, 'A quincentenary: the battle of Northampton, July 1460', *Northamptonshire Past and Present*, 2, 1960, pp. 21–5. See also M. Ingram, *The Battle of Northampton 1460*, 2015.

23. H.T. Riley, ed., *Registrum Abbatis Johannis Whethamstede*, 1872, pp. 376–8.

Chapter Two

1. H.T. Riley, ed., *Registrum Abbatis Johannis Whethamstede*, 1872, pp. 381–2. W. and E. Hardy, ed., *Recueil des Chroniques et Anchiennes Istories de la Grant Bretaigne par Jehan de Waurin*, vol. 5, 1891, p. 325.

2. J.S. Davies, ed., *An English Chronicle of the Reigns of Richard II, Henry IV, Henry V and Henry VI*, 1856, pp. 106–7.

3. J. Stevenson, ed., *Annales Rerum Anglicarum, Letters and Papers Illustrative of the Wars of the English in France*, vol. 2, 1864, p. 775.

4. In the English Civil War, Sandal Castle could only garrison a small contingent of men in cramped conditions.

5. H. Ellis, ed., *Edward Hall's Chronicle*, 1809, p. 250.
6. D. Defoe, *A Tour Through the Whole Island of Great Britain*, vol. 3, Letter 9. See also K. Dockray and R. Knowles, *The Battle of Wakefield*, p. 26.
7. J. Leland, 'Itinerary, 1558', *Yorkshire Archaeological and Topographical Journal*, 10, 1889, p. 242.
8. J. Gairdner, ed., 'Gregory's Chronicle' in *The Historical Collections of a Citizen of London*, 1876, p.208.
9. J.S. Davies, ed., *An English Chronicle of the Reigns of Richard II, Henry IV, Henry V and Henry VI*, 1856, pp. 106–7.
10. J. Strachey, ed., *Rotuli Parliamentorum*, vol. 5, 1767, pp. 375–9.
11. William Neville, Lord Fauconberg, was Warwick's uncle.
12. J. Stevenson, ed., *Annales Rerum Anglicarum, Letters and Papers Illustrative of the Wars of the English in France*, vol. 2, 1864, p. 775.
13. J. Gairdner, ed., 'Gregory's Chronicle' in *The Historical Collections of a Citizen of London*, 1876, p. 211.
14. H. Ellis, ed., *Edward Hall's Chronicle*, 1809, p. 251.
15. *Ibid.*
16. J. Gairdner, ed., 'Gregory's Chronicle' in *The Historical Collections of a Citizen of London*, 1876, p. 211.
17. *Ibid.*
18. *Chevauchée* is a French term used to indicate an armed ride through enemy territory. In the Hundred Years War it involved acts of pillage, rape and widespread devastation in the name of chivalry.
19. H.T. Riley, ed., *Croyland Abbey Chronicle*, 1854, p. 423.
20. J. Gairdner, ed., 'Gregory's Chronicle' in *The Historical Collections of a Citizen of London*, 1876, p. 212. It seems reasonable to suppose that William Gregory's detailed account of the battle and the defences employed by the Yorkists is not that of a casual observer.
21. H.T. Riley, ed., *Registrum Abbatis Johannis Whethamstede*, 1872, pp. 388–92.
22. J. Gairdner, ed., 'Gregory's Chronicle' in *The Historical Collections of a Citizen of London*, 1876, pp. 213–14.
23. *Ibid.*, p. 212.
24. *Ibid.*, p. 214.
25. See, 'The Rose of Rouen' in *Archaeologia*, 29, pp. 343–7.

Chapter Three

1. J. Stevenson, ed., *Annales Rerum Anglicarum, Letters and Papers Illustrative of the Wars of the English in France*, vol. 2, 1864, p. 775.

2. A.H. Thomas and I.D. Thornley, eds, *The Great Chronicle of London*, 1938, p. 195.

3. J. Stevenson, ed., *Annales Rerum Anglicarum, Letters and Papers Illustrative of the Wars of the English in France*, vol. 2, 1864, p. 777.

4. J.A. Giles, ed., 'Hearne's Fragment' in *Chronicles of the White Rose*, 1834, p. 8.

5. A.B. Hinds, ed., *Calendar of State Papers and Manuscripts in the Archives and Collections of Milan*, vol. 1, 1912, p. 61.

6. J.A. Giles, ed., 'Hearne's Fragment' in *Chronicles of the White Rose*, 1834, p. 8–9.

7. It is likely that Fauconberg commanded between 8,000 and 10,000 men considering that Edward Earl of March entered London with 8,000 troops from Mortimers Cross.

8. See, G. Perjes, *Agrarian Production, Population, Army Provisioning and Strategy in the Second Half of the 17th Century 1650–1715*, 1963, p. 84. Also see J. Keegan and R. Holmes, *Soldiers: A History of Men in Battle*, 1985, pp. 221–40.

9. E. Hardy, ed., *Recueil des Chroniques et Anchiennes Istories de la Grant Bretaigne par Jehan de Waurin*, vol. 5, 1891, p. 336.

10. See, 'The Rose of Rouen' in *Archaeologia*, 29, pp. 343–7.

11. For the contracting of troops in the 'wars' see, K.B. McFarlane, *The Nobility of Late Medieval England*, 1973., M. Hicks, *Bastard Feudalism*, 1995., W.H. Dunham, *Lord Hastings' Indentured Retainers 1461–1483*, 1955, A.W. Boardman, *The Medieval Soldier in the Wars of the Roses*, 1996, pp. 61–92.

12. J. Gairdner, ed., *The Paston Letters*, vol. 6, 1904, p. 85.

13. A. Raine, *York Civic Records*, Yorkshire Archaeological Society, Record Series, 1, 1939, p. 135.

14. J.E. Winston, *English Towns in the Wars of the Roses*, 1921, p. 61.

15. *Ibid.*, p. 50.

16. *Ibid.*, p. 23.

17. A. Raine, *York Civic Records*, Yorkshire Archaeological Society, Record Series, 1, 1939, pp. 135–6.

18. Dorset County Record Office, 'Bridport Muster Roll', 1457, B3/FG3.

19. J. Gairdner, ed., 'Gregory's Chronicle' in *The Historical Collections of a Citizen of London*, 1876, pp. 214.

20. The confusion over the bridges and bridge breaking in the wars and Towton is dealt with in Chapter Seven.

Chapter Four

1. Some historians regard the skirmish with Fitzwalter's men as the battle of Ferrybridge. Evidence suggests that there was in fact a skirmish at dawn and a main battle on 28 March.

2. A.B. Hinds, ed., *Calendar of State Papers and Manuscripts in the Archives and Collections of Milan*, vol. 1, 1912, p. 61.

3. J. Gairdner, ed., 'Gregory's Chronicle' in *The Historical Collections of a Citizen of London*, 1876, p. 216.

4. J.A. Giles, ed., 'Hearne's Fragment' in *Chronicles of the White Rose*, 1834, p. 9.

5. H. Ellis, ed., *Edward Hall's Chronicle*, 1809, pp. 254–5.

6. *Ibid.*, p. 255.

7. E. Hardy, ed., *Recueil des Chroniques et Anchiennes Istories de la Grant Bretaigne par Jehan de Waurin*, vol. 5, 1891, pp. 337–8.

8. H. Ellis, ed., *Edward Hall's Chronicle*, 1809, pp. 254–5.

9. C. Forrest, *The History of Knottingley*, 1871, pp. 127–8.

10. *Ibid.*, p. 17.

11. G.L. Harriss and M.A. Harriss, eds, 'John Benet's Chronicle for the years 1400–1462', *Camden Miscellany*, 24, 1972, p. 230.

12. H. Ellis, ed., *Edward Hall's Chronicle*, 1809, p. 255.

13. *Ibid.*, p. 250.

14. *Ibid.*, p. 255.

15. E. Hardy, ed., *Recueil des Chroniques et Anchiennes Istories de la Grant Bretaigne par Jehan de Waurin*, vol. 5, 1891, p. 338.

16. C. Forrest, *The History of Knottingley*, 1871, p. 105.

17. *Ibid*, p. 102.

18. E. Hardy, ed., *Recueil des Chroniques et Anchiennes Istories de la Grant Bretaigne par Jehan de Waurin*, vol. 5, 1891, p. 338.

19. J.A. Giles, ed., 'Hearne's Fragment' in *Chronicles of the White Rose*, 1834, p. 9. It is more than likely that the duration of the two battles of Ferrybridge and Towton were mistaken by the

chronicler for one, hence the notion that the battle lasted for a full day and a half (see Chapter Eight).

Chapter Five

1. J. Leland, 'Itinerary, 1558', *Yorkshire Archaeological and Topographical Journal*, 10, p. 243.

2. See, R. Brooke, 'The field of the battle of Towton', a paper read before the Society of Antiquaries in 1849, in *Visits to Fields of Battle in England of the Fifteenth Century*, 1857. pp. 112–13, and H. Cary, *A History of the Civil Wars of England between the two Houses of Lancaster and York*, vol. 1, London 1641.

3. J. Leland, 'Itinerary, 1558', *Yorkshire Archaeological and Topographical Journal*, 10, p. 243.

4. The Tudor chronicler Edward Hall, who may have visited the battlefield, states, 'But in the mean way there was a little brook called Cock, not very broad but of great deepness' and this was the cause of the multiple drownings. See H. Ellis, ed., *Edward Hall's Chronicle*, 1809, p. 256.

5. See J. Lang, *Corpus of Anglo-Saxon Stone Sculpture, Volume 3: York and Eastern Yorkshire*, 1991. Most likely this was a wayside cross located at an important road junction or an ancient boundary stone.

6. R. Brooke, 'The field of the battle of Towton', a paper read before the Society of Antiquaries in 1849, in *Visits to Fields of Battle in England of the Fifteenth Century*, 1857, p. 115.

7. J. Leland, 'Itinerary, 1558', *Yorkshire Archaeological and Topographical Journal*, 10, p. 243.

8. *Ibid.*

9. R. Brooke, 'The field of the battle of Towton', a paper read before the Society of Antiquaries in 1849, in *Visits to Fields of Battle in England of the Fifteenth Century*, 1857, p. 123.

10. W. Wheater, *The History of Sherburn and Cawood*, 1865, p. 70.

11. J. Leland, 'Itinerary, 1558', *Yorkshire Archaeological and Topographical Journal*, 10, p. 243.

12. R. Brooke, 'The field of the battle of Towton', a paper read before the Society of Antiquaries in 1849, in *Visits to Fields of Battle in England of the Fifteenth Century*, 1857, p. 91. Bloody

Meadow has been the subject of a recent archaeological survey, but no human remains have been found there. However, is highly likely that the Hungate family cleared most of these bones from the battlefield as noted by Leland, see above.

13. *Harleian MS 795*, British Library.

14. R. Whittaker, *Leodis and Elmete*, 1816, p. 156. It is perhaps coincidental that both Dacre and Clifford were killed by arrows after unclasping their 'bevors', therefore the two incidents may really only reflect one death if Edward Hall is to be believed.

15. J. Leland, 'Itinerary, 1558', *Yorkshire Archaeological and Topographical Journal*, 10, p. 243.

16. F. Drake, *Eboracum*, 1736, p. 111.

17. Bronze Age artefacts have been found close to Castle Hill confirming the presence of ancient habitation on the plateau from the earliest times.

18. H. Ellis, ed., *Edward Hall's Chronicle*, 1809, p. 255.

19. J. Leland, 'Itinerary, 1558', *Yorkshire Archaeological and Topographical Journal*, 10, p. 243.

20. J. Strachey, ed., *Rotuli Parliamentorum*, vol. 5, 1767, pp. 477–8.

21. E. Hardy, ed., *Recueil des Chroniques et Anchiennes Istories de la Grant Bretaigne par Jehan de Waurin*, vol. 5, 1891, pp. 339–40.

22. Pharsalia (in Thessaly) was a battle fought between Pompey and Julius Caesar in 48 BC. Towton was likened to this chiefly by Victorian writers.

Chapter Six

1. See, 'The Rose of Rouen' in *Archaeologia*, 29, 1824, pp. 343–7. Evidence shows that the battle began 'affter ye none' but the hour is not given. In the fifteenth century it was usual to give the hour, e.g., 'seven of the clocke affore none ... one of the clocke after none ... 3 of the clocke at after none' and so on. See H. Kurath, S.M. Kuhn, R.E. Lewis, J. Reidy, M.J. Williams, eds, *Middle English Dictionary*, 1952, p. 1046.

2. A.B. Hinds, ed., *Calendar of State Papers and Manuscripts in the Archives and Collections of Milan*, vol. 1, 1912, p. 62.

3. A.H. Burne, *Battlefields of England*, 1950, p. 105.

4. See V. Fiorato, A. Boylston and K. Knusel, eds, *Blood Red Roses*, 2000, pp. 47–52 for a detailed breakdown of ages at death of the Towton soldiers. Estimates confirm that men between fifteen and fifty fought in the battle.

5. J. Gairdner, ed., *The Paston Letters*, vol. 3, 1904, pp. 267–8.

6. H. Ellis, ed., *Edward Hall's Chronicle*, 1809, p. 255.

7. Prickers and scourers were used in battle for killing deserters, killing and pursuing routed troops, securing food, scouting in enemy territory and so forth.

8. H. Ellis, ed., *Three Books of Polydore Vergil's English History*, 1844, pp. 110–11.

9. J. Keegan, *The Face of Battle*, 1976, pp. 113, 326.

10. G.E. Corrie, ed., *Sermons by Hugh Latimer, Bishop of Worcester, 1555*, 1844–5, p. 167.

11. H. Ellis, ed., *Edward Hall's Chronicle*, 1809, pp. 255–6.

12. H. Ellis, ed., *Three Books of Polydore Vergil's English History*, 1844, p. 111.

13. G. Brereton, ed., *Froissart's Chronicles*, 1968, pp. 88–9.

14. M. Jones, ed., *Philip de Commynes, The Memoirs for the Reign of Louis XI, 1461–1483*, 1972, p. 71.

15. H. Ellis, ed., *Edward Hall's Chronicle*, 1809, p. 256.

16. E. Hardy, ed., *Recueil des Chroniques et Anchiennes Istories de la Grant Bretaigne par Jehan de Waurin*, vol. 5, 1891, p. 340.

17. P. Makin, *Provence and Pound, Bertrand's Propaganda*, 1978, pp. 43–9.

18. H. Ellis, ed., *Three Books of Polydore Vergil's English History*, 1844, p. 111.

19. W.H. Stevenson, ed., *Records of the Borough of Nottingham*, vol. 2, 1883–5, p. 377.

20. H. Ellis, ed., *Three Books of Polydore Vergil's English History*, 1844, pp. 223–4.

21. M. Jones, ed., *Philip de Commynes, The Memoirs for the Reign of Louis XI, 1461–1483*, 1972, p. 181.

22. A.B. Hinds, ed., *Calendar of State Papers and Manuscripts in the Archives and Collections of Milan*, vol. 1, 1912, p. 64.

23. E. Hardy, ed., *Recueil des Chroniques et Anchiennes Istories de la Grant Bretaigne par Jehan de Waurin*, vol. 5, 1891, p. 340.

24. J. Bruce, ed., *Histoirie of the Arrivall of Edward IV, 1471*, 1838, pp. 28–30.

25. J.A. Giles, ed., 'Hearne's Fragment' in *Chronicles of the White Rose*, 1834, p. 9.

26. H.T. Riley, ed., *Croyland Abbey Chronicle*, 1854, p. 426.

27. A.B. Hinds, ed., *Calendar of State Papers and Manuscripts in the Archives and Collections of Milan*, vol. 1, 1912, p. 62.

28. J. Bruce, ed., *Histoirie of the Arrivall of Edward IV, 1471*, 1838, pp. 20–1.

29. J.A. Giles, ed., 'Hearne's Fragment' in *Chronicles of the White Rose*, 1834, p. 9.

30. H. Ellis, ed., *Three Books of Polydore Vergil's English History*, 1844, p. 111.

31. H. Ellis, ed., *Edward Hall's Chronicle*, 1809, p. 256.

32. M. Jones, ed., *Philip de Commynes, The Memoirs for the Reign of Louis XI, 1461–1483*, 1972, p. 187.

33. H.T. Riley, ed., *Croyland Abbey Chronicle*, 1854, p. 425.

34. H. Ellis, ed., *Edward Hall's Chronicle*, 1809, p. 256.

Chapter Seven

1. J. Gairdner, ed., 'Gregory's Chronicle' in *The Historical Collections of a Citizen of London*, 1876, pp. 217–18.

2. *Ibid*, p. 198.

3. F. Drake, *Eboracum*, 1736, p .306.

4. H.T. Riley, ed., *Croyland Abbey Chronicle*, 1854, p. 425.

5. The execution of certain knights after the battle is proof that Edward IV wished to punish both traitors and valued Lancastrian captains. Archaeological and forensic evidence may prove that these individuals are the ones found in the Towton Hall graves?

6. A.B. Hinds, ed., *Calendar of State Papers and Manuscripts in the Archives and Collections of Milan*, vol. 1, 1912, p. 66. If the State Papers are correct and the 20,000 alluded to is the number of men that remained in Edward's army, this is a good indication that the Yorkists probably lost approximately 5,000–8,000 men at Towton.

7. J. Gairdner, ed., 'Gregory's Chronicle' in *The Historical Collections of a Citizen of London*, 1876, p. 218.

8. Shakespeare, *Richard III*, Act I, Scene IV.

9. J. Strachey, ed., *Rotuli Parliamentorum*, vol. 5, 1767, p. 545.

10. J. Gairdner, ed., *The Paston Letters*, vol. 3, 1904, p. 274.

11. J. Ross, 'The Battle of Towton (1461): a 550-year retrospective,' in *Magazine of The Friends of the National Archives*, vol. 22, no. 2, 2011.

12. J. Gairdner, ed., *The Paston Letters*, vol. 3, 1904, p. 102.

13. F. Drake, *Eboracum*, 1736, p. 111.

14. R. Whittaker, *Leodis and Elmete*, 1816, p. 157.

15. *Ibid.*

16. R. Brooke, 'The field of the battle of Towton', a paper read before the Society of Antiquaries, 1849, in *Visits to Fields of Battle in England of the Fifteenth Century*, 1857, p. 95.

17. *Ibid.*

18. Ridge and furrow field systems have been identified on several parts of the battlefield near Renshaw Wood, extending from Towton and Saxton villages and beside Saxton Grange.

19. M. Strickland and R. Hardy, *The Great Warbow*, 2005, p. 31.

20. J. Strachey, ed., *Rotuli Parliamentorum*, vol. 5, 1767, p. 478.

21. V. Fiorato, A. Boylston and K. Knusel, ed., *Blood Red Roses*, 2000, pp. 90–102.

22. *Ibid.* Detailed analysis and a complete inventory of the injuries sustained can be found in *Blood Red Roses*.

Chapter Eight

1. A.B. Hinds, ed., *Calendar of State Papers and Manuscripts in the Archives and Collections of Milan*, vol. 1, 1912, p. 64.

2. H. Ellis, ed., *Three Books of Polydore Vergil's English History*, 1844, p. 111.

3. J.S. Davies, ed., *An English Chronicle of the Reigns of Richard II, Henry IV, Henry V and Henry VI*, 1856, p. 109.

4. K. Dockray and R. Knowles, *The Battle of Wakefield*, pp. 5–6.

5. See A. Boardman, *The First Battle of St Albans*, 2006, p. 40.

6. See H.T. Riley, ed., *Croyland Abbey Chronicle*, 1854, p. 425 and J.S. Davies, ed., *An English Chronicle of the Reigns of Richard II, Henry IV, Henry V and Henry VI*, 1856, p. 110.

7. F.W.D. Brie, ed., *The Brut Chronicle*, vol. 1, 1906, p. 533. H. Ellis, ed., *Edward Hall's Chronicle*, 1809, p. 255.

8. A.H. Thomas and I.D. Thornley, eds, *The Great Chronicle of London*, 1938, p. 217.

9. L. Boatwright, M. Habberjam and P. Hammond, 'Richard III and the men who died in battle,' *Ricardian Bulletin*, Autumn 2007, p. 20.

10. M. Habberjam, 'Towton Memorial Chapel', *Ricardian Bulletin*, Autumn 2003, p. 26. Also see Harleian 433 in the *Register of Grants for the Reigns of Edward V and Richard III*, folio 38 which states, 'Warraunt to the Receivor of [the Duchie of] Pounfret [Pontefract] for the contaction of the summe of xl li. [40 pounds] for the building of the chapelle of Towton.'

11. J. Leland, 'Itinerary, 1558', *Yorkshire Archaeological and Topographical Journal*, 10, p. 243.

12. M. Habberjam, 'Towton Memorial Chapel', *Ricardian Bulletin*, Autumn 2003, p. 26.

13. *Ibid.*, p. 27.

14. W. Wheater, *The History of the Parishes of Sherburn and Cawood*, 1882, p. 70. Dom. (*dominus* lord) Robert Burdet – a Dominican chaplain.

15. G.E. Kirk, 'Saxton Church, Lead Chapel and Towton Chapel', *Ricardian*, 1960, p. 48.

16. For the excavation work carried out on the grave see V. Fiorato, A. Boylston and K. Knusel, eds, *Blood Red Roses*, 2000, pp. 29–35.

17. F. Drake, *Eboracum*, 1736, p. 111. The suggestion by Drake may prove that the chapel was to the north of the 'original' village not the present layout of Towton.

18. Full descriptions of the tomb are given in, R. Whittaker, *Leodis and Elmete*, 1816, p. 156 and in F. Drake, *Eboracum*, 1736, p. 111.

19. P. Cross, *Saxon*, no. 55, The Sutton Hoo Society, July 2012, pp. 8–10.

20. R. Brooke, 'The field of the battle of Towton', a paper read before the Society of Antiquaries in 1849, in *Visits to Fields of Battle in England of the Fifteenth Century*, 1857, p. 126.

21. 'Letter to Colonel Gascoigne about Lord Dacre's Tomb 1882', Lotherton Hall Archives, Leeds Museums and Galleries. Thanks to Stephanie Davies and Brian Hull.

22. T.D. Whitaker, *The History and Antiquities of the Deanery of Craven*, 1812, p. 366.

23. W. Wordsworth, *The Poetical Works: In Four Volumes*, Vol. 3, 1832.

24. F. Drake, *Eboracum*, 1736, p. 111.

25. Parish Records, Sherburn-in-Elmet, burials 1754–1778 (including notes and memoranda 1787), Borthwick Institute for Archives, University of York.

26. J. Gairdner, ed., 'Gregory's Chronicle' in *The Historical Collections of a Citizen of London*, 1876, p. 216.

27. M. Strickland and R. Hardy, *The Great Warbow*, 2005, p. 31.

28. *Ibid.*, p. 278.

29. L. Thorpe, trans., *The Journey Through Wales and The Description of Wales*, 1978, p. 113.

30. Subsequent writers, including Polydore Vergil and Edward Hall, copied from these earlier estimates.

31. A.B. Hinds, ed., *Calendar of State Papers and Manuscripts in the Archives and Collections of Milan*, vol. 1, 1912, p. 61.

32. H.T. Riley, ed., *Croyland Abbey Chronicle*, 1854, p. 425.

33. *Ibid.*

34. The whereabouts of Dintingdale (Duntyngdale) has been variously approximated, but evidence of it (and that it was a crossroads) can be found in J. Stevenson, ed., *Annales Rerum Anglicarum, Letters and Papers Illustrative of the Wars of the English in France*, vol. 2, 1864, p. 162.

35. This was a normal manoeuvre in medieval warfare whereby archers, comprising the vaward, would screen the mainward and rearward as they took up position on the battlefield.

36. The City of York had a population of about 10,800 in the reign of Edward III. It is a conservative estimate that about ten per cent of this figure fought at Towton. See *Archaeologia*, 20, 1824, p. 525 and A. Raine, York Civic Records, Yorkshire Archaeological Society, *Record Series*, 1, 1939, p. 135.

37. J.A. Giles, ed., 'Hearne's Fragment' in *Chronicles of the White Rose*, 1834, p. 8–9. The chronicle indicates that the army was comprised mainly of Welshmen and Kentish men. Also see, A.B. Hinds, ed., *Calendar of State Papers and Manuscripts in the Archives and Collections of Milan*, vol. 1, 1912, p. 64.

38. *Ibid.*, p. 66.

39. H. Ellis, ed., *Three Books of Polydore Vergil's English History*, 1844, p. 111.

40. H.T. Riley, ed., *Croyland Abbey Chronicle*, 1854, p. 425.
41. H. Ellis, ed., *Edward Hall's Chronicle*, 1809, pp. 255–6.
42. J. Stevenson, ed., *Annales Rerum Anglicarum, Letters and Papers Illustrative of the Wars of the English in France*, vol. 2, 1864, p. 775.
43. J. Bruce, ed., *Histoirie of the Arrivall of Edward IV*, 1471, 1838, pp. 6–7.
44. J. Gairdner, ed., 'Gregory's Chronicle' in *The Historical Collections of a Citizen of London*, 1876, p. 217.
45. J. James, *A History of Bradford and its Parish*, 1866, p. 44.
46. T.T. Empsall, 'The Bolling Family', *The Bradford Antiquary*, vol. 2, 1895, p. 118.
47. *Ibid.*, p. 121.
48. D. Defoe, *A Tour Through the Whole Island of Great Britain*, vol. 3, Letter 9.

Appendix 2

1. Henry VI.
2. Edward IV.

Appendix 4

1. J. Raine, ed., *Testamenta Eboracensia*, vol. 3, Surtees Society, 1865, p. 337.
2. P. Routh and R. Knowles, *The Medieval Monuments of Harewood*, 1983, p. 92.
3. *Calendar of Patent Rolls 1461–1467*, Public Record Office, 1897, p. 24.

Select Bibliography

Primary Sources
Annales Rerum Anglicarum, Letters and Papers Illustrative of the Wars of the English in France, vol. 2, ed., J. Stevenson, 1864.
'John Benet's Chronicle for the years 1400–1462', eds, G.L. Harriss and M.A. Harriss in *Camden Miscellany*, 24, 1972.
Brut, *The Brut Chronicle*, 2 vols, ed., F.W.D. Brie, 1906.
Calendar of Patent Rolls 1461–1467, Public Record Office, 1897.
Calendar of State Papers and Manuscripts in the Archives and Collections of Milan, vol. 1. 1385–1618, ed., A.B. Hinds, 1912.
Commynes, Philip de, *The Memoirs for the Reign of Louis XI, 1461–1483*, ed., M. Jones, 1972.
The Coventry Leet Book, ed., M.D. Harris, 1907–13.
Croyland Abbey Chronicle, ed., H.T. Riley, 1854.
'Bridport Muster Roll', 1457, Dorset County Record Office, B3/ FG3.
An English Chronicle of the Reigns of Richard II, Henry IV, Henry V and Henry VI, ed., J.S. Davies, 1856.
Eboracum, ed., F. Drake, 1736.
Friossart, *Froissart's Chronicles*, ed., G. Brereton, 1968.
The Great Chronicle of London, eds, A.H. Thomas and I.D. Thornley, 1938.
'Gregory's Chronicle' in *The Historical Collections of a Citizen of London*, ed., J. Gairdner, 1876.
Hall, Edward, *Hall's Chronicle*, ed., H. Ellis, 1809.

Harleian MS 433, British Library.

Harleian MS 795, British Library.

'Hearne's Fragment' in *Chronicles of the White Rose*, ed., J.A. Giles, 1834.

Histoirie of the Arrivall of Edward IV, 1471, ed., J. Bruce, 1838.

Latimer, Hugh, *Sermons by Hugh Latimer, Bishop of Worcester, 1555*, ed., G.E. Corrie, 1844–45.

Leland, J., 'Itinerary, 1558' in *Yorkshire Archaeological and Topographical Journal*, 10, 1889.

'Letter to Colonel Gascoigne about Lord Dacre's Tomb 1882', Lotherton Hall Archives, Leeds Museums and Galleries.

Parish Records, Sherburn-in-Elmet, burials 1754–78, Borthwick Institute for Archives, University of York.

The Paston Letters, 1422–1509 A.D., ed., James Gairdner, 3 vols, 1872–75.

Plumpton Letters, ed., T. Stapleton, 1839.

Records of the Borough of Nottingham, vol. 2, ed., W.H. Stevenson, 1883–5.

Registrum Abbatis Johannis Whethamstede, ed., H.T. Riley, 1872.

'The Rose of Rouen' in *Archaeologia*, 29.

Rotuli Parliamentorum, vol. 5, ed., J. Strachey, 1767.

Testamenta Eboracensia, ed., J. Raine, vol. 3, Surtees Society, 1865.

Three Fifteenth-Century Chronicles, ed., J. Gairdner, 1880.

Vergil, Polydore, *Three Books of Polydore Vergil's English History*, ed., H. Ellis, 1844.

Waurin, Jehan de, *Recueil des Chroniques et Anchiennes Istories de la Grant Bretaigne*, vol.5, 1891, eds, W. and E. Hardy, 1891.

Worcester, William, *Annales Rerum Anglicarum*, ed., Stevenson, 1864.

York Civic Records, ed., A. Raine, *Yorkshire Archaeological Society, Record Series*, 98, 1939.

Secondary Sources

Amyot, T., 'Remarks on the Population of English Cities in the time of Edward the Third', *Archaeologia*, 20, 1824.

Armstrong, C.A.J., 'Politics and the Battle of St Albans, 1455', *Bulletin of the Institute of Historical Research*, vol. 33, no. 87, 1960.

Attreed, L., *York House Books 1461–1490*, 1991.

Barnard, F.P., *Edward IV's French Expedition of 1475*, 1975.

Boardman, A.W., *The First Battle of St Albans, 1455*, 2006.

Boardman, A.W., *The Medieval Soldier in the Wars of the Roses*, 1996.

Boatwright, L., Habberjam, M., and Hammond, P., 'Richard III and the men who died in battle,' *Ricardian Bulletin*, Autumn 2007.

Bogg, E., *Lower Wharfedale*, 1904.

Brooke, R., 'The Field of the Battle of Towton', a paper read before the Society of Antiquaries, 1849.

Brooke, R., *Visits to Fields of Battle in England*, 1857.

Brooke-Little, J.P., *Boutell's Heraldry* (revised edition), 1973.

Burne, A.H., *Battlefields of England*, 1950.

Cross, P., 'The ritual of horse burial – Sutton Hoo and beyond', *Saxon*, The Sutton Hoo Society, July 2012.

Defoe, D., *A Tour Through the Whole Island of Great Britain*, vol. 3, Letter 9.

Dockray, K., *Henry VI, Margaret of Anjou and the Wars of the Roses*, 2000.

Dockray, K., and Knowles, R., *The Battle of Wakefield*, 1992.

Drake, F., *Eboracum*, 1736.

Dunham, W.H., 'Lord Hasting's Indentured Retainers 1461–1483', *Transactions of the Connecticut Academy of Arts and Sciences*, September 1955.

Empsall, T.T., 'The Bolling Family', *The Bradford Antiquary*, vol. 2, 1895.

Fiorato, V., Boylston, A., and Knusel, C., eds, *Blood Red Roses*, 2000.

Forrest, C., *The History of Knottingley*, 1871.

Gillingham, J., *The Wars of the Roses*, 1981.

Goodman, A., *The Wars of the Roses*, 1981.

Goodman, A., *The Wars of the Roses: The Soldiers' Experience*, 2005.

Gransden, A., *Historical Writing in England*, ii, 1982.

Griffiths, R.A., *The Reign of King Henry VI*, 1981.

Habberjam, M., 'Towton Memorial Chapel', *Ricardian Bulletin*, Autumn 2003.

Hampton, W.E., *Memorials of the Wars of the Roses*, 1979.

Hardy, R., *Longbow*, 1976.

Hicks, M.A., *Bastard Feudalism*, 1995.

Hicks, M.A., *Warwick the Kingmaker*, 1998.

Jack, R.I., 'A quincentenary: the battle of Northampton, July 1460', *Northamptonshire Past and Present*, 2, 1960.

Jacob, E.F., *The 15th Century, Oxford History of England*, 1961.

James, J., *A History of Bradford and its Parish*, 1866.

Johnson, P.A., *Duke Richard of York 1411–1460,* 1988.

Jones, M.K., 'Somerset, York and the Wars of the Roses', *English Historical Review*, vol. 14, no. 411, April 1989.

Keegan, J., *The Face of Battle*, 1976.

Keegan, J., and Holmes, R., *Soldiers: A History of Men in Battle*, 1985.

Keen, M.H., *Chivalry*, 1984.

Kingsford, C.L., *English Historical Literature in the 15th Century*, 1913.

Kirk, G.E., 'Saxton Church, Lead Chapel and Towton Chapel', *The Ricardian*, 1960.

Kurath, H., Kuhn, S.M., Lewis, R.E., Reidy, J., Williams, M.J., eds, *Middle English Dictionary*, 1952.

Lander, J.R., *The Wars of the Roses*, 1965, revised 1990.

McFarlane, K.B., 'Bastard Feudalism', *Bulletin of the Institute of Historical Research*, 20, 1943–45.

McFarlane, K.B., *The Nobility of Late Medieval England*, 1973.

McGill, P., *Heraldic Banners of the Wars of the Roses*, 1990.

Makin, P., *Provence and Pound, Bertrand's Propaganda*, 1978.

Markham, C., 'The Battle of Towton', *Yorkshire Archaeological and Topographical Journal*, 10, 1889.

Maurer, H.E., and Chron, B.M., eds, *The Letters of Margaret of Anjou*, 2019.

Myers, A.R., *English Historical Documents, 1327–1485*, 1969.

Oman, C., *The Art of War in the Middle Ages*, vol. 2, 1924.

Oman, C., *The Political History of England 1377–1485*, 1920.

Perges, G. *Agrarian Production, Population, Army Provisioning and Strategy in the Second Half of the Seventeenth Century 1650–1715*, 1963.

Pollard, A.J., *North-Eastern England During the Wars of the Roses*, 1990.

Pollard, A.J., 'Percies and Nevilles', *History Today*, Sept. 1993.

Ramsay, J.H., *Lancaster and York*, 1892.

Ross, J., 'The Battle of Towton 1461: a 550-year retrospective', *Magazine of The Friends of the National Archives*, vol. 22, no. 2, 2011.

Routh, P., Knowles, R., *The Medieval Monuments of Harewood*, 1983.

Scofield, C.L., *Life and Reign of Edward IV*, 1923.

Smith, M.E., 'Henry VI's Medical Record: A Preliminary Survey', *The Ricardian*, no. 43, December 1973.

Smurthwaite, D., *The O.S. Guide to the Battlefields of Britain*, 1984.

Storey, R.L., *The End of the House of Lancaster*, 1966.

Strickland, M., and Hardy, R., *The Great Warbow*, 2005.

Thorpe, L., *The Journey Through Wales and The Description of Wales*, 1978.

Wheater, W., *The History of Sherburn and Cawood*, 1865.

Whitaker, T.D., *The History and Antiquities of the Deanery of Craven*, 1812.

Whittaker, R., *Leodis and Elmete*, 1816.

Winston, J.E., *English Towns in the Wars of the Roses*, 1921.

Wolffe, B., *Henry VI*, 1981.

Woolgar, C.M., *The Great Household in Late Medieval England*, 1999.

Wordsworth, *The Poetical Works: In Four Volumes*, Vol. 3, 1832.

Young, P., and Adair, J., *Hastings to Culloden*, 1979.

Index

About the Author

Andrew Boardman has written extensively on British military history. In 1992, he formed the Towton Battlefield Society and wrote the first major work about the battle two years later. His special interest is the medieval period, and when a mass grave was unearthed in Towton village in 1996, Andrew was consulted and formed part of the team from Bradford University that investigated it.

He has been a consultant on many TV documentary series for the BBC, Channel 4, Sky One and Yesterday Channel, and lectures on the battles of the Wars of the Roses and related subjects.

To date, Andrew's other non-fiction work includes *The Medieval Soldier in the Wars of the Roses*, *Hotspur: Henry Percy Medieval Rebel*, *Blood Red Roses* and *The First Battle of St Albans 1455*. He lives in Yorkshire, writes a weekly newsletter called History Mondays, and has recently published two historical novels with military themes.

twitter.com/wotroses
linkedin.com/in/awboardman/
historymondays.substack.com